THE CHICAGO PUBLIC LIBRARY

SOCIAL SCIENCES AND HISTORY DIVISION

FORM 19

Accreditation of Teacher Education:
The Story of CATE 1984–1989

Gordon Macintyre

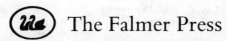 The Falmer Press

(A member of the Taylor & Francis Group)
London • New York • Philadelphia

UK	The Falmer Press, 4 John Street, London WC1N 2ET
USA	The Falmer Press, Taylor & Francis Inc., 1900 Frost Road, Suite 101, Bristol, PA 19007

© D.G. Macintyre 1991

First published 1991

British Library Cataloguing in Publication Data
McIntyre, Gordon
  Accreditation of teacher education: the story of CATE
  1984–1989
  1. Great Britain. Teachers. Professional education
  I. Council for the Accreditation of Teacher Education
  370.71

  ISBN   1–85000–980–5
         1–85000–981–3 pbk

Library of Congress Cataloguing-in-Publication Data
MacIntyre, Gordon.
    Accreditation of teacher education: the story of CATE,
  1984–1989 / Gordon MacIntyre.
       p.   cm.
    Includes bibliographical references and index.
    ISBN 1–85000–980–5: —— ISBN
        1–85000–981–3 (pbk.)
    1. Teachers colleges—Great Britain—Accreditation.
  2. Teachers-Training of—Great Britain.   3. Council for the
  Accreditation of Teacher Education (Great Britain)   I. Title.
  LB2060.A2M33   1991
  370′.71′0941—dc20   90–25668
                                                          CIP

Jacket design by Caroline Archer

Typeset in 10½/12 Bembo by
Graphicraft Typesetters Ltd., Hong Kong

*Printed in Great Britain by Burgess Science Press, Basingstoke
on paper which has a specified pH value on final paper
manufacture of not less than 7.5 and is therefore 'acid free'.*

Contents

Contents

PART THREE: OTHER ASPECTS OF THE CRITERIA

PART FOUR: 'WHAT CATE DID'

APPENDICES

Preface

I owe it, I think, to my former colleagues on the Council for the Accreditation of Teacher Education (CATE) and to the staff of the institutions whose courses we reviewed to offer a justification for this book, and I might first explain how I came to be a member of the Council. The Department of Education and Science (DES) and Welsh Office Circular which established CATE gave it a role in respect only of England and Wales. The Department of Education for Northern Ireland (DENI) subsequently issued a paper about how the institutions of initial teacher training in that province might be associated with the accreditation exercise. One of the bodies consulted was the Northern Ireland Advisory Committee on Teacher Education (ACTE), of which I was the Chairman. The education community in Northern Ireland values the currency in Britain of teaching qualifications conferred in the province, and ACTE had therefore no doubt that some formal arrangement was desirable, but members were also very conscious of many differences in the education system of which an accrediting body would need to take account. Various possibilities were canvassed, such as a separate CATE or a Northern Ireland sub-committee on what was then the University Grants Committee (UGC) model. But the solution eventually adopted was to have CATE's terms of reference enlarged to include Northern Ireland while asking the DES to accept the nomination of an additional member who could act in an informal sense as a Northern Ireland representative. When this was agreed the DENI asked me to be that link person. (There would also be an assessor to CATE from the DENI Inspectorate.) I was told that my being on the staff of the Open University was incidentally attractive to the DES.

Thus it happened that some nine months after it began work I found myself a member of CATE with an opportunity for participant observation of what was clearly one of the most significant developments in teacher training in the United Kingdom since the Second World War. With no very clear idea at first of what use I should make of them, I kept my own notes to supplement the official record of what went on. As our work proceeded I began to see how these might be organized, and after CATE's term was finished at the end of 1989 I completed the job of writing them up in book form.

Insider accounts of recent events, which were at the time confidential, are commonplace in some fields of activity, notably government and politics, but unusual in education. I have considered whether producing an account of this kind is to betray a trust. My conclusion, which I hope will be endorsed, is that the intrinsic interest and relevance of the material for those in education, and in particular for those concerned with the training of teachers, is sufficient to outweigh such scruples. I have no axe to grind, and I have tried as carefully as I can to present a truthful, though inevitably partial, account of the events in which I took part. This is no exposé of political malpractice, devious bureaucrats or incompetent institutions. For the members of CATE, struggling to perform to the best of their ability an almost impossibly complex and difficult task, I had the utmost admiration. No one should be surprised if we each brought attitudes and special interests which at times influenced the direction of our work, or if we developed a strong corporate ethos; that is the way such bodies work. I also found the representatives of the institutions we met impressive for their thoughtful and sensitive approach to the professional preparation of the next generation of teachers for the country's children. No one should be surprised if in their different circumstances they adopted different methods and structures; that too is part of the story.

I have been unable to see how a useful account of CATE's work could have been written without the specific references I have made. It will be apparent from my narrative that when these are to courses reviewed by CATE's Group A I am writing from greater direct knowledge of the relevant papers and discussions than when one of the other Reporting Groups was most immediately involved; in the latter case I am largely dependant on my comprehension of the situation as presented to the Council by the respective Convenors. If imperfect understanding or the need for concision has caused any of these references to be inaccurate or misleading I ask for pardon. But in many instances both courses and personnel will have changed since the events described in these pages, and it should be obvious that there is no basis in my allusions to aspects of courses which caught the attention of CATE for any ranking or assessment of the institutions concerned. Clearly there are dangers in this undertaking, but I believe that greater understanding of 'what CATE did' and the principles which it evolved must be helpful to those now engaged in the field both in this country and elsewhere, and that such an account as this will be of some value to future historians of teacher education. It is in that spirit that I offer my story of CATE, 1984–1989.

Acknowledgments

I am indebted to all those mentioned in this book for their contribution to my continuing education, and in particular to the members and officers of CATE for the fellowship which I enjoyed for four-and-a-half years. Sir Clifford Butler has kindly given me his recollections of the role of ACSET in the genesis of CATE. I am grateful to the Director of the University of London Institute of Education for permission to quote in chapter 24 from an internal Institute document. I should especially like to thank my secretary, Mrs Maureen Watters, for patiently instructing me in the skills of wordprocessing and for her ready assistance on the printer.

Gordon Macintyre
December 1990

Notes and Abbreviations

1   Initial teacher training (ITT) is provided in England, Wales and Northern Ireland by universities and 'public sector institutions' — polytechnics and colleges, usually designated colleges or institutes of higher education (CHE or IHE). A few of the colleges are voluntary — i.e., church-provided. When CATE began its work courses leading to Qualified Teacher Status (QTS) were of two kinds — consecutive and concurrent. The consecutive version was a one-year course for graduates leading to the Postgraduate Certificate in Education (PGCE). The concurrent courses, which might be of three or four years' duration, combined professional training with undergraduate studies leading usually to a Bachelor of Education degree (BEd), though sometimes to a BA or BSc with a Certificate of Education; concurrent courses could be general or with honours. The PGCE route was used mainly, but not exclusively, by intending secondary (11–18) teachers; BEd degrees were provided mainly but not exclusively by public sector institutions.

2   In the ITT context there is an inherent ambiguity in the use of the word 'course', and it is not one which can be removed in this book. 'Course' may mean the programme of study followed by all the students in an institution working towards a particular qualification — for example, a BEd; or it may mean a route followed by some of these students — for example, those intending to teach primary children in the upper age-range, those taking history as a main subject of study; or it may mean an element within the programme — for example, curricular studies, multicultural education. Confusion among these usages has been avoided as much as possible in the ensuing text.

3   In the text of this book the following simplifications have been adopted.
    i   No distinction is made between general and honours BEd degrees, since this was not relevant to the process of accreditation.

(In practice non-honours degrees became increasingly uncommon and three-year BEds became extinct.)

ii The term UDE (University Department of Education) is normally used to refer to the department of a university responsible for providing ITT, though in some cases it is actually known as a school or faculty of education.

iii Reference is made to 'the Secretary of State' to indicate the political authority in England and/or Wales. In fact Circulars affecting education are usually issued jointly by the Department of Education and Science (DES) and the Welsh Office and refer to the Secretaries of State — i.e., those in charge of these two Departments. Authority to approve ITT courses rests in England with the Secretary of State for Education and Science, in Wales with the Secretary of State for Wales, and in Northern Ireland (under direct rule) with the Department of Education for Northern Ireland (DENI).

Other Abbreviations Used in the Text

ACSET	Advisory Committee for the Supply and Education of Teachers
ACTE	Advisory Committee on Teacher Education (Northern Ireland)
APU	Assessment of Performance Unit
BPS	British Psychological Society
CATE	Council for the Accreditation of Teacher Education
CDT	Craft, design and technology
CI	Chief Inspector
CNAA	Council for National Academic Awards
FE	Further Education
GCSE	General Certificate of Secondary Education
GRIST	Grant-related in-service training
HMI	Her Majesty's Inspector/Inspectors/Inspectorate
HMSO	Her Majesty's Stationery Office
INSET	In-service education of teachers
IT	Information technology
LEA	Local education authority
NAB	National Advisory Body for Local Authority Higher Education
NAHT	National Association of Head Teachers
NaPTEC	National Primary Teacher Education Conference
NASUWT	National Association of Schoolmasters/Union of Women Teachers

NATFHE	National Association of Teachers in Further and Higher Education
NCATE	National Council for Accreditation of Teacher Education (United States of America)
NNEB	National Nursery Examination Board
NUS	National Union of Students
NUT	National Union of Teachers
OU	Open University
PCFC	Polytechnics and Colleges Funding Council
PE	Physical education
PESC	Public Expenditure Survey Committee
PIT	Pool of inactive teachers
PSE	Personal and social education
RE	Religious education
SCETT	Standing Committee for the Education and Training of Teachers in the Public Sector
SCOP	Standing Conference of Principals
SI	Staff Inspector
SRHE	Society for Research into Higher Education
TEFL	Teaching English as a foreign language
TES	Times Educational Supplement
TESL	Teaching English as a second language
TESOL	Teaching English as a second or other language
THES	Times Higher Education Supplement
TVEI	Technical and vocational educational initiative
UCET	Universities Council for the Education of Teachers
UGC	University Grants Committee
UPTEC	Undergraduate Primary Teacher Education Conference
WAB	Welsh Advisory Body for Local Authority Higher Education

Part One

CATE at Work

Chapter 1

Background (Our Heroine Is Born)

Unlike Aphrodite, CATE did not spring from the sea but rather from a particular historical situation, and some awareness of this context is necessary in order to understand why the Council was established. The famous speech delivered by James Callaghan as Prime Minister at Ruskin College in October 1976 presaged an era in which education was to figure more prominently on the political agenda than for at least thirty years. The service was beginning to be seen by politicians as consuming a large and growing proportion of national resource yet not to be delivering the goods in terms of either the country's economic performance or satisfaction on the part of parents and employers. Governments were now to become much more concerned about standards and accountability, and in practice this meant becoming much more interventionist. Gone were the days when, as Bernard Donoughue recalls Harold Wilson observing in the sixties, the DES was little more than a postbox between the local authorities and the teachers' unions. Teacher training was especially vulnerable to critical scrutiny both because it could be held responsible at one remove for many of the alleged shortcomings of the schools and because it was perceived to be in a state of confusion and uncertainty in organization and in method.

Insofar as this was true it was scarcely surprising, for since the Second World War the system had been subjected to a series of extraordinary upheavals. Even before the war ended the emergency training scheme had been launched as a crash programme to cope with the raising of the school leaving age to 15, and in the next few years there was also an expansion of permanent training institutions to meet the needs of the bulge in the birth-rate. A second and less foreseeable rise in births after 1955 and the tendency for young people to stay longer at school led to a further rapid expansion in 1958–60. The Teachers Certificate course was lengthened in 1960 from two years to three and the balance of training was altered from secondary to primary. From 1964 the BEd was introduced. The James Committee reviewed the whole system during 1970–

72. In 1972 a White Paper proposed an expansion of teacher education outside the university sector and the CNAA began validating BEd degrees, but in the following year a DES Circular presaged the first contraction, for the birth-rate was falling again. As a result there were two successive reductions in the number of colleges through merger or closure. In the meantime the BEd degree was being fundamentally rethought and recast and Certificate courses began to be phased out. In 1982 there was a third round of cuts, depriving more colleges and polytechnics of their teacher training intakes and causing reductions in teaching staff. In little more than a decade the number of public sector institutions providing initial training in England and Wales had roughly been halved.

James Callaghan had called for a great debate to begin on education. In 1977 the DES published a Consultative Document which purported to sum up the regional conferences and other consultations which were initiated by his speech. It was a somewhat bland document, but with regard to the initial training of teachers (ITT) it noted 'fairly widespread misgivings' on these issues:

(i)   whether entrants to the teaching profession have a sufficient command of the English language and are adequately numerate;

(ii)   whether teachers have an adequate appreciation of the world outside the education system, particularly the importance of industry and commerce to the national well-being and the problems facing an industrial society like ours in an increasingly competitive world;

(iii)   whether existing courses of teacher education give enough attention to the role of teachers in a multicultural society;

(iv)   whether existing courses of teacher education furnish students with the essential intellectual mastery of the subjects they will teach;

(v)   whether they provide students with sufficient practical guidance to enable them to become effective teachers capable of directing children's work and of ensuring their good discipline. (DES, 1977)

The proposals for addressing these issues did not extend to course accreditation but many of the criteria produced seven years later for CATE had a very obvious derivation from the concerns identified at the time of the Great Debate.

There were similar indicators. In 1978 and 1979 the DES published surveys by HMI of primary and secondary education in England respectively. Both of these reported a considerable amount of teaching that was inadequate in its subject content. (It may be noted at this point that some of the documents quoted in this chapter relate to England and Wales and some only to England. The education system in Northern Ireland had not been subjected to a similar process of inspection and survey.) In 1981 another paper followed from discussion of the secondary survey in England; this was *Teacher Training and the Secondary School*. It suggested that 'hidden' shortages in schools (subjects being taught by teachers not adequately qualified in them) raised three issues concerning initial training. These were the question of how best to attract and select good candidates, the matter of second subject courses, which were sometimes taken by students with no background in the subject beyond 'O' level, and the relevance to the secondary curriculum of the degrees held by PGCE students. The paper also advocated more attention being paid in training to the contribution which each subject could make to the whole curriculum in order to achieve better continuity and greater coherence across the educational disciplines. On methodology it called for colleges to consider the influence on students of the teaching methods they experienced there — to avoid passive learning and to promote a repertoire of teaching styles. Attention was called to the importance of the personal and social development of pupils, of professional skill in assessment and of an informed and flexible attitude to the needs of the less able. Again there was much here that was picked up by the 1984 criteria.

1982 saw the publication of a DES discussion paper which was based on a survey of newly-trained teachers carried out by HMI during the previous year (*The New Teacher in School*). This found that one teacher in ten revealed insecurity when they were teaching subjects for which their training had supposedly prepared them and 'nearly one in four are in some respects poorly equipped with the skills needed for teaching' — situations described as 'disturbing'. The commonest weaknesses were 'failure to assess pupils' work and to match teaching methods and materials to their needs, particularly where there was a wide range of ability, aptitude or cultural background'. The authors pointedly remarked: 'one is bound to ask why, when there is no shortage of applicants for teaching posts, as many as a quarter of the teachers in the sample should be markedly deficient in a number of the teaching skills which they might have been expected to acquire through their training.' Surprise was also expressed at the fact that, 'after initial selection for training followed by a period of between one and four years of further assessment for suitability as a school teacher, a number of teachers who are temperamentally ill fitted for the task still find their way into the classroom'. The first recommendation therefore was that 'the training institutions should carry out a more effective process of "quality control"' (DES, 1982).

It is very clear from these documents that at this period a number of strong concerns was building up in the Inspectorate. The Secretary of State asked the Advisory Committee on the Supply and Education of Teachers to consider the structure and content of initial training courses and whether changes were needed. To assist ACSET a further discussion paper was prepared by HMI in 1982, and after extensive consultation a revised version of it was published in January 1983 under the title *Teaching in Schools: The Content of Initial Training*. Referring to the findings of the earlier documents, it drew attention to the variety of styles and patterns of training then current and observed:

> Notwithstanding the value of institutional freedom in profession-al matters, and the value of variety and experiment in the curriculum of teacher education, there is a widely recognized need for agreed guidelines on the content of training, and for the guarantee of an acceptable level of preparation in the subject or aspect of the curriculum which a teacher offers to teach. In an earlier survey...the time allocated to subject studies ranged from 22 to 50 per cent of the total undergraduate taught programme. Recent analysis of course submissions showed that this range has not narrowed in recent times. (DES, 1983)

Although it was not published until May 1987, it is not irrelevant to refer also to the HMI survey *Quality in Schools: The Initial Training of Teachers*, for it was based on visits to a sample of public sector institutions during the period January 1983 to January 1985, and its findings must have begun to colour official thinking at the time when CATE was established. This survey also discovered great variation in the time devoted to specialist subject study, and at the formal presentation of the document in London a Staff Inspector remarked that this was bound to attract the attention of the Secretary of State. The same SI reported as another principal finding of the survey that a marked defect in primary training was the lack of what he called transformer courses, designed to help students apply their specialist subject to children's learning. As late as June 1988 CATE received an HMI review of ITT in UDEs, *Education Observed* 7, which was to some extent a counterpart to the earlier survey of public sector institutions and which also related largely to the situation before our influence was brought to bear. CI Alan Marshall suggested that the message was: 'Good stuff; pity about the autonomy' — by which he meant not of institutions but of tutors. HMI had observed one meeting of all the tutors in a UDE concerned with a group of students at the end of which the chairman had said, 'That was very valuable — we must meet again some time.' *The Content of Initial Training* had concluded in 1983:

It seems right to expect all initial training courses, while retaining their individual philosophy and style, to achieve a minimum standard of effective mastery of the main teaching subjects for all their students, and to ensure that the preparation of every intending teacher should include an agreed minimum range of professional content, appropriate to the phase in which the student will teach. (DES, 1983)

ACSET's advice was included as an annex to the White Paper, *Teaching Quality*, which followed in March 1983. Recognizing no doubt both the need for some external influence on ITT and the political unattainability of a general teaching council, the Committee believed that the Secretary of State should establish criteria which he would take into account in deciding whether or not to approve ITT courses. These should relate to the initial selection of students, to the level and amount of subject content, to professional content and to links between training institutions and schools. It also expressed the view that ACSET itself provided an appropriate forum in which to develop such criteria. The White Paper, having covered some now familiar ground about the importance of teachers' personal qualities and of the match between their qualifications and what they were called upon to teach, announced the Government's acceptance of ACSET's advice. The Secretary of State proposed to promulgate criteria against which he would in future assess ITT courses before deciding whether to approve them. These criteria would be drawn up after consultations channelled through ACSET, and would relate both to professional and academic content of courses and to good working relationships with schools. Once they were published, he would initiate a review of all existing courses, and might withdraw approval from those which did not conform to the criteria.

In spite of the undertaking to consult, the White Paper went on to give some fairly detailed guidance, in which the hand of the HMI was discernible, about the nature of the criteria. Three broad requirements which they should impose would be that training should include at least two full years' course time devoted to subject studies at a level appropriate to higher education, adequate attention to teaching method and close links with practical experience in school. In order to satisfy the last of these requirements a sufficient proportion of each institution's staff should have enjoyed recent success as teachers in schools. Strong pointers were also given to means of improving the selection of students for training (White Paper, 1983).

The outcome from the discussions which followed was the publication on 13 April 1984 of DES Circular No. 3/84, *Initial Teacher Training: Approval of Courses*. It announced acceptance by the Secretary of State of a further recommendation from ACSET:

that, in order to obtain consistency in the assessment of courses, a single Council should be established to advise on the approval of teacher education courses both in the universities and in the public sector. [The Secretaries of State] have therefore decided to establish a Council for the Accreditation of Teacher Education with the following terms of reference: 'to advise the Secretaries of State for Education and Science and for Wales on the approval of initial teacher training courses in England and Wales'. (DES, 1984a)

The Council would be asked to review all existing courses and to scrutinize proposals for new ones. This job should be complete within three to four years, and the Council's future would then be considered. An annex to the Circular set out in seventeen paragraphs the criteria which the Council was to apply in giving its advice about the approval of courses. For ease of reference these are referred to hereafter in this book as the Criteria.

I hope that this historical introduction has served two purposes. The first is to make plain that CATE and the Criteria which it was charged to enforce did not burst suddenly upon the educational scene. They arose directly from perceived shortcomings in teacher education which had been identified and intensively discussed for at least seven years beforehand. 'There is no question,' said Tim Eggar, MP, Education Minister, in November 1990, 'but that teacher training in the 1970s and early 1980s was in a mess.' The second point is closely related. It was natural that the phrase 'the CATE Criteria' should slip into use, and as a shorthand reference it did no harm; but it was profoundly misleading if it was taken to mean, as it sometimes was by people who should have known better, that the Criteria were CATE's invention. They were not; they were promulgated by the Secretary of State on the advice of a representative professional body, and CATE had no role except to apply them. From time to time as the Council proceeded with its work we received representations from concerned groups which wanted the Criteria to have something or something more to say about their particular field of interest, be it health education, music, American studies, religious education, consumer education or psychology. Our answer had always to be the same: we had no power to vary the Criteria by addition, modification or omission. Only the Secretary of State could do that, as in due course he did.

Chapter 2

The Council: Members and Officers

The Council for the Accreditation of Teacher Education met for the first time on 24 September 1984. The venue, as for all subsequent meetings of CATE, was Elizabeth House in London, the somewhat unprepossessing office block beside Waterloo Station which housed the DES. Here it occupied in succession two suites of rooms, both of which tended to be chilly in winter and in the summer to offer a choice between stifling heat and an inability, if the windows were opened, to hear ordinary conversation above the noise from the railway.

By the time I attended my first CATE meeting in July 1985 the Council had clearly become a friendly, closely knit and hard working body. It was no less evident that this was due in large measure to the informal yet incisive style of its Chairman, Professor William Taylor, CBE, then Principal of the University of London and shortly to become Vice-Chancellor of the University of Hull. Then aged 55, he was a slim, tallish man with an alert manner, extraordinary energy and a very sharp mind; he was also a man of great personal kindness. First names were in regular use, and as we assembled for our meetings or helped ourselves to our buffet lunches Bill Taylor was ready with an affable and interested word for everyone and a comment or anecdote about every subject which might crop up. Impromptu witticisms and apt allusions from the chair could also be expected to relieve the formal business. When Mary Hallaway left the Council a month or two before the end of its term she responded to Bill's thanks and best wishes by observing that while she had not felt of CATE days 'Oh good!', she had known that they would be enjoyable and stimulating. This was the ethos which Bill was so skilful at creating. He was a masterly chairman, making each contribution to discussion seem both welcome and valuable, and often expressly inviting comment from those likely to be able to illumine a particular topic; yet the very manner in which he would scan the table to see who else might wish to speak had the effect of deterring any intervention that was not going to be reasonably cogent and to the point. His authority sprang in part, of course, from his being as head of a university the most elevated personage among us, but also from his unrivalled experience of the field and grasp of the issues. He would usually give a fairly firm lead in debate, but was also adept at detecting how opinion was moving, and appeared genuinely ready to modify his position. His summings up were rarely challenged as the expression of a consensual view.

The person who, next to the Chairman, probably had most to do with setting the tone of CATE's work was its first Secretary, Ernest Grogan. He was a seconded civil servant and, in the event, he retired eighteen months before our term expired. Ernie was a gentle and humorous man, in whose speech the traces of his Hampshire origins could still be faintly discerned. He had, of course, no professional background in teacher training, and his influence, as it seemed to me, encouraged a firm application of the letter of the Criteria. At the same time he went out of his way to be helpful to the institutions with whom we dealt, through informal as well as formal contacts, and even those whose philosophical differences with CATE were sharpest would pay tribute to the personal courtesy which they had received from Ernie. Like the Chairman, he took pleasure in contributing to the Council's social cohesion — for example, by producing an enormous iced cake for our meeting in September 1987 with the inscription 'Happy Birthday CATE' (we were 3), and on 1 April preceding his retirement by circulating a spoof memo about a reconstitution of the Council as the United Chocolate, Cocoa, Air and Trite Chunter Office (UNCHOCOATRICO) in which we all reappeared under ingenious anagrams of our names — Chairman, Mr Wally Italio. It was especially helpful from my point of view that when I joined the Council I was allocated to Group A, since Ernie himself acted as its Secretary, and I learned much from him.

The Circular, which announced the establishment of CATE, had stated that it would be for the Council itself to determine its working methods, and it included the suggestion that since visits by Council members to individual institutions would be among the sources of information from which the Council would draw, it might establish working parties for this purpose. A paper presented to the first meeting proposed specifically that since it would be expensive and difficult to arrange formal visits by the whole Council smaller reporting groups should be established to make such visits and prepare reports for consideration by full Council; these might be reconstituted after a year in order to facilitate the sharing of experience and the maintenance of common approaches and standards. There was general support for the idea of setting up reporting groups, and a paper for the second meeting suggested that the groups should be three in number. Since the original Council comprised eighteen members in addition to the Chairman this arrangement resulted in groups of six, each with a balance of interests and experience.

It soon became apparent why I was asked to join Group A. One of its six members had already ceased to attend meetings. This was Councillor Frank Cogan, the Chairman of Hertfordshire County Council and one of two local authority members originally appointed; he resigned in the following year. The Group had suffered another loss, for at my first Council meeting the Chairman announced that Peter Snape had felt it necessary to step down as its Convenor. He was General Secretary of the Secondary Heads Association (SHA), then much involved with a protracted industrial dispute on the part of many in the teaching profession, and a few months later he resigned from the Council altogether. Group A also included two of the three members of the Council who had been appointed as non-educationalists; these were Michael Dixon, education correspondent and later columnist for the *Financial Times*, and Peter Ward, the UK Personnel Director for Hewlett Packard. The structure and terminology of teacher training is surprisingly complex and esoteric, and it was not always easy for Michael and Peter — or for the Council's third industrial member, who was Angus Clark, the Director of Personnel for Sainsbury's — to participate fully in some of the more technical aspects of discussion. Their other problem was that regular attendance at meetings appeared to be more difficult than for the rest of us; Michael Dixon in particular was liable to be detained by the exigencies of his journalistic deadlines, and this contributed further to Group A's manpower problems.

The two remaining members of the Group at this time provided a nice contrast in styles. Dr David Shadbolt, the Principal of Worcester College of Higher Education, had agreed to become Convenor in succession to Peter Snape. A brisk, wiry man with a shock of white hair, he was meticulous in his preparation for our meetings, and would fire off his detailed conclusions about the lengthy submissions we had received with such rapidity that the rest of us were sometimes struggling to keep pace with his references or to initiate a slightly more extended discussion of some of the points at issue. When we met with representatives of the institutions he was similarly business-like to the point of slight excitability, and it was on occasion not unamusing to observe a marked deflation of confidence on the part of members of a newly arrived delegation who had just arranged their papers on the table before them when they were asked to explain a discrepancy in the number of hours of subject study tabulated on page 43 of their Document C with the diagram of course structure in Appendix II of Document F. But at least they knew that we had read their papers with care, and interviews were always conducted in a thoroughly professional manner.

Tony Becher, Professor of Education at the University of Sussex, had a much more relaxed manner and a sense of humour which was at times slightly boisterous, but behind it was a robust mind and a keen nose for humbug. On the whole, however, Tony's approach was to assume that an institution probably knew what it was doing and should be allowed to get on with it unless it was manifestly in default of the Criteria; he was prone to be especially sympathetic towards the universities. Discussion was rarely dull when Tony was around, and David Shadbolt too had a lively sense of fun. Michael Dixon, having been an observer of the educational scene for a good many years, had a fund of stories on which he would embark with great gusto. Meetings of Group A were thus fairly convivial. We had a number of in-jokes, one of which was based on the exotic life-style of Peter Ward, whose apologies for absence often arose from business trips abroad and who had from time to time to withdraw from meetings in order to speak to New York on his portable phone.

We were by chance the only one of the three Reporting Groups which was totally male in composition, and this remained the case after the first general change of Convenors, when Bill Wright was moved across from Group C to be our leader. Bill was then the Chief Education Officer for the City of Wakefield, and consequently an employer rather than a trainer of teachers. He was himself a historian, and these two aspects of his background tended to colour his attitude. His approach to the submissions we received from institutions was a kind of dogged determination to get to the bottom of what they were doing and how they were doing it, and on this he was prepared to spend a great deal of time. The result could be a rather niggling preoccupation with points of detail but it also meant that he occasionally spotted significant problems that the rest of us had missed. Bill too had a good sense of humour, of a dry and ironic bent. Meeting as frequently as we did and over so long a period it was natural that we developed a close sense of group identity. In 1988, when we were told of our impending reinforcement by two lady members, I observed to Tony Becher that this might have implications for Group A's atmosphere of a slightly seedy gentlemen's club. 'Slightly seedy!' exclaimed Tony: he thought 'totally degenerate' would be nearer the mark. However, the advent of Anne and Lesley did nothing to diminish the Group's *joie de vivre* and we continued secretly to congratulate each other that we had not been called upon to serve on either of the other Groups, which we suspected, perhaps quite unjustly, of undue solemnity.

Since Group Convenors had a special role at Council meetings the Convenors of the other two Groups were among other members who appeared most prominent when I first joined CATE. At this time they were Andrew Collier for Group B and Dr Hester Mary Hallaway for Group C. Andrew had in common with Bill Wright that they were the two tallest men on the Council and also — until Bill retired in 1988 — the two Chief Education Officers, in Andrew's case for Lancashire. Appearing youthful for so senior a post in the educational world (though, like the rest of us, he grew older in service), he had an impressive air of calm authority. He was one of those who was ready to enter into discussion at the level of the principles underlying the Criteria, and though no less committed to them than anyone else he was on occasion prepared to express views that were not wholly in accord with the Chairman's. Mary Hallaway might have been cast as everyone's idea of a headmistress of the traditional school — smartly if sensibly dressed, brisk and alert, cultivated yet formidable, with a nice turn of astringent phrase. She was in fact the Principal of the Catholic Trinity and All Saints' College in Leeds. She retired from this post at Easter of CATE's final year, and in the autumn returned to university teaching in Africa. In preparation for this she set about learning to ride a motor-bicycle.

When Bill Wright became Convenor of Group A similar changes resulted in Derek Mortimer and Renford Bambrough taking over Groups B and C respectively. Derek had been from the outset of my observation a prominent contributor to discussion. When appointed to CATE he was Assistant Director of Wolverhampton Polytechnic, and he later became Principal of Suffolk College of Higher and Further Education. He was a fluent speaker with a very clear mind. Contributions made by Renford tended more towards brevity, with at times a certain epigrammatic flavour. Unlike Derek, he was not involved with teacher training, but he was a doughty upholder of the Criteria. As a fellow of St John's College, Cambridge, he rather enjoyed the role of the Council's resident philosopher. In an article published in January 1990 he suggested that part of the reason for his membership and that of Dr Bernice Martin might have been to assist the Council with the conceptual questions which it encountered.

For the third phase of the Council's work, when I was myself Convenor of Group A, Bernice was my opposite number on Group B. A Reader in Sociology at Bedford College, London, she had also been a constructive contributor to the early development of the Council's thinking, but was absent for the academic year 1986/87 when she was in the States. She had a relaxed style and a good wit. Dr Marian Giles Jones, the third Convenor of Group C, had perhaps been appointed to represent unofficially a Welsh interest on the Council in rather the way that I was expected to do in relation to Northern Ireland. Her role changed during her time on CATE: from being initially Senior Mistress and Head of Modern Languages in a school in Gwynedd she became lecturer in Modern Languages in the Department of Education of the University of Wales in Bangor. In the CATE context she took a special interest in language issues.

Another Council member who changed job during the life of CATE, and incidentally also ceased to work in a school, was Peter Scott, a prominent member of the Association for Science Education, who moved from being Head of the City of Leeds School to being a Principal Inspector for Lincolnshire. A similar fate befell Peter Griffin, who had been Headteacher of a Junior School in Cardiff, and when CATE began work was on secondment to serve as President of the NUT; he became an Adviser for South Glamorgan. Neither of the Peters was prevented by these moves from being able to contribute a school's perspective to our discussions, but the only founder member who continued to be a practising teacher throughout the life of CATE was Pat Mullany, and he figured on our membership list not as a primary school teacher but in his capacity as Chairman of Doncaster Education Committee. Though probably the youngest member of CATE, Pat had a serious illness in 1987 which kept him out of action for a few months.

The remaining founder. member of CATE was Dr David Hargreaves, then Chief Inspector for the Inner London Education Authority. However, he resigned so early in the Council's life that our paths never actually crossed in this connection. Thus within about eighteen months CATE had lost three of its original nineteen members and gained only me. In October 1986 we were joined by two further members who were both serving heads, Michael Pipes and Dr David Winkley. Michael was then Headmaster of the City of Portsmouth Boys' School; he was also President of the National Association of Head Teachers, and towards the end of CATE's term he took early retirement from teaching in order to become Managing Director of the NAHT's Trading Company. David was Headteacher of Grove Junior School in the Handsworth district of Birmingham, where there was a very high proportion of children of Asian origin on the role; he was active in establishing a politically independent national centre for action research in primary education. Both Michael and David were men of considerable ability and experience.

Three months later the Secretary of State appointed another local authority representative, who could be seen as a replacement for Councillor Cogan. Alistair Lawton was Deputy Leader of Kent County Council — a senior member of a Conservative county to balance Pat Mullany from a Labour borough. Alistair was a wise and experienced man, but unfortunately, like Pat, he suffered a serious illness, which kept him away for about a year, and his health never fully recovered. In July 1987 the Chairman told Council that he had suggested to the DES the appointment of three additional members to provide an extra person for each Reporting Group. He hoped that these appointments, if agreed, would help to strengthen the representation on the Council of serving classroom teachers, polytechnics, and perhaps women. However, some time elapsed before there were any developments. In November we were told that the Department was still looking for good people who were in sympathy with CATE's work. The minute read that progress was constrained 'by the need to establish that particular individuals would be able to make effective and appropriate contributions to the work of the Council'.

This raises a point which needs to be addressed: to what extent was the membership of CATE packed? Writing in *The Times* in March 1990, a few weeks after our eventual demise, Professor Alec Ross referred to bodies such as CATE consisting of 'officials, hired executives and nominated individuals of the approved persuasion' (Ross, 1990). There is no doubt that the initial misgivings felt by many involved in teacher education about the criteria for accreditation were exacerbated by the fact that they were to be applied by a council with membership, as Professor Edwards of the University of Newcastle has put it, 'which seemed light in knowledge of what was being accredited' (Edwards, 1990) and which was nominated by the Secretary of State. The allegation of relative unfamiliarity with teacher education was certainly true of some members, not least myself, and I suppose it is possible that ministers had some awareness of the general orientation of those who were asked to serve on CATE. There was also a sense, as Andrew Collier once remarked, in which we had all subscribed to the Criteria by agreeing to do so. Nevertheless I have no doubt that several members started out with a degree of scepticism about at least some aspects of the exercise on which we were engaged, and discussion of any point of principle or application threw up a range of attitudes and opinions. Whatever the basis of selection in particular cases, members of CATE were not yes-men or -women, as I hope this account will demonstrate. If we had an ideology in common, it seemed to me to be a strong belief in the importance of teacher education and a commitment to its improvement in the interests of the children in the schools rather than any predetermined view concerning the means by which this should be brought about.

In January 1988 the manpower situation became more pressing as a result of the resignation of Peter Ward, who had taken another job; but by the early summer it began to look as if the Secretary of State had decided against any further appointments. However, in July our number was increased by the appearance of Miss Lesley Abbott and Mrs Anne Cattoor, whose accession to Group A has already been mentioned. Their appointments enhanced not only the representation of those areas to which the Chairman had referred a year earlier, but also our expertise in the education of younger children: for Lesley was Principal Lecturer in Early Years at Manchester Polytechnic, while Anne was Head of Tudor First School in the London Borough of Merton. In spite of the disadvantage of joining our ranks so late, they both picked up the threads of our activity remarkably quickly. Lesley had a quiet and thoughtful approach, yet proved an able advocate for her specialist field; while Anne would come to our meetings straight from her school with a flow of tales from the mouths of her infants, and CATE's kitchen was enlivened by her donations of children's art. As late as November 1988 the third new member came on the scene in the person of Mrs Ann Rees, Vice-Chairman of the National Executive of the Pre-School Playgroup Association and a company director. A final and even more surprisingly late appointment to the Council was made in February 1989, when Julian

Greatrex, a consultant, was appointed; but he was able to play little part in our proceedings.

At the Council meeting in June 1988 we said goodbye to our Secretary, Ernie Grogan. Had CATE existed for only its originally expected duration, his 'terminal secondment' would have given him just time to round our business off, but his retirement now left us with eighteen months still to go. Thus we came under new management with the secondment from her post as Senior Education Officer for Further and Higher Education in East Sussex of Mrs Gillian Murton. To take over as Secretary at this point in the Council's life was no easy assignment, not only because Ernie had been so well liked a colleague, but because of the complexity of our work and the fact that it was now so dependent on an accumulation of case law. It said a great deal for Gillian's ability and dedication that the transition was remarkably smooth, and indeed for Group A, which continued to be serviced by the Council Secretary, there was a noticeable improvement in the manner in which helpful agendas were received in good time and full notes of our meetings produced. Gillian was a tall, strongly built, white-haired woman with a confident manner which enabled her to keep Group A in order with firm good humour. My assumption of the role of Group Convenor occurred just after she came into her CATE post, and our partnership thereafter, at least from my point of view, was both efficient and congenial.

Throughout the Council's life a determining factor in what it could attempt to do was the fact that it had the smallest secretariat with which it could have been expected to operate. Apart from an administrative officer, the Secretary had only two assistants, each of whom acted as secretary to one of the other two Reporting Groups. The first two officers in these roles were John Doe and (joining a little later) Mrs Shirley Bidewell. In 1986 they were succeeded by Stephen Dance and Mrs Valerie Orton; and when Stephen in turn moved on, midway through 1989, Group B was serviced for the last six months by Ms Heather Briant. All these were notably competent and dedicated civil servants.

The other groups of personnel associated with CATE were our assessors from the Inspectorate and from the DES. Full Council meetings were normally attended by the Chief Inspector for teacher education, a post held successively during the life-time of CATE by Mrs Pauline Perry and Alan Marshall. Pauline was plausibly credited with a major role in the genesis of CATE, having had much to do with the production of the HMI paper, *Content of Teacher Education*. She certainly played a notable part in steering our work for CATE's first two years. As the *TES* reported, 'Mrs Perry's diminutive stature contains a considerable amount of energy, intellect and charm' (Spencer, 1986). However, the occasion of this comment was her appointment in the autumn of 1986 to become, at the South Bank, the country's first woman Director of a Polytechnic. By the time her successor joined us our procedures were fairly well established, but Alan Marshall furnished us with helpful and good humoured advice for the remainder of our term. His own background was in CDT, and he was particularly prone to probe proposals for courses in that field. Alan took early retirement from the Inspectorate which coincided with the dissolution of CATE (Mark 1) on the last day of 1989. A number of Staff Inspectors acted as assessors to the Reporting Groups, but as most of them are still in service their anonymity is respected in these pages.

Our representatives from the DES came from the Teachers Supply and Training Branch of the Department, colloquially referred to as 'Branch'. At Council level we were well served successively by three Assistant Secretaries from TST Branch — Mrs Imogen Wilde, David Love and for the final and longest period John Whitaker — who contrived to convey to us the background of current thinking in the Department while at the same time respecting our professional independence. John Whitaker in particular was deeply committed to the success of our endeavours, and gave us much quiet help. More junior members of Branch normally attended Group meetings and served as links with higher places.

Chapter 3

Defining Accreditation

A fundamental aspect of the Council's work which had to be understood and established from the outset was that its responsibility was limited to accreditation, and that this was distinct from the processes of course approval and academic validation, for which responsibility rested elsewhere. This distinction was expounded at the first meeting in an agenda paper which after discussion and refinement became Catenote 1, published in January 1985 and widely circulated. The explanation given there was in summary this.

ADMINISTRATIVE COURSE APPROVAL is agreement — in the case of UDEs by what was then the University Grants Committee, in the case of public sector institutions by the Secretary of State — that a course shall have a share of the intake to initial teacher training, with numbers, age phase, and secondary school subject being specified.

VALIDATION is the process leading to ACADEMIC APPROVAL — agreement by a university authority or by the CNAA as appropriate that a course meets certain standards for the purpose of leading to an academic award.

ACCREDITATION is the process of determining that a course is suitable for the professional preparation of teachers and hence for the award of Qualified Teacher Status (QTS) on its successful completion. This process concludes with 'SCHEDULE 5 APPROVAL' by the Secretary of State.

CATE's job, therefore, was to recommend in the light of the Criteria whether Schedule 5 approval should be given to an ITT course, or, if the course were already running, whether it should be renewed. CATE had no executive responsibility in this process. The Catenote also pointed out that accreditation did not apply to institutions but to courses; where an institution ran several courses these would therefore be considered separately, though normally at the same time.

In spite of this attempt at clarification, confusion about the various kinds of approval was not wholly removed and difficulties arose from time to time concerning the order in which they should be given. To cover the situation where a new course was proposed but CATE was not in a position to review it, perhaps because an HMI report was not available, the Secretary of State could give temporary approval. Otherwise the sequence indicated above was the sensible one, though it was recognised that in practice the processes of validation and accreditation might sometimes need to be pursued at virtually the same time. However, in September 1985 Council decided in connection with one course that no decision on the nature of a recommendation to the Secretary of State should be made until the outcome of its submission for validation was known. This line was upheld in a number of similar instances, members considering that it would place the CNAA in an invidious position if an institution could go along and say in effect, 'CATE thinks this course is all right, so please don't make any difficulties by messing it about now'. Nevertheless, in a natural desire to get institutions off their agenda when they had completed course reviews, Reporting Groups did continue to bring to Council proposals concerning unvalidated courses. The practice came to be that in these circumstances Council would determine the nature of its recommendations but they would not formally be conveyed to the Secretary of State until validation was complete.

We continued virtually until the end of our term to encounter evidence that the distinction between professional accreditation and academic validation was not always clearly grasped. Other kinds of demarcation had to be maintained too. When the Secretary of State decided in the spring of 1987 that two institutions, whose courses we had already begun to review, were to lose their intakes to teacher training, the view was taken that our independence had been preserved by not being consulted on the matter; and shortly afterwards the Chairman told Council that he had declined on our behalf to comment on a report from the UGC/WAB concerning the future of ITT in Wales since the issues which it raised about the roles of institutions were outside our terms of reference.

Grey areas of relevance sometimes arose in our dealings with institutions. On one occasion when Bill Wright was Convenor of Group A he drew attention to a comment in the papers of an institution whose representatives we were about to meet that they did not always find 'A' levels to be an essential prerequisite for success in the relevant subject studies. Tony Becher pointed out that this was not related to the Criteria. 'We can still ask', said Bill. 'Yes', replied Tony, 'and they can still say, "Mind your own business."' Later, when I was Convenor, I sometimes introduced into our discussions with institutions a topic that was not strictly pertinent with the prefatory remark that we did not see this particular issue (for example, education for mutual understanding in Northern Ireland) as being problematic, but that we should be interested to hear a little more about it. Whatever our guests thought on these occasions, I never received the retort imagined by Tony, but even HMI seemed occasionally to forget our proper role. On another occasion Group A was informed that a local Inspector had nothing to add to what we had already been told about a course 'except that the general health of the institution needs close attention'. We had to say that we found this observation neither helpful nor to the point. Our field of competence had clear limits and we had no wish to overstep them.

Chapter 4

Obtaining Information

Circular 3/84 set out certain principles for the Council's operation. It would be expected to draw on all relevant information, and this was in every case to include the findings of HMI visits to the institutions under review. Reports on public sector institutions would be published, and those on UDEs, which HMI would visit by invitation, would be made available to the Council by the Secretary of State. (The provision for invitations by the universities, to which HMI have no right of entry, was of course a nice example, depending upon one's point of view, of scrupulous protocol or creeping centralization: the reality was that without the report which would result from an invitation to inspect there would be no accreditation and in the long run no UDE. No university declined to invite, and a few volunteered to let their reports be published.) In addition the Council would have assessors from the Inspectorate who would make available 'HMI knowledge of teacher training institutions'. At the first meeting of CATE CI Pauline Perry pointed out that HMI reports on individual institutions would reflect the much broader role of the Inspectorate, but would cover particular points that would be relevant to the Council's evaluation of courses.

Although, as noted in chapter 2, the heavy demands which would be entailed by members of CATE themselves visiting institutions were part of the original rationale for breaking the Council into groups, there was at first a division of opinion about visits as part of the accreditation process. Some members feared that the Council's credibility would suffer without them; others doubted both their practicality and their value. Full inspections of teacher training institutions were estimated to require an average of seventy HMI days, and there was a danger that short and less thorough visits by members of CATE might actually be counter-productive. The general view was that the Council should not commit itself at the outset to a rigid policy on visits, though it was at first assumed that it would never without a formal visit contemplate a recommendation that accreditation should be withheld. On the other hand it would be necessary to avoid giving the impression that a visit must imply such an intention.

When the Reporting Groups got down to work thought began to be given to other kinds of information which would be required about the courses to be reviewed and how it should be collected. The Council was on record in its first Catenote as saying that it wished to impose the least possible administrative burden on institutions. It was agreed that in setting a review in motion the Secretary would send to an institution —

A   A covering letter to the Principal.

B   A form requesting basic data about each course being submitted for accreditation — the award to which it led, its length, the age-range at which it was directed, the validating body, and the like. This became known as Cateform 1.

C   A digest of the Criteria to assist institutions in demonstrating that they were all being satisfied.

It was further agreed that the documents available to Reporting Groups in respect of each institution would be as follows.

1   The relevant HMI report.

2   A note prepared by Teachers Branch of critical comments made in the report.

3   A copy of the Secretary's letter to the head of the institution.

4   The institution's response to the HMI report. (In the case of public sector institutions the DES routinely asked the LEA or governing body to state what action was proposed in the light of a report. CATE asked that universities should also be given the opportunity to comment.)

5   Any HMI comments on the institution's response. (In practice these were given verbally, as is described in chapter 6.)

6   A commentary on the institution's response prepared by Teachers Branch. (In practice this rarely if ever materialized.)

7   Criterion-related abstracts from the HMI report prepared by the CATE Secretariat. (These became known as Cateform 2, but were discontinued midway through the Council's term.)

8   The institution's completed version of Cateform 1.

9   Whatever information and material the institution saw fit to present in order to demonstrate that each course satisfied the relevant Criteria.

In March 1985 the Groups met for the first time with all these papers before them, and it was apparent that the material was voluminous. The secretariat was asked to devise a system for indexing it, and this was introduced, but the problem of data overkill, as is described in chapter 5, was never satisfactorily resolved.

It had been agreed to indicate in Catenote 1 that where information available to the Council from an institution or otherwise was sufficient for its purposes neither a meeting nor a visit would always be necessary; and when the Reporting Groups looked at papers from the first set of institutions their preliminary conclusion was that in one or two cases this was the position. However, in July 1985 the Chairman reported to Council receipt of an objection from one of them. The Council's decision in respect of the University of Newcastle had been to declare a readiness to recommend approval of their PGCE courses in a year's time subject to certain conditions being fulfilled. Part of the University's complaint now was that it had neither been visited nor invited to send representatives to a meeting. Council's reaction was to reaffirm that it was not its policy to convene a meeting with every institution at the time of the first review of its courses. Thereafter, however, a meeting with representatives of every institution became standard practice. Group A once considered breaking with this rule; we had been allocated Cambridge UDE and the HMI report was so laudatory that there appeared to be few points for us to raise. However, we decided that if an exception was to be made it ought not to be this one lest we appeared to be assuming that an ancient seat of learning must be all right.

While meetings with institutional representatives became automatic, visits remained unusual. When the first of the Northern Ireland institutions came on stream the other members of Group A came over and we briefly went round them all to introduce ourselves and gain some sense of the circumstances in which they were working. This, however, was rather a special case, and it was the only visit that Group A made; the other Groups may have made at most two or three each, and always when there was some good reason for doing so. The only other occasion when Council discussed the question in principle was in October 1987. We had received some negative feedback from a local committee which considered our practice of summoning institutions to Elizabeth House to be a bureaucratic procedure. The Chairman remarked that he thought nevertheless there was now a better understanding of the difference between CATE, with its tiny secretariat, and the CNAA, with all the manpower and resource which it had at its command. It appeared that we were about to move on to the next item on the agenda when CI Alan Marshall asked if we were not prepared to consider the point about visiting institutions rather than always having them come to us. While pointing out that occasional visits had been made, several members drew attention to the impossible amount of time that would be required of us if visits were to become a regular part of our proceedings, and Ernie Grogan observed that members were not inspectors. However, Alan did not let the matter drop; he said he was surprised by the reaction he had received, adding how important he had found it during his ten months in his present role to get a feel for context, and how he had been struck by the tremendous diversity among institutions. His point was understood, but some members saw it as actually easier to maintain a professional relationship if we did not make personal visits, and Bill Wright reiterated the argument that our credibility would suffer if we spent half a day in an institution and then pretended to know all about it. There was also the risk of criticism from institutions whose courses we had reviewed without visits if we changed our procedure at that stage. Existing practice was endorsed, and the issue did not surface again.

Chapter 5

The Reporting Groups in Action

When papers were sent from CATE to nine institutions in January 1985 it was intended that the latter should constitute the first of a series of 'rounds', of which there might be three in a year, each comprising up to five institutions per group. In the event, however, this tidy system was soon modified in favour of a more flexible rolling programme. For the first year or two our dependence on HMI reports resulted in some delay, caused not so much by manpower problems in the Inspectorate as by printing hold-ups in HMSO. When a report had become available, and the Secretary had obtained the other necessary documents, the institution would be allocated to one of the three Reporting Groups. This was done mainly in the light of the Groups' relative workloads at the time, though Group A dealt with all the Northern Ireland submissions, and Group C, of which Marian Giles Jones was a member, with the Welsh ones except for that of which she herself joined the staff; obviously no Group reviewed the courses of an institution with which any of its members had a close association. The distribution which eventuated from this process is shown in appendix 3.

Examination of the paperwork concerning any institution might well figure more than once on the agenda of the relevant Group before members felt ready to arrange through the secretariat to meet with its representatives. Though scrutiny of the written submissions in relation to each of the Criteria was bound to be a fairly complex exercise, it has to be said that it was made more difficult by the mass of material which many institutions submitted, often leaving us to do most of the work of digging out the relevant information from numerous parts of documents which might well have been written for other purposes, such as course handbooks or validation papers. Group A reported an early and flagrant example of this, and Council endorsed the Group's intention to identify as far as was possible from available data any further information required and then to ask the university concerned not only to provide this but to present the original material again in a criterion-related format; the secretariat undertook to make even clearer to institutions in future that this was what was required for all courses.

Nevertheless, pleas for more terse and specific responses continued to be made. Until the Council's last eighteen months all members were sent the papers for every institution (thereafter it was agreed that unless by request we should each receive only those for our own Group), and of course members of CATE had to prepare for meetings in their own time. Renford Bambrough was clearly not speaking only for himself when he once declared it quite unreasonable that members should have to wade through mountains of paper in order to sift out the 10 per cent that was relevant. Peter Scott called it saturation bombing. Even after four years of CATE activity the problem persisted, and I recall pointing out that one college's submission to Group A equated to a medium-length novel; Tony Becher observed that it was as if the authors had taken the headings of the Criteria as triggers for pieces of extended writing. On another occasion, when we had before us a particularly diffuse and badly organized submission from a large and prestigious university, Gillian Murton wondered aloud if part of the problem was that no one in the institution really had an overview of the course.

The Council itself met on about eight occasions each year, and normally the Groups would meet twice between meetings of Council. Groups also met for an hour or so on the morning of Council meeting days, but this was to tidy up the proposals they would be making later and deal with minor items of business; there was never enough time then to meet a delegation. Since it was not always easy within this schedule to find mutually convenient dates for meetings with institutions, enforced delay could make our task more complex. A Group would typically be at various stages of review with up to half a dozen institutions at any particular time. After a day in London we each became reimmersed in our normal work, and it was not easy to keep the details of every submission fresh and distinct in one's mind. At times, to be honest, there was an element of repetition in our discussions, especially since those attending consecutive meetings were unlikely to be exactly the same set of Group members.

As one means of easing these problems Groups developed a degree of specialization among their members, with one person taking a lead on student selection, another on staff development, and so forth. At least one Group applied this technique to the scrutiny of the papers. All, I think, did so in preparing for meetings with institutional representatives, so that the Convenor could pass the questioning from one member to another as we moved through the areas for discussion; the secretariat would have notified the institution of these in advance. However, this approach had its limitations; it was seldom that all Group members were present for any particular meeting, and it often happened that someone who had expected to be there and had been assigned a role in discussion was

prevented at the last moment from attending, so that his area of questioning had to be taken over by somebody else. The Convenor in particular
had to be ready to step into any breach.

Meetings with institutions did not occur on every Group day — not
infrequently we would spend all our time discussing documents —
though occasionally we would meet one institution in the morning and
another in the afternoon, which was heavy going. A typical day's business started at 10.30 am with paperwork for several institutions taking us
through to a light lunch; after lunch we would hold a meeting, for which
we had made final preparations during the morning, with representatives
from one institution. It was unusual for fewer than four such representatives to turn up, and twice that number was not unknown, so that the
CATE members were often outnumbered by the visitors. It was understandable that institutions should wish to come armed with all the expertise they might need in order to deal with our enquiries, but since several
people often wanted to contribute to the response to a question we tended
to get rather more detail than we needed, and meetings usually lasted for
a couple of hours. If possible, before we dispersed around 4.00 pm, we
would exchange impressions about the interview we had just conducted.
It would often happen that we would have agreed with our visitors at the
end of the meeting that it would be helpful for them to follow up with
some supplementary information in writing — perhaps on an issue about
which they had not brought with them all the detail we required, or on
one that needed further reflection. This could result in another bombard-
ment of paper, and sometimes several written exchanges and discussions
in Group were called for before members felt ready to make their proposals to Council.

At every Council meeting a major part of the business was the
presentation by each of the three Group Convenors of proposals from
their respective Groups. Since proposals had often been finalized only at
the short Group meeting immediately preceding Council it was common
for some of them to be tabled, but the principle was established that no
proposal should be entertained unless the relevant institution had been
named in the agenda. This was to ensure that members not in the
proposing Group had an opportunity to scan the papers in advance. I
doubt very much whether any of us had time to do this on a regular
basis, but the procedure was designed to help make a reality of the
convention that recommendations were made to the Secretary of State in
the name of the Council as a whole. In practice the onus was on the
Convenors in introducing their proposals to draw attention to any unusual features of a course, aspects with which they had had difficulty or
points of principle or interpretation about which a general Council view
appeared to be required. When the Convenor had completed this introduction the Chairman would first invite supplementary comment from
other members of the proposing Group and then ask for questions or

comments from other members of Council, or indeed from the Council assessors. Occasionally a straightforward proposal would be accepted without discussion. Often, however, the ensuing debate was both lengthy and detailed; it was an additional burden on the Convenors that they never knew what unforeseen point would be picked up by somebody or recognized as relevant to another Group's current preoccupations. Sometimes the outcome was an agreement by the originating Group to take a proposal back for second thoughts or further enquiry. In any case there was no doubt that members tried hard by these means to ensure that the Groups were applying a consistent approach, and that there was an agreed CATE policy towards all contentious issues.

Yet in spite of these conscious efforts problems did arise. At the Council meeting in March 1986 Derek Mortimer reported having heard from two sources that one of the Groups was now regarded in the system as a soft touch. CI Pauline Perry said she had heard that too. Discussion ensued as to how this piece of folklore might have arisen. A possible explanation was that by chance one Group had dealt with a larger number of secondary PGCEs than the others, for already it had become apparent that these were on the whole the more straightforward type of course: most of the major problems were arising with primary BEds. However, the more important question was how to prevent the appearance or reality that there actually were differences of standard or approach among the Groups. A possible step would be for the membership to be reshuffled, but the consensus was against this, for the Groups were now felt to be coherent and learning to work together. Other suggestions were for regular meetings of the Group Convenors to explore issues of common interest and for occasional attendance by members as observers at meetings of Groups other than their own. In practice, however, the former of these things rarely and the latter scarcely ever happened — we simply did not have enough time. The idea which seemed most promising was that the position of Group Convenor should change hands periodically, and as indicated in chapter 2 there were two such general rotations, made after consultation by the Chairman, in the autumn of 1986 and again in the early autumn of 1988.

Nevertheless, anxieties still occasionally surfaced. At a meeting of Group A in the spring of 1987 David Shadbolt was distinctly grumpy because the institution of which he was Principal was getting a rough ride from Group B on staff development, and he felt that the Council was not being consistent. Ernie Grogan conceded that there were differences among the Groups in the areas on which they concentrated, and Group B was particularly hard-line on this issue. Someone surmized that this might be because it included several teachers. Differing emphases among the Reporting Groups were mentioned again at a Group A meeting a year later; Group B was still said to be strong on staff development and Group C on subject studies. Ernie reported, with evident disapproval, that

Group C regularly called for validation documents. Prompted by Bill Wright, the Chairman raised the issue at Council and the alleged pre-occupations of Groups B and C were mentioned, rather, as it seemed to me, to the surprise of the members of these two Groups. However, everyone took seriously the question of the messages being received by the system if different standards were indeed being applied. Members agreed that for the most part we did not know what went on in other Groups. Similar points were made in discussion as on the last occasion: reshuffling Group membership might help, but for personal and practical reasons a majority was clearly against it. Renford Bambrough rounded off the debate by declaring in mock magisterial style, 'It is not necessary that it should happen; therefore it is necessary that it should not happen.'

The general issue was not discussed again, and the composition of the Groups changed only through the addition of one or two new members. But right up to the end of CATE's life, and indeed especially in its last year or so, questions would be raised at Council, either at the instigation of a Group or as a result of members commenting on other Groups' proposals, where it was apparent that divergencies were appearing and a common line was needed. Notable examples were what constituted acceptable forms of renewed classroom experience for tutors, how serving teachers needed to be represented in student selection, how much contact time should be expected within the minimum period of study of language and mathematics teaching, how courses with an unusually high level of 'exceptional entry' should be monitored, our approach to particular subjects of study, and requirements for new types of course in areas of teacher shortage. These are referred to in greater detail in the appropriate chapters.

Chapter 6

HMI in Action

I have said something in chapters 2 and 4 about CATE's formal relationship with the Inspectorate, and in particular about the status of HMI reports as prerequisites of institutional review. It was also agreed at the outset that whenever possible HMI would attend the meetings of the Reporting Groups as assessors. The exception was any occasion when we met with representatives of an institution. The deliberate absence of HMI from these encounters was intended to reflect and emphasize our mutual independence.

The reality, however, was rather more complex. One of the first institutions to be reviewed was Birmingham Polytechnic, and in September 1985 Group A presented to Council a clutch of proposals concerning its courses which was duly accepted. Two of these were for positive recommendations in respect of the primary and secondary PGCEs. However, when Group A met in January 1986 we received a note to inform us that the Department had been considering independently of the Council what its own action should be on the LEA/Polytechnic's response to the HMI report. In this connection the Department had obtained the advice of the Inspectorate, which was understood to include serious reservations about certain aspects of the primary PGCE. The Primary SI with ITT responsibility appeared along with our usual HMI Assessor to explain these reservations, and it was put to us that in the light of what he had to say we might wish to reconsider our original conclusions about the course. The nature of the reservations and the action subsequently taken upon them are described in chapter 15, but this incident was an early indication of the influence of the Inspectorate on CATE's proceedings, and indeed of its dependence on the HMI perception of what was actually happening on the ground. In this instance the Group was given to understand that it had been misled by a skilful presentation. Had it not been for the fact that the Council's recommendation to the Secretary of State had not yet been formally communicated to the Polytechnic the episode would have been even more embarrassing.

A somewhat similar incident occurred some three months later when Group A met on the morning of the April 1986 Council. It had been our intention to put a positive proposal to Council about all the courses at Portsmouth Polytechnic, but the SI now reported reservations which derived in part from CNAA minutes. This of course raised an issue of principle: were these admissible evidence to bring before CATE? We had been at pains to assert that accreditation was a different exercise from validation. But HMI were assessors to the CNAA as they were to CATE, and CATE was heavily reliant on the guidance given by the Inspectorate. The Chairman, who was attending the Group meeting for this important question, illustrated the difference between the familiarity with the work of an institution which was available to the Inspectorate and that which members of CATE could possibly achieve by referring to the number of man days which was devoted to a full inspection. Clearly there had to be some mechanism for updating HMI judgments in order to avoid situations like this and the one which had arisen at Birmingham Polytechnic. It might be said that taking more up-to-date information into account was like accepting new evidence after the trial — no doubt an unfortunate analogy, the Chairman accepted; but CATE was now embarking on second phase reviews (see chapter 7) in which it had to be concerned with the effectiveness of institutions' responses to conditions required of them as opposed to simply being satisfied, as with earlier cases, that they were doing at least something about the Criteria. If HMI were to issue formal updating reports, with a requirement to publish and a right granted to institutions to make a considered response, this would create a problem for CATE because of the subsequent delay. It seemed better to establish that when a Reporting Group began to consider an institution's submission this should be a signal to HMI to provide the Group with any updating information or new factors such as CNAA judgments. This kind of HMI input should be in the form of a commentary on an institution's response, particularly with regard to new or revised courses, and would therefore be more closely related to the Criteria than the original inspection report.

With regard to the submission now before us it was agreed to withdraw our proposal in respect of the primary BEd course. When this was explained to Council later in the day CI Mrs Perry stated that at first HMI had deliberately made no further input into CATE discussions after the initial inspection report since they were concerned to maintain our independence; they did not wish to appear to be implying, 'We know things that you don't.' But in the case of the two polytechnics with which Group A had been dealing they had become concerned about the way the discussion was going because of slightly distorted information from the institutions. The one now before us had put on a good performance and persuaded the Group. Some reservations were expressed by members about using validating information in this way, since it was confidential as between the institution and the CNAA. Andrew Collier argued, however, that it was perfectly proper for HMI to suggest a line of questioning which a Group might pursue, since it would still be CATE which was making the judgment. The Chairman, in summing up, adopted a metaphor from assessing restaurants in the good food guides: the chef might have changed. Pauline Perry said HMI would welcome an opportunity for making an input to Reporting Groups' work subsequent to the inspection report. (Speaking at the local committees conference in December 1986, Pauline said that she herself had at first been reluctant to accept the updating role on the purist view that nothing should be said about an institution behind closed doors which was not on the record. She had been overruled, but the compromise was that institutions were told if updating was being provided.).

From this time onwards it became standard practice, at least in Group A, that when we began consideration of the paperwork for any institution we would turn first to our assessor from the Inspectorate, who would have been alerted to our business in advance by the secretariat, and ask for his or her guidance: indeed successive Convenors became rather irritated if such a contribution was not available when it was needed. At the local committee conference already mentioned Pauline Perry explained the function of HMI at Reporting Group meetings as being to interpret 'HMI-speak'; the guidance provided would normally take the form of a gloss on the initial report, drawing attention to key issues, commenting on the institution's own submission, especially any aspects which were deemed to require probing, and drawing on any recent observations from the local Inspector about how things were moving and about any new developments. A nice example of the specific interpretation of HMI-speak was provided for Group A when we were giving preliminary consideration to an institution about which the Inspectors' report referred thus to an unusual feature:

> This is a potentially valuable component but its purpose is not yet fully understood by all tutors and interpretations of the course outline vary considerably.

'In other words', said our SI, 'they don't know what they're doing.' Updating in general was the more desirable because especially during the earlier part of our term it was common for the printed HMI report which we had before us to be based on a visit made two or three years previously. A supplementary verbal report was always helpful, therefore, and the assessor was often present at subsequent discussions to answer questions or express a view on our conclusions as we gradually moved towards them. There was a desire on all sides to avoid a repetition of the early *contretemps*, though, as the sequel will show, this was not always achieved.

The flavour of some HMI involvement in our work may be conveyed by illustration (obviously I can speak only for what I myself observed). A month after the second polytechnic episode which has just been described Group A was due to meet representatives of Bishop Grosseteste College. Prior to the meeting we were going through the paperwork, which included a supportive letter from the Bishop of Lincoln in his capacity as Chairman of the College Governors. The SI asked us how we reacted to the third paragraph of this letter. It was evident that none of us had seen anything particularly significant in this episcopal communication. When we looked at the passage to which our attention was drawn it referred to the Governors' belief that continuous review was more effective than 'any more simplistic appraisal of, for example, the proportion of time given to subject study and school based study'. It appeared that in the mind of the SI this sentiment was attributable to the influence of the College's 'strong-minded' Principal, who was on record as being philosophically opposed to the subject studies criterion. She also asked us if we thought the Council would be taking an interest in how the local committees were working. Again it seemed that no one at first quite saw her drift, but she went on to observe that three of the committees had now 'defied' CATE — Middlesex and Kingston Polytechnics, and now Bishop Grossetseste (though this was not strictly true, even allowing for a degree of overstatement in the use of the verb 'defy', since the Bishop was writing on behalf of the Governors). The University of Sussex was also mentioned as being in the opposition camp.

At the end of May 1986 a Council meeting coincided with publication of a report in the journal *Education* of attacks made on CATE at an educational meeting. This was referred to in conversation at the end of Group A's preliminary meeting. 'Well', said Tony Becher smilingly, 'you don't *have* to agree with the Criteria — you *can* be rude about them'. 'No', said our SI blandly, in apparent agreement; 'if you don't like them you can get out of teacher training'. In July of that year Group A was due to meet representatives of Sheffield UDE. We were running through the points to be raised with them when the SI drew our attention to the fact that they organized their 36-week PGCE course in three terms of 14, 14, and 8 weeks respectively. This, she observed portentously, was an 'odd' arrangement which she thought we might investigate. When she withdrew shortly afterwards, David Shadbolt pointedly waited until the door had closed and declared that he was not going to stand for this kind of nit-picking, though he knew why she was doing it (protecting herself, he thought, from above). Tony Becher said he would resign if we had to ask questions like that. The question, however, was raised during our subsequent meeting, and received a satisfactory answer.

In the light of these incidents it seemed a little ironic that a few days later, when Group A was meeting prior to the July 1986 Council, the same SI expressed a worry about the extent to which HMI were getting drawn into the Council's work. What prompted this remark was that during our interview in the previous week with representatives from Kingston Polytechnic David Shadbolt had suggested that a paper urgently required for this day's Council should be sent to the SI. That had apparently led to the Dean of the Faculty of Education ringing her up and saying he understood she had the final yea or nay about their submission. She had been at pains to disabuse him. We agreed that in future we should avoid such misunderstandings by asking for all papers to be sent to the secretariat. Nevertheless, Peter Ward observed to me that day that he had noticed an 'evolution' in the relationship of the Council to the Inspectorate. I took a later opportunity to ask him what he meant by this. He said he thought the Inspectorate were using us as a front!

A barbed observation reported by Patricia Santinelli of the THES in the following month indicated a view of the situation from one on the receiving side. 'CATE is relying heavily on inspectorate reports', she wrote, 'and in return HMI is examining or has examined courses with CATE criteria in mind. Their joint effect on institutions was described by one head of department as sitting on an iceberg waiting to be rescued by the Titanic' (Santinelli, 1986). The local committee conference in December 1986 also provided an opportunity for the expression of views from the field. Leonard Marsh, the 'strong-minded' Principal of Bishop Grosseteste College, said he thought it regrettable that HMI, because of CATE, were now looking at courses as an arithmetical exercise; it was very unfortunate to find experienced professionals with a hidden calculator in their pockets. Professor Maurice Galton of Leicester UDE felt that some HMI had too narrow a vision, confined to their own subject, and that dialogue with them was limited because they seemed worried that they might be quoted to CATE.

The situation was such a sensitive one that tensions between the Inspectorate and Reporting Groups were bound to surface from time to time. HMI (and DES) intervention in the case of Kingston Polytechnic is described in chapter 14. In January 1988 reference was made in full Council to the difficulties which had arisen for Group A over a proposed addition to Bath UDE's concurrent degree in design and technology and which are described more fully in chapter 16. The Chairman said he would consider with Branch and with HMI the procedures for HMI input between initial consideration of a course and a recommendation on it being sent to the Secretary of State. CI Alan Marshall had three points to offer there and then. (i) HMI evidence was not the only evidence available to CATE; (ii) it did not necessarily relate to things as they were at the time of review, nor was it necessarily consistent with other evidence; and (iii) while HMI were happy to provide evidence asked for by Reporting Groups, they were not an arm of the Reporting Groups. The Chairman pointed out that if a second HMI report on an institution was adverse there was no obligation on CATE to review the course or courses again:

this had implications for arrangements after CATE. At the time, it may be added, this dispassionate discussion of the principles involved scarcely did justice to Group A's feelings about the position in which we had been placed.

At the second conference for local committees, in May 1988, CI Alan Marshall referred to the schizophrenia from which HMI suffered since their role was both to give advice and to make an independent evaluation of work on the ground. He listed the various stages of HMI involvement in the process of course development. First, they were called upon to advise on the provisional allocation of numbers to institutions. They were sometimes consulted by institutions — and would like this to happen more often — about course design, though they had no part in the process of course approval. At the stage of course validation their views were invited by the CNAA (though not by the universities). At local committee level local Inspectors normally attended as assessors and he was anxious for them to be fully involved. HMI were now advising the DES when there was an application for temporary approval of a course. HMI inspected courses, as of right or by invitation. In the accreditation process their role was strictly advisory to CATE; but acceptance of CATE recommendations was not automatic, and here again HMI advised Branch, which advised the Secretary of State. At the Council's special meeting in February 1989, described in chapter 30, Alan explained that now that the initial round of inspections of all the ITT institutions in England, Wales and Northern Ireland was complete HMI had embarked on a new round of inspection of certain aspects of ITT — currently, for example, preparation for primary teaching. HMI would of course need to make a formal visit of the original kind if new institutions wished to start ITT courses, but this was not very likely in present circumstances. The Inspectorate would therefore be concentrating on the production of summary reports on a variety of issues.

For the Council meeting in July 1989 he produced a paper on HMI and CATE which covered much the same ground as his remarks to the local committees conference. It was not clear why this statement was given to us when we had only about five months to run, except perhaps that arrangements for our successor body were then being carefully considered. The paper drew attention again to the different modes in which HMI worked — as advisers (to the providers of ITT, to local committees, to CATE Reporting Groups, to CATE itself, and to the DES) and as evaluators. Introducing the paper at the meeting, Alan referred to it as an account of the Janus-like Inspectorate, acknowledging that some might prefer the description 'two-faced'. The paper explained the role of local or link HMI in advising institutions about course proposals — an 'honest broker' — though at a later stage HMI would be required to make evaluative judgments. The Chairman drew attention to one paragraph which touched on the familiar problem of updating information: HMI would make available to groups such information as they derived from non-reporting visits or further scrutiny of documentary evidence. 'If such evidence is offered to CATE by HMI, or requested, the main principle which operates is that the institution shall know whenever possible of that advice. There is no "secret" advice to CATE.' Bernice Martin said she was a little worried by this passage. Did it mean that everything an HMI Assessor said to a Group in private he or she had already told the institution? And why 'whenever possible'? Alan replied that if an Inspector were asked a question by a Group he couldn't run off and phone the institution to tell them what he was going to say before he said it; but in principle this was the rule they worked to. The Chairman observed that there were still some sensitivities in the situation, but it was a miracle that the relationship had worked so well.

This was the last occasion on which it was discussed in general terms. Alan Marshall's paper had concluded:

> HMI attaches great importance to its work in support of Council. The relationship of HMI to CATE, at all levels, is that of professional adviser. That task is a useful offshoot to HMI's main duty, namely: providing professional advice to the Secretary of State and DES. HMI seeks to be as helpful as possible, but not to be intrusive. CATE may well call for more advice than HMI is in a position to offer. That inability might come, if at all, from a clear need to respond to other priorities and in consequence to have to limit the time spent on ITT.

Nothing I observed in my years on CATE suggested that this was not an accurate statement of principle and intent. On the great majority of occasions when we looked for it the guidance we received was genuinely helpful — not least, in Group A, from the Northern Ireland Inspectorate. But even HMI are human, and I have perhaps said enough in this chapter and in various references in my later account of the application of the Criteria to show that at times the line between advice and intrusion became a little blurred.

Chapter 7

Outcomes of Course Reviews

A discussion paper prepared for the Council's first meeting raised the question of possible forms of accreditation. It accepted that in the first phase of CATE's operations it was unlikely that every course reviewed would be able to satisfy all the Criteria fully. The Council might therefore wish to consider the possibility of accreditation conditional upon further satisfactory progress being made in respect of specified Criteria — this might be for a time limit of two years, and would be appropriate only where the Council was satisfied that the institution concerned was genuinely committed to rapid progress in the necessary direction. Where, on the other hand, the Council was not prepared to give a particular course accreditation in any form the institution would need to be told that accreditation was being withheld subject to a review of the position in, say, a year's time; if that review in turn failed to provide satisfactory evidence of improvement the Council might then make a formal recommendation to the Secretary of State for the withdrawal of approval from the course. This was essentially the formulation which was embodied in Catenote 1. When the Council had completed consideration of a course the recommendation being made to the Secretary of State would be formally notified to the institution.

By April 1985 the first Group proposals were before Council and several of these took the conditional form envisaged in the Catenote. The Council's assessors pointed out, however, that if a course had received Schedule 5 approval this would continue to apply until it was formally withdrawn or renewed, and the Secretary of State had no power to give conditional approval. It would therefore be necessary in these cases for the Council itself to inform institutions of its readiness in principle to recommend Schedule 5 approval subject to the requisite progress being made; and in accepting the need for this procedure the Council recognized that it would also have to indicate to institutions the nature of the progress required. In the same way, when the Council was unable to signal its provisional readiness to make a recommendation for Schedule 5 approval, but was nevertheless prepared to reconsider the whole course after a specified period, it would be necessary for the institution to be informed directly with full reasons for the Council's concern. Thus recommendations made formally to the Secretary of State would only be for either confirmation or withdrawal of Schedule 5 approval, and in these cases reasons for the recommendation would also be given to institutions in consultation with the Reporting Group Convenors. The assessors for their part undertook that the Department would be as flexible as possible in deciding whether revisions to a course called for reconsideration of an existing Schedule 5 approval so as not to inhibit improvements made in relation to the Criteria.

At the following meeting there was further discussion of the form in which proposals should be formally approved by the Council. It was agreed that in the interests of consistency they should be presented as far as possible in standardized terms which were consistent with the wording of the Criteria: it was important that the Council should not appear to be imposing conditions not explicitly justified by Circular 3/84. Letters from the secretariat to the institutions could, however, be couched in less formal terms and could offer guidance as to how the conditions might be met. The outcome of the former decision was that conditional proposals were normally worded as follows:

> That subject to certain conditions being met within one year, the Council will then be prepared to recommend to the Secretary of State the renewal of the Schedule 5 approval of this course/these courses. The conditions are that substantial further progress is made towards:

— and the conditions followed as a series of numbered points.

As early in the Council's life as December 1985 the Chairman reported that increasingly institutions were requesting advice about their courses in advance of a CATE review; this trend seemed likely to continue. It was agreed that the limited resources available to the Council would normally make it impossible to meet such requests. The feeling was that institutions seeking this kind of informal advice should be invited to consult HMI, though it would be important to warn them that views expressed by members of the Inspectorate could not prejudge those of the Council. Like other procedural questions this one tended to recur, and it did so next in October 1986 in the context of rather unfriendly comments made about CATE by the Select Committee of the House of Commons. Renford Bambrough suggested that one strand of criticism on the part of institutions arose from our unwillingness to offer advice in advance of submissions. The Chairman said he had thought of asking for a professional secondment from the DES of someone who might undertake this role with a degree of independence. This was discussed at some length. One of the more incisive contributions came from the Inspector Assessor from Northern Ireland, who argued that it would create an invidious situation if courses ostensibly based on 'our' advice were then not approved. This seemed to be the general view, and the Chairman dropped the idea.

In April 1987 there was a report to Council from several members who had recently attended a SCOP conference on CATE and the accreditation of teacher education. Mary Hallaway said she had undertaken to pass one point on to us because it had been made so strongly; this was that people whose courses had not yet been 'Cated' felt a considerable deprivation in not being able to discuss the issues in advance. They understood our problems in this regard but the feeling was still there. The Chairman pointed out that people did phone the Secretary informally and he reminded us of our earlier agreement to refer institutions for guidance to their local HMI, even though it was accepted that Inspectors' knowledge of CATE's requirements varied. CI Alan Marshall undertook to come back to Council about this after consulting colleagues. There was a worry that if prior advice were permitted it would become general practice and if Council members made written comments to institutions they would be quoted back to us. In July Council was told that an internal memorandum to HMI on ways of giving further assistance to colleges was in preparation. Thus matters were left until the end of CATE's life. From the Council's point of view the reasons for the stance which it took seemed compelling; yet it was understandable that it should look to the field like the deliberate rejection of a more positive and interactive role in favour of remaining an examining body.

The point had arisen in a slightly different form in April 1986 when the secretariat brought a paper to Council arising from the fact that the Reporting Groups were by that time beginning 'second reviews' — beginning, that is to say, to look at revised submissions in respect of courses to which they had earlier given only conditional approval. The Chairman suggested that we must now be clear whether our role was to say 'yes' and 'no' or to be engaged in a continuous process of educational influence. He suggested that our terms of reference obliged us to be nearer to the yes/no end of the continuum. The initial round of courses considered had led to one of four outcomes:

(i)   yes;

(ii)   yes if (certain conditions were met);

(iii)   no but (come back in a year's time);

(iv)   no.

Now as we embarked on the second reviews it had to be recognized that Groups would have to operate flexibly — for example, conclusions might occasionally need to be further postponed while course development continued; nevertheless we must be prepared to move closer to (i) or (iv). In other words, if in our professional judgment the decision should be 'no' we ought to be ready to act accordingly. The DES Assessor added that the Secretary of State would prefer a hard line where possible.

In July 1986 the Chairman returned to the theme by suggesting that the Council might in practice find a recommendation to withhold or withdraw approval difficult to make; he wondered whether it would be possible to have a fifth form of outcome. I suggested that a softer option which was not inconsistent with anything CATE had already said could be found by employing another phrase from Catenote 1, namely that the Council was 'unable to recommend either full or conditional approval'. The Chairman said that this was the form of words which he had in mind. Derek Mortimer saw no point in raising this now as the issue was hypothetical; the Chairman suggested that we leave the matter for the time being but note that a fifth outcome was possible. The reason for these discussions seemed a little puzzling unless on the assumption that Branch believed one or two courses ought to be closed and was afraid that when it came to the crunch we should duck it. In practice, as the sequel will show, Council did on a number of occasions face up to not making even a conditionally positive recommendation, though usually expressed as making no recommendation rather than an explicitly negative one.

Another issue of principle arose in January 1987 when Derek Mortimer brought forward on behalf of Group B proposals in respect of a CHE. These included positive recommendations for their BEd courses, but the Group wished to add riders to the approvals in which, while tactfully commending certain aspects of the institution's work, the Council would convey that it hoped for further improvement in others. This led to lengthy discussion, first about wording. Michael Dixon thought that 'hoped' was rather weak. Someone suggested 'urged', but Derek thought that that was too urgent. We settled in the end for 'wishes to encourage the College...' But the wider question was whether we should be making this kind of addendum at all. Mary Hallaway said she had always thought in terms of a pass/fail model (though, she might have added, one in which resits were permitted). And if, as Derek had said, 'would wish' was too strong an expression, why, asked the Chairman, say anything at all? Derek thought that 'attitudinally' the institution needed reinforcment. 'Keep it up', suggested the Chairman; just so. But some members felt that the laudatory part of the proposed comments, to which Derek had referred as 'gold stars', were also dangerous and inappropriate. The Chairman as usual was concerned about the messages which would go out to the system. On the other hand it was suggested that all we were doing was to give the Secretary guidance about what he might convey to the institution.

The Chairman remarked that the Council had never sought to approve the actual text of letters which went to institutions, and that this was useful as it meant that if necessary we could distance ourselves slightly from the Secretary's wording. The discussion fizzled out somewhat inconclusively with the Chairman observing wryly that new members would see that our recommendations were subject to textual exegesis normally reserved for writing of greater literary merit — or rather, perhaps, since Ernie Grogan pretended to be offended by this aspersion on his labours, to 'works' of greater literary merit. But the minute recorded that the Council had:

> considered the extent to which formal notifications to institutions of Council decisions should also contain additional comments which were not formal conditions of approval. The distinction was drawn between aspects of courses which barely met the Criteria (for the mention of which there was abundant precedent) and aspects which were considered to represent especially good practice (which had not hitherto been the subject of comment). It was agreed that although the Council might wish to return to this question, the present practice should be continued in appropriate cases.

The question was not in fact addressed again in exactly this form, though the issue of good practice came in for extensive discussion, as is recorded in chapter 29. 'Reinforcing' comments continued occasionally to be made in letters from the secretariat at the instigation of a Group. These were not necessarily recorded in Council minutes, but Group Convenors, in introducing proposals to which a rider was to be added, would normally inform Council of what was intended.

A further procedural aspect of the outcome of course reviews arose once or twice when an institution asked that our deliberate omission of a particular subject strand from a positive recommendation should be reconsidered. There was no provision in our procedures for appeals, and Council therefore felt a little uneasy about entertaining them. In practice the appropriate Reporting Group would reassure itself that its original proposal had been well founded and consistent and would seek confirmation of this view from Council; but latterly we decided to advise institutions to address any further appeal to the Secretary of State, whose role it was to make the decisions. In only one instance that I can recall (see chapter 13) did Council consciously change its mind about a recommendation, and that was at the instigation of HMI after some reconstruction of the course.

A final point concerning outcomes was whether there should be some time-limit for accreditation. The discussion paper prepared for the Council's first meeting suggested that five years might be appropriate, perhaps with course reports within that period and automatic review at the end. This was discussed at some length. There was general agreement that there must be a limit; but while some members felt that five years might be too long (the Criteria themselves might have been amended before then), there was a counter-argument that in the interests of continuity and stability institutions should not be required to seek re-accreditation after too short an interval. Questions also arose about review or reporting arrangements. Pauline Perry drew attention to the dangers of applying too heavy a hand to courses after they were accredited; institutions should not be made to feel that CATE was perpetually hovering over their shoulders. The formulation eventually adopted on this point in Catenote 1 was that after the Council had made a positive recommendation it might at any time decide to undertake a further review of the course.

> It is not intended that this should occur during the three to four years of the Council's existing remit unless significant changes are proposed relevant to the Criteria...The recommendation will be on the understanding that any such changes which may be proposed are reported to Council by the institution. (CATE, 1985a)

As Mary Hallaway once observed, it was a matter of 'Scout's honour'. Sometimes, of course, an institution would conscientiously report changes which were really very minor. In April 1989, when we were trying to speed our work up in anticipation of our demise, Council agreed that Reporting Groups should use their discretion in deciding whether to refer such changes to the Council for transmission to the Secretary of State.

As time passed, we became increasingly conscious that we had no continuing contact with courses for which the review had been completed early. In May 1988 the Chairman commented to a meeting convened with a number of other bodies that CATE had no mechanism for keeping an eye on courses after they had received the Secretary of State's approval; he thought this was an issue that might have to be addressed when arrangements beyond the Council's current term were being considered. CI Alan Marshall remarked that HMI certainly could not embark on another massive round of all the institutions in the country — a follow-up cycle would take another eight years! He added that there were checks and balances in the existing arrangements — indeed a network of hurdles for course approval which needed rationalization. What we had was something that had been pummelled into shape rather than conceived as a totality. (He was referring here to the procedures described in chapter 6.) As to monitoring, the Secretary of State could not in his view do it by massive machinery; it could only be done by light sampling. All institutions were different — context was always important; and one of his colleagues added that while some parts of the process were covered by reading paper it could not all be done that way. I describe in chapter 30 the solution to this problem eventually adopted for the period after our term ended. In the meantime I refer next to another aspect of the evolving situation — the results of return visits by HMI to institutions which had been inspected prior to CATE review.

Chapter 8

Second Inspection Reports

By 1988 it began to happen that institutions which had earlier been the subject of formal inspection, CATE review and decisions about their courses by the Secretary of State would receive second formal visits by HMI. At the November Council the Chairman referred to an account which had appeared in the press of an HMI report on Birmingham Polytechnic. 'A teacher-training faculty', Sarah Bayliss had written in the *TES*, 'has been criticized by Her Majesty's Inspectorate, two years after its courses were approved by the Secretary of State for Education under the "CATE" system... The report implies that there was a small flurry of activity to arrange school experience around the time of the previous HMI and CATE visits. This then went into decline.' (Bayliss, 1988) The slight inaccuracy in the reference to a CATE visit did not prevent the implication from being clear. The Chairman said he had spoken to Branch about how to handle the situation and was going to discuss it with the Convenors after the meeting. When we held our post-Council get-together it was evident that he felt quite strongly about what he regarded as a breach of faith. It appeared that copies of three second-phase reports had now been sent to the Secretary and others would follow; how were they to be taken into account? It seemed that HMI themselves had not yet given this much thought. If a second report related to an institution which was still under review the answer was fairly clear; the more difficult situation arose when, as with Birmingham Polytechnic, accreditation had already been granted. My own inclination was to wait for the Secretary of State to refer back to us any such cases which he considered to require another look, but the Chairman thought our position would be undermined if we appeared to be unconcerned, and with specific regard to Birmingham Polytechnic we should write and ask them what was going on. In December he reported that he had done so, in fairly strong terms. (The substance of this case is dealt with in chapter 24. Group A, which was then dealing with some outstanding issues relating to the institution, postponed further consideration until satisfaction had been given.)

In April 1989 Group A received what was now being called a milestone report, based on an HMI visit in the spring of the previous year, on Essex IHE, an institution with which we had already dealt. The report contained some critical comment and while not all of this related to the Criteria there were statements about links with schools which were relevant. We considered what response, if any, we should make. The SI confirmed that the institution would be required to make its own response to the DES. While this would oblige the institution to give some attention to HMI's comments Gillian Murton was not sure that a copy of its response would come to CATE as it would in the case of an initiating report, or that we had the right to ask for it. Tony Becher thought that, just as at first review, we should not take any action without having access to the response, and took the view that we should not get involved at all unless we could envisage having such strong reservations that we might want to recommend withdrawal of accreditation. Bill Wright on the other hand considered that our terms of reference gave us a continuing role in relation to courses submitted to us. I suggested that I should raise the matter at Council as one of principle, and this was agreed.

In doing so I contrasted the Essex case with that of Birmingham Polytechnic about which the Chairman had taken action; what we had encountered on this occasion was in a grey area where criticism was not all Criteria-related and where it was not likely to lead to withdrawal of approval. I suggested that there were three possibilities — to do nothing (relying on the procedures for the institution to respond), to await the response before taking action, or to write immediately. Other Groups might meet similar situations and we needed to take a common line. Group B reported that they had had a somewhat similar experience, though different in detail. The Chairman favoured my third course, and Bill Wright repeated his contention that we had warrant for continued involvement. The final decision was that Reporting Groups should decide whether second-stage reports contained sufficient evidence of departure from the Criteria to justify presenting it to Council for action. In matters of lesser concern Groups would be free to make appropriate comment to institutions direct.

This became standard practice for the remaining months of our term. In July, for example, Group A considered a milestone report on St Martin's College. Like any such document it contained a few critical comments, but the general view was that it was a good report, and our SI seemed happy. I sought Gillian's advice on the proper procedure if we did not consider there was anything to which attention needed to be drawn. She thought it would be appropriate for me as Convenor to make a verbal statement to Council to that effect, and this was duly done. The last occasion on which milestone reports were discussed in principle was at a Convenors' meeting in September 1989. Gillian's note drew attention to the fact that this round of HMI reports had been concerned with aspects of the work of a sample of institutions rather than with their total range of ITT. She pointed out that these reports could present various dilemmas for Reporting Groups — determining their relevance if a course review was in progress, what weight to attach to them in view of the fact that the availability of a second report on one institution but not on another was largely fortuitous, and whether Criteria-related criticisms in such reports justified thorough reassessment of changes in a course which might otherwise have been regarded as minor ones. We did not really have time to carry this debate much further forward. The feeling was that these reports might be expected to be picked up in a more comprehensive manner by our successor body, which was to have a more explicit monitoring role.

Chapter 9

Progress and Winding Up

At the beginning of the Council's term so much preliminary work had to be done in clearing the ground that CATE made rather a slow start to its essential job of reviewing courses. Having met for the first time in September 1984, members were not in a position to begin course reviews until March 1985, and it was the end of May before the first proposals came forward from the Reporting Groups. By the end of 1986 we found that numerically we were about half-way through the ninety-seven in-stitutions then in the field, but we still had 62 per cent of the courses to look at and many that had been reviewed would need to be considered again. The Chairman foresaw that it would be 1989 before we had completed our assignment, yet ways of speeding up the process did not present themselves. He felt that an increase in membership in order to form a fourth Group would not be productive as it would merely add to the load at full Council meetings.

By April 1987 the good news, as the Chairman put it, was that HMI reports had been received on nearly two-thirds of the institutions; the bad news was that CATE had completed business with only thirteen of them. 'We're being pretty rigorous', he observed. It was also becoming clear that the situation was constantly changing; new courses were always on the way and we should never be able to draw a line in the sense that the process would be completed. However, it was not so bad as suggested in a recent press report that we were disastrously behind our timetable; and the DES Assessor could see a time coming when the bulk of the work would be done, probably before the allocation for the early 1990s. A hopeful note was also struck by Ernie Grogan, who suggested that as our work progressed an increasing number of courses would be found accept-able at first review. As indicated in the penultimate chapter, this did prove to be the case.

At the end of July 1987 the Secretary of State accepted that the CATE exercise was going to take longer than the three to four years originally envisaged; he wrote to members to extend our appointments to the end of 1989. Having summarized the current situation, Kenneth Baker's letter stated that all those courses which had existed when the Council started its work should have received at least one round of scrutiny by that time. By then too the Department hoped to have been able to assess some of the effects of the exercise and to decide what should be the arrangements for the longer term. In September we were told that HMI reports had still to be received on twenty-two institutions. By November the series of inspections of English institutions was complete, and the last report was expected by Easter of the following year.

When we met after the 1988 summer break Gillian Murton had taken over as Secretary and she pointed out in a paper that there were problems about the categorization of CATE's work. Confusion was arising because the number of proposals for modifying courses was increasing and institutions on which it was thought that work had been completed were reappearing for further review. She therefore introduced a new categorization of institutions with the following results:

Substantial part of submission recommended	47
Substantial part deferred or approved conditionally	7
Substantial part currently under review	18
Initial submission awaiting review	7
Initial submissions awaited	14
TOTAL	93

This clearly more helpful approach was also rather alarming, since it showed that with only fifteen months to go before our extended deadline we had been able to make positive recommendations in respect of barely half the institutions and had not even made a start on reviewing nearly a quarter of them. In November 1988 we received a further report which used similar categories except that at the request of Branch they were quantified in respect of courses rather than of institutions. The picture which emerged was that of 331 courses we had now substantially completed a review of 161; a review had not begun on about seventy-eight. Our workload for 1989 was therefore pretty formidable. Even midway through our final year the number of institutions with which we had more or less completed business had risen to only sixty-five (roughly two-thirds).

The Chairman was, of course, concerned about this situation. When he sat in on the first meeting of Group A after the 1988 summer break and spoke of the danger of the last phase of CATE's work having the atmosphere of the condemned man's breakfast he had in mind partly the need for post-CATE arrangements to be known soon if institutions were to go on taking us seriously. But at a meeting of Group Convenors in

November he remarked that the year we had to run was still a year — there was nothing worse than being seen as a lame duck; and in January 1989 he asked Council how we were to avoid planning blight. He thought we should have to move towards giving sharper and more incisive responses; sometimes we should be prepared to say, 'This course is no good for the following reasons'. We could no longer say, 'Put it right in a year'. The DES Assessor commented that adjustment on the part of institutions was possible in the case of most of the Criteria, and Reporting Groups were now experienced at coaxing them into the box; the major exception was the requirement for main subject study to be in the taught curriculum. Perhaps the Council could sweep up the remaining courses on that basis. Planning blight, he felt, would affect our work only if the criteria to be applied after our demise were to be radically different. Bernice Martin commented that institutions differed in their responsiveness to the present criteria: some needed positive discipline, others only a shot across their bows. The Chairman said he took it there was agreement that we should try to speed up: Convenors and the secretariat would have to work closely on this.

It was, however, left unclear how the objective was to be achieved, and in fact we came as close as we did to wholly completing our assignment — as close indeed as it was possible to do — simply by meeting even more frequently during 1989 and attacking our programme with determination. We did not move to more summary judgments but continued doggedly with our established procedures except that for the first few months of our final year when conditions were attached to a positive recommendation they were couched in terms of progress being made within six months rather than a year. The context in which the remainder of our work was to be conducted became clearer in May 1989 when the DES made it plain through the publication of the *Consultative Paper on Future Arrangements for Accreditation* that there would be a successor body with a similar role to ours and that the criteria which it would be charged to enforce would not be radically different from those with which we had worked. This provided a helpful assurance of continuity.

In September 1989 we were told that it had been agreed with Branch that CATE would aim to complete its review of all courses that were running, including as far as possible those given temporary approval for a 1989 start. By now we were in no position to check on progress made even within a six-month period. Group A had one course before it where at an earlier stage we should have adopted the formula of progress within a year, and the Chairman agreed that it would now be reasonable to revert to that stance; from then on we began, when occasion warranted it, to ask for reports 'to the reconstituted Council'.

After we had met for the last time Gillian sent us a valedictory progress report as at 31 December 1989. We had by then reviewed 394 courses (excluding some resubmissions, which would have taken the figure over 400) in ninety-three existing institutions. This was no mean achievement. The substantial part of the submissions of ninety institutions had been positively recommended; for only three had we declined to recommend approval.

Chapter 10

Appearance and Reality

I have now given a fairly full account of how CATE worked, the procedures adopted to discharge its task and its efforts to do this thoroughly and consistently. I shall go on to discuss the particular problems which it encountered in applying the Criteria. Yet a preliminary question must arise and did occasionally trouble us — could we be sure that when we reviewed the courses submitted to us we were dealing with reality and not appearances? It is a question posed by Education Minister Tim Eggar in November 1990 as 'whether CATE Mark I was bamboozled and whether courses have not changed.' (DES, 1990b)

I have explained that visits to institutions by CATE members were a rarity, and when they did take place they were not quasi-inspections. There were strong reasons for this, but even if there had been nothing to make extended visits impractical the majority of us were not qualified to assess what we saw, and there was in any case a sense in which we were not directly concerned with quality. As Eric Bolton, the Senior Chief Inspector, said in a conference speech in January 1985, considering the question from the Inspectorate's point of view:

> It is possible for a course to appear to satisfy all the criteria and yet be regarded by HMI as poor or inadequate in important ways. It is also possible that some courses could be judged good by HMI, but fail to satisfy some of the criteria set down. (Bolton, 1985)

Most of the Criteria could be satisfied at various levels of effectiveness, and many of them were really proxy measures: if, for example, a student devoted at least 100 hours to study of the teaching of mathematics in primary schools she was likely to have a firmer grasp than if she spent less time on it, but there was still no guarantee of any particular standard having been reached.

CATE was dependent in the first instance on the written word. I have described some of the problems inherent in this process. At its worst it was a search for a needle of hard fact in a haystack of verbiage. But on the other hand we could hardly have rested content with a two-line memo from a head of institution certifying that all the Criteria were being met. We needed some descriptive confirmation of how it was being done, and in interpreting that we could and did seek the guidance of our professional advisers in the Inspectorate, who had had an opportunity to observe what was happening on the ground. (Eric Bolton again: 'The first task of HMI inspecting teacher training courses, or anything else, is always the same: to decide what they think of it in terms of the standards of learning being achieved.').

Our other source of confirmation that all was well was our meeting with the institution's representatives. Part of the difficulty here was on our side of the table. It was hardly feasible in the nature of the situation that we could clearly predetermine what responses to our questions we should regard as satisfactory, but the result was that the process of reaching collective conclusions after interviews were over was often rather subjective and sometimes obfuscated by imperfect or conflicting recollections of what our visitors had actually said. It was in practice left to the member of the Group asking the questions about a particular aspect to decide how far he or she would press them, and there was an almost unavoidable tendency for us to be somewhat preoccupied before our own turn for questioning came with the issues that we each had to raise and slightly to turn off afterwards. Thus to a degree our judgments were bound to reflect the extent to which we received an impression of competence and good intent.

And this was the other side of the problem — what Bill Wright once referred to as the credibility of witnesses. Sometimes the impression carried away from these meetings was at variance with that created by the papers we had previously received — a delegation might appear a good deal better organized than its documentation, or occasionally vice versa. My own prejudice was in favour of the more apparently reflective groups who were prepared to admit that they had not yet got everything quite right but were seeking in a perceptive way to do better. Nevertheless it was clearly possible that we could be misled, and a form of halo effect was hard to avoid. The Chairman mentioned to Council in April 1988 hearing anecdotes that things were not as they seemed. It had to be acknowledged, he added, that if a delegation came to meet a Group well briefed, speaking with one voice, well turned out and agreeable in manner the Group would be more likely to accept their case than if the reverse were true. I have already quoted instances where HMI believed that we were in effect having the wool pulled over our eyes, and in chapter 29 I shall recount another somewhat startling intervention by HMI in the context of our attempt to identify good practice: the reality, we were told, did not match the rhetoric. There was also the occasionally disturbing evidence which began to emerge when HMI returned to institutions that had already been 'Cated'.

I do not believe that we were often confronted by deliberate deception. But when the future of people's institutions and of their own jobs were at risk it was only to be expected that they would present what they were doing in the most favourable light. Only HMI might have been in a position to say, 'It's not quite like that', and by conscious decision they were not present at our meetings with institutional representatives. Equally, of course, a poor impression made at interview might have obscured sound work going on back at base. Gross errors of judgment by CATE could have been corrected by advice given to the Secretary of State before he announced a decision on a course. As the civil servants like to say, there were checks and balances in the system. But in principle the problem of distinguishing reality from appearance seemed intrinsic to the process of accreditation as prescribed by DES Circular 3/84.

Part Two

Subject Studies

Chapter 11

Subject Studies

Chapter 1's brief summary of events preceding the establishment of CATE took as its starting point the Great Debate which followed the Callaghan speech of 1976, but the aspects of the Criteria commonly referred to as subject studies related to a number of interlocking issues of which some had been current in varying forms in discussions of teacher training for a much longer period. These issues included the antithesis between the 'personal' and professional education of the student, the respective advantages of concurrent and consecutive approaches to academic and professional course content, the effect on these of different forms of validation, and with regard to primary education the question whether teaching should be more child-focused than subject-focused. The complex history of these controversies cannot be traced here. But criteria are a form of quality control and to understand why particular criteria were adopted one must be aware what faults or omissions they were designed to correct. Enough was said in Chapter 1 to indicate how prior to 1984 HMI had highlighted a number of concerns which must have had a strong influence on Government thinking. Three of these had an especially close bearing on the subject studies criteria which were promulgated in that year — in summary:

(i)   that in some cases students' main subjects of academic study were insufficiently related to the school curriculum, so that there was a lack of match between their qualifications and what they were supposed to be teaching;

(ii)   that partly for this reason and partly because in some courses too little attention was given to academic study some teachers had too slight a knowledge base;

(iii)   that some courses did not prepare students adequately to apply their subjects of academic study in the classroom.

This was the background to the most famous and controversial of the Criteria — that

> the higher education and initial teacher training of all intending teachers should include the equivalent of at least two full years' course time devoted to subject studies at a level appropriate to higher education. (DES, 1984a)

Moreover, the initial degrees of entrants to PGCE courses should be 'appropriately related to the work of primary or secondary schools (whichever is relevant)'. Relevance to the school curriculum was prescribed for BEd courses also but two distinctions were made between those for the primary years and those for secondary teaching. In the latter 'the two years should be spent in the study of one or two subjects within the secondary curriculum as it is at present or as it may be expected to develop in the foreseeable future'. In the former, however, 'a wide area of the curriculum might constitute the student's specialism and the time allotted to this part of the course should include the application of the subjects concerned to the learning and developmental needs of young children'.

In March 1985, after the first experience by the Council's Reporting Groups of considering responses from the institutions allocated to them, the interpretation of this section of the Criteria was one of the points which came up for discussion when notes were being compared. It was agreed that it would not be possible to accept as an element in the required two full years of subject study time spent either on educational or professional studies or, in the case of primary BEd courses, on general curriculum studies. On the other hand it was recognized that although the scope for flexibility here was limited, members would need to evaluate individual circumstances very carefully in order not to inhibit course developments that were genuinely aimed at meeting the Criteria. There was an expectation in the field that many existing primary BEds would fail to meet them. A further discussion took place at the following meeting; members compared specific examples encountered among the first round of institutions with the aim of ensuring consistency of approach and it was decided that it would be desirable to issue guidelines in the form of a Catenote. A draft prepared for the May 1985 meeting and based on the work of HMI was thought to be a sound basis for a publication, but a large number of amendments were proposed and the secretariat was asked to revise the paper. In July 1985 a few more improvements were suggested and it was agreed to publish a final version which incorporated these. Catenote 3, *Subject Studies*, was distributed at the beginning of August 1985.

Having quoted from the relevant paragraphs of the Criteria, the Catenote drew attention to the distinction between primary and secondary BEd courses in respect of methodology. In the case of BEd courses for primary teachers there was a requirement that the course time devoted to subject studies should include their application.

> In this case, therefore, such 'applications' or methodology work contributes to the required equivalent of at least two full years of subject study...However, in the case of secondary courses, the requirement...relating to the methodology of teaching the chosen subject specialism, or curricular area, is additional to the requirement...and does not contribute to the two full years. (CATE, 1985c)

This was followed by a section on the level of subject studies, rehearsing the rationale for this being 'intellectually demanding' and stressing that subject studies should not be 'pursued in ways too narrowly related to their application in the classroom'. The two years need not be uninterrupted: the requirement was in effect for half of a four-year course, and there was no single organizational model. Joint teaching with other undergraduate students would sometimes be possible.

With regard to specialist studies for secondary teachers the Catenote drew attention to the indication in the Circular that these should be pursued only in one or in two subjects, and in the latter case attention was also drawn to a subsequent DES circular letter (DES, 1984b) which prescribed that when the pattern adopted was a main subject and a subsidiary subject or curricular area the time and attention devoted to the latter must amount to at least a third of that given to the main subject. Referring to subject studies for primary teachers, the Catenote asserted that:

> Collectively, the staff of a primary school should command a range of subject specialisms covering as much as possible of the school curriculum. This does not imply the replacement of the class teacher by the specialist. It does mean that adequate specialist expertise in each aspect of the curriculum should, when required, be available. (*ibid*)

Thus was introduced into CATE policy the notion of subject leaders or consultants in primary schools which had a warrant in the White Papers, *Teaching Quality* and *Better Schools*, though not explicitly in the Criteria themselves. Schools could not always be staffed so that teachers' individual specialisms covered the whole curriculum, and therefore there was a case, as provided in the Criteria, for specialism in 'a wide area of the curriculum', and examples given of subject clusters were science, maths and technology; music, drama and art; or history and geography. (In July 1987 the Chairman remarked how it had been borne in on him that the

Criteria were predicated on schools being of a certain size, though LEAs has found it difficult politically to close small schools. A Staff Inspector said it was with smaller primary schools in mind that the Criteria referred to specialism in an *area* of the curriculum.) Less time would be devoted to subject studies for primary than for secondary teachers because of the requirement that courses for the former should include application, but:

> this in no way detracts from the need for the specialist subject studies themselves to be pursued at the level of rigour appropriate to an undergraduate course. The Council's view is that these studies should normally account for at least three-quarters of the two years' minimum time allocation. (*ibid*)

The last point, which was consistently applied by Reporting Groups, was an interpretive enlargement of the Criteria. Appended to the Catenote was an annex which summarized in schematic form the requirements relating to subject studies in undergraduate courses of initial teacher training for primary and secondary teachers respectively.

There was no doubt that the Chairman himself was strongly in support of the case for academic subject studies and he maintained that in most comparable countries there was a similar trend towards a stronger knowledge base for intending teachers. In March 1986 he spoke in his recently acquired role as a grandfather. His granddaughter would be going to school in four-and-a-half years' time (though in fact we were told later as an example of the move towards 'early years' that the young lady first did so two days after her fourth birthday); he wanted her to be taught history or science or whatever by people who understood the epistemology and traditions and methodology of these subjects. But unease was felt in many quarters about the effects of the subject studies criteria, especially on preparation for primary school teaching. Strong opposition from UPTEC had been reported in May 1985. After the Council meeting in April 1986 some members met with representatives of the Society for Research in Higher Education to discuss a number of matters arising from a recent conference they had held on the impact of CATE. They considered that the content of subject specialism might be inappropriate for students in training for teaching, especially if colleges had to bring in academic help from universities. To this the reply they were given was that it was for institutions to choose the people they used. But the SRHE considered that the emphasis on subject specialism was pushing the preparation of primary teachers — and therefore primary education — in a direction which secondary education needed to move away from. Moreover, the time now pre-empted by subject studies in order to comply with the Criteria meant less time for professional studies; the experience of students was being changed; there was a lack of integrative activity, of opportunity to show how theory and practice interrelate.

These trenchant criticisms met with a courteous if bland response, but they were not isolated; CATE was seen by many as adopting an insensitive and mechanistic approach. At the May 1986 Council the Chairman mentioned having been on the previous evening at a meeting in Cheltenham at which he had been asked, 'Can so many people be so wrong?' A deputation from the CNAA told us they were bothered by the way Catenote 3 seemed to be doing damage to institutions which were trying to get away from the academic/professional divide and forcing them down the road to specialism. In the course of the discussion the Chairman said it would indeed be worrying if the Criteria were making teaching qualifications less professional. 'But they are!' our visitors responded. The 3:1 ratio between subject study and application in courses for primary teachers was difficult to reconcile with the way validation had developed: institutions were satisfying CATE only by making arbitrary definitions. They asked us if we were disturbed by the undernourishment of professional education. They were worried by the extent to which the Criteria were preventing course evolution. CATE was enforcing a departure from a frame of reference provided by peer evaluation and as a result courses were being repackaged; a certain amount of 'creative accounting', they suggested, was going on in order to demonstrate that courses complied with the Criteria. Bernice Martin observed that the labels 'pedagogic' and 'academic' were not intended to be arbitrary distinctions; what was constraining institutions from merging them professionally? The Chairman also pointed out that initial training could not do the whole job of producing fully professional teachers: it was only the start of a process which also included induction and in-service education. In that case, the CNAA deputation responded, the expectations of headteachers would need to change; they must be prepared for the ability to organize classroom teaching being squeezed out of initial training. The Chairman could not accept that argument; the curriculum even of 5-year-olds must be about something. The CNAA said it seemed a pity that all that was separating us was perhaps half a year's subject study.

Meanwhile, for the May 1986 Council meeting which had preceded this encounter the Chairman had written a paper on 'the acceptability of "non-curricular" BEd subjects' — a problem which had by then begun to exercise the Council. Could we recommend the accreditation of courses with a specialism in subjects other than those customarily recognized as contributing directly to the primary school curriculum? He referred to the relevant part of the Criteria and to the HMI discussion paper, *The Content of Initial Training*, which had stated explicitly that 'every BEd degree should offer subjects for study which are directly relevant to the school curriculum' (DES, 1983). He went on to point out that it was by no means easy to determine from the name given to a subject offered for study whether or not its content had curricular relevance in the primary school, and he gave examples of BEd subjects currently on offer — some admittedly in subsidiary elements — which might not be regarded as featuring in the primary school curriculum (American studies, classics, economics, health studies, law, philosophy, third world studies). The paper then dealt in detail with the special case of psychology, as described in Chapter 14, and in doing so suggested that the two years of subject study in the primary BEd might be regarded as fulfilling three main purposes:

(i)   the ability to make a specialist contribution in the primary school;

(ii) the opportunity to benefit from pursuing study of a subject in depth in a manner appropriate to higher education; and

(iii) as a means of acquiring knowledge directly relevant to the content of the primary curriculum.

(He suggested when he introduced the paper that this had not been expressed before in quite this form.)

His conclusion was that it was not feasible to make a blanket judgment about the suitability or otherwise of 'non-curricular' subject studies for accreditation purposes. Aspects of the content of some of them might be directly relevant to what primary teachers are called upon to do, just as PGCE candidates with 'non-curricular' degrees might bring valuable knowledge and skills to teaching. The main requirement in both cases was for men and women who had pursued in depth subjects that had direct relevance to the curriculum as it is and as it is likely to develop. CATE should be willing to consider 'non-curricular' subjects on their merits, though this flexibility needed to be accompanied by recognition on the part of institutions of the continued priority that should be given to curricular relevance. It would be neither practicable nor desirable to draw up a list of approved subjects: Reporting Groups would need to make judgments about curricular relevance on the basis of careful scrutiny of course content and balance. The paper concluded by reminding the Council that the issue was one of some sensitivity in the field, and it was important that the Council's views should not be misunderstood.

In the discussion which ensued at the Council meeting Bernice Martin made the point that there was one perspective from which there was need for greater clarity on the matter — namely, that of sixth-formers who intended to teach when they came to choose the subjects they were going to follow. An SI who was in attendance that day said that schools were changing: the idea that loving children was good teaching was giving way to curriculum-led teaching. She thought most courses with questionable titles had an acceptable content, and agreed that they needed to be looked at individually. This view was echoed by the Branch Assessor. The Chairman repeated that we should be flexible if the institutions were sensible. Tony Becher pointed out that there were checks in the system through the market economy — whether students got jobs. But there was a general recognition, reflected in the minutes, that in the end a subject specialism could be accepted by the Council only on the ground that it met the Criteria. At the following meeting the Branch Assessor reaffirmed the DES view that in deciding whether individual subject specialisms were acceptable CATE would need to judge how far the content of the study contributed to knowledge of a specific curriculum subject or area.

However, the position we had now reached made at least one member of the Council uneasy. Andrew Collier wrote a paper for the meeting in September 1986 which he headed 'CATE and the Curriculum'. It was prompted by recent decisions by the Council to endorse French but not psychology as a suitable subject of study for primary BEds and to cast doubt on the suitability of personal and social studies as a second subject specialism for a secondary PGCE. He argued that if subject specialisms were to be strictly limited to a defined primary curriculum then we must have an agreed definition of the curriculum, and if there were optional subjects such as French then there would need to be a strict national quota of places. But on the other hand it could be argued that any of the subjects mentioned could make a contribution to the school curriculum in terms of skills and practical value. The Criteria were neither clear nor consistent on the matter. If CATE was going to take a fairly broad view of them then further formal statements from the Secretary of State about the curriculum might not be needed, but if we were to take the narrow view which the recent decisions indicated then it was essential that such decisions should be taken against clear criteria for the primary and secondary curricula. CATE was not constituted to determine the school curriculum, and it was important that it should not take on that role, particularly through a series of *ad hoc* decisions on individual courses. The Council should therefore consider seeking clarification from the Secretary of State concerning the intention of the subject studies criteria and a statement of the school curriculum against which recommendations should be made.

In initiating the debate which this paper generated the Chairman made it fairly clear that he thought the Council had behaved properly in the decisions it had so far made, and in his view there was not a major problem. He did not see any inconsistency in our recommendations about French and psychology, for French appeared on some primary school timetables whereas psychology did not. Personal and social studies should, he believed, be pursued mainly through in-service education — 'Beware the 23-year-old specialist', he observed — though awareness and sensitivity should be encouraged through educational and professional studies in initial training. Derek Mortimer said that in relation to the curriculum we should be looking at the purposes rather than the titles of courses. Andrew reminded us of the White Paper, *Better Schools*, and suggested that we should use and be seen to use that as a guide. The DES Assessor expressed the view that we ought to be concerned with what was taught as opposed to what ought to be taught. 'Peace studies?' asked Andrew gently.

The Chairman said there was no question about the appropriateness of some non-curricular subjects in preparation for teaching — sociology was one such; but as a Council we should stick to national guidelines and avoid statements about the curriculum and hidden epistemology. Though a number of somewhat conflicting views had been expressed during the discussion (Bill Wright argued that mathematics and psychology could both be relevant to the primary curriculum), the Chairman summed up in Prime-Ministerial fashion by thanking Andrew for raising this important subject, and asking if he was content that the Council should minute carefully the various points that had been made and in particular cases should scrutinize course content. Sensing, I think, that the Chairman did not wholly sympathize with his views, Andrew did not press the matter further, except to say that he would look at the minute when it was produced.

The minute read as follows:

As a result of extensive discussion of the points raised in Mr Collier's paper, the Council concluded that its responsibility was to apply the subject studies criteria rather than to define or determine the contents of the school curriculum. It was therefore especially important that the Council should not be seen to be attempting to determine the school curriculum through its recommendations. In exercising its responsibilities, the Council might in some cases need to look beyond subject titles in order to determine whether particular programmes of study were designed to develop students' strengths in curriculum subjects. This in turn might call for judgments as to what constituted the curriculum — either as it was at present or as it might be expected to develop in the foreseeable future. In the more difficult of these cases, the Council would need guidance on which to base and justify its decisions. It was agreed that in the absence of an explicit definition of the curriculum, the Council should first have regard to the policy statements contained in the White Paper, *Better Schools*. Reporting groups would therefore need to ensure that their proposals were demonstrably in line with those statements, and Group proposals would then need especially careful consideration by the full Council. It was agreed that the Council would need to return again to this matter as the practicability of this approach was tested in Reporting Groups.

Before the next meeting of the Council took place the secretariat distributed some passages from the 1985 White Paper 'for members' information and guidance'. The passages selected were paragraphs 60–75 on the organization and content of the curriculum and paragraphs 159–167 on match between teachers' qualifications and their teaching programmes. The elements in the primary curriculum on which the Government believed there was wide agreement, and which were spelt out in that document, closely foreshadowed the content of the National Curriculum which was enacted three years after its publication. Andrew Collier was not present at the October 1986 meeting of the Council at which the minute was ratified, so he had no opportunity to comment. My own subsequent observation was that neither in Group A nor at Council was reference ever again made to *Better Schools*, and the reconsideration of the issue which was presaged in the minute never took place. Concentration on course content, however, did become the Council's normal basis for its recommendations.

In July 1987, when a proposal came forward in respect of Essex IHE, we were given a small insight into the difficulties which beset some institutions. An SI remarked that this was a college caught in the swing from one bandwagon — 'No', she said, interrupting herself, 'I oughtn't to use that word' — from one emphasis to another. It appeared that they had had a strong subject emphasis, then had moved to a more professional approach, and now had had to go back. A year later a similar comment was made by Group B about Bulmershe CHE: it had moved to a 'professional' degree, and in the changed climate was now coming back again, though at that stage not far enough.

A curious incident emerged at a meeting of Group A in February 1988. Ernie Grogan told us that the last batch of recommendations from CATE to the Secretary of State had included subject studies in anthropology, archaeology and environmental studies, which Kenneth Baker had approved in spite of some reservations, though not outright opposition, from Branch. However, Mr Baker had written to Ernie to say that he shared the doubts expressed by Branch about these courses, adding that he trusted CATE would not approve any more. Although Ernie said he had told the Chairman, who had agreed that it was ominous, this was not reported at full Council. Group A found it rather startling, especially with regard to environmental studies, and Tony Becher said he would resign rather than be told what to do by the Secretary of State. This was the only instance of direct political 'interference' of which I heard. Our SI advised us to take our stand on the Criteria, and I think I may say that we were not intimidated.

Yet opposition to the subject studies criterion did not die out. After the Council meeting in June 1988 a number of us stayed on to meet representatives from SCETT. They told us that they had conducted a survey of their members which revealed almost as much concern about the insistence on two years of subject study as there had been at the start of CATE's term. It came especially from those involved in training for the early years of schooling, and was not so much a matter of opposition to subject studies as of anxiety about the time left for other things, and in particular the possibility of responding to new demands. (The Kingman Report on the teaching of English language had earlier been mentioned, as had proposals for assessment.) Renford Bambrough replied that stimulating and effective teaching was most likely to come from teachers who were themselves still learning and had lively recollections of what it is like to learn. He added a question about the PGCE: if adequate professional studies could be packed into one year there, why could they not be dealt with adequately in the longer time available in the BEd? The visitors answered that there was a case for an extended PGCE. Renford continued by pointing out that some course elements had in fact been dropped — theoretical psychology, sociology, and philosophy; and though he personally was very keen on philosophy he recognized that institutions had to establish priorities. The reply to this was that it was more serious if what had to be cut was child development and how children learn. A member of the deputation stressed that they had actually been surprised that concern was still so strong in this area, but they were reporting what they had found.

Confirmation of the currency of these concerns was provided at the following meeting, in July 1988, when we had before us a paper on the education and training of teachers for work in primary schools from the National Primary Teacher Education Conference. It called for a review of the Criteria, and in particular for a relaxation of the subject studies requirement in order to allow more time for general curriculum and professional work. David Winkley said he did not think their case was made out; the evidence, though very marginal, suggested that in their first year teachers trained by the BEd were slightly superior to those with PGCEs. Anne Cattoor said it would take a long time to establish that in a primary school the staff should turn for help to a colleague as a subject co-ordinator rather than to the head. Andrew Collier thought the NaPTEC document dangerous because it could be used to argue against any particular academic discipline for primary teaching. Michael Pipes believed the general view now was that the influence of CATE was good, but the subject studies criterion was the last bastion to fall. Lesley Abbott argued that subject studies must be related to the child, but the Chairman reminded us that before CATE there had been tremendous variation in the amount of application associated with subject study: it had often depended on the predilections of a head of department. Derek Mortimer observed that the argument had shifted from subject studies *per se* to the right balance in the initial training curriculum, and the Chairman drew attention to the scope for flexibility within the Criteria. This was the last occasion on which there was any extended discussion of the principles involved.

Chapter 12

Aspects of Implementation

Relevance of Initial Degrees

Cateform 1 requested institutions to supply a list of the first degree subjects of their most recent PGCE intake to each secondary subject method group and to each primary course. This information was a starting-point at most Group meetings with institutional representatives for discussion about how they fulfilled the requirement to satisfy themselves that the content of candidates' initial degrees was appropriately related to the work of schools. The level of *prima facie* match between first degrees and the school curriculum varied considerably from institution to institution, and in part no doubt this reflected differing philosophies about the generalizability of intellectual disciplines. But it was noticeable that when we pointed to particular examples (graduates admitted to primary PGCE courses with degrees in law or planning or engineering or languages) it frequently transpired that the individual in question had turned to teaching as a mature entrant after experience in employment which would itself be valuable in a school context. Another paragraph of the Criteria declared that such experience should count in a candidate's favour and we often heard that these mature students had much to offer to the profession. In the case of secondary methods courses the question which we were occasionally prompted to ask was whether there was a sufficient commonality among the first degrees to constitute a shared base for applications work; but again we usually received fairly reassuring answers to such enquiries.

'A Level Appropriate to Higher Education'

Though clearly an important aspect of the subject studies criterion, the specific requirement that undergraduate courses should be at a level appropriate to higher education was not one which it was usually necessary or appropriate for CATE to investigate. As Ernie Grogan had from time to time to remind Group A, the courses which came before us had received academic validation, or were in process of being validated, and we had therefore to assume that they were sound in that respect. When we met representatives of the CNAA in May 1986 they wondered aloud how CATE thought itself equipped or set about trying to assess the level of subject studies.

However, at a fairly early stage in our work Group C did make bold to query what was going on in one of the universities. HMI had noted as a distinguishing characteristic of the primary BEd at Durham the integration of subject studies with other undergraduate work in the University. Six subjects were on offer, and the BEd students took two for a term each in their first year and spent a further term, not necessarily in the same subject, in each of the second and third years. It was therefore possible for a student's year and a half of subject study to comprise short courses in four different subjects. HMI had been critical of this arrangement on grounds of inadequacies in time, rigour and methodology, and though the University had defended its integrative system the Group saw conflict with the Criteria not only in inadequate preparation for curricular leadership but in failure to achieve the required level of study. They had asked for more information but the University had declined to provide this on the grounds that it was the sole concern of their Senate.

Council agreed that the lack of coherence and progression in this model could not be reconciled with the Criteria and that the Group should renew its request. In conveying this to the Vice-Chancellor Ernie was to make it clear that CATE was not seeking to derogate from the Senate's responsibility for the validation of the individual units available to students but that our concern was with the course of study as a professional preparation for teaching, and in order to satisfy the Criteria a substantial repackaging of the relevant elements of the course would be required. This approach did elicit more information from the UDE; members of the Group subsequently visited the University, and after a year's deferment they reported in July 1987 that they had no difficulty in proposing a recommendation for approval of what was now a new primary BA in Education. Students were to spend almost all their time during the first two years of the four-year course studying their academic subjects in the University and subject choice was restricted to ensure that it formed a coherent programme suitable for an intending primary teacher. The Vice-Chancellor had gone out of his way to indicate that the changes had his personal support.

As will appear in some of the later chapters, doubts about academic progression sometimes arose in modular degrees, though clearly there was no conflict between the Criteria and modular structures *per se*. CATE looked for evidence that students' choice was guided according to some principles which ensured both a coherent curricular base and an acceptable guarantee of 'degree-worthiness'.

Two Full Years' Course Time

The need to establish that two full years' course time were actually devoted to subject studies arose with every concurrent course of training which CATE considered. The structure of such courses varied enormously and in every instance we had to disentangle the element of subject study from whatever form of course organization was in use and assess its length against the degree total. Although institutions were asked to supply us with this information it often came in extraordinarily complex tabulations which made it difficult to be certain that we were arriving at the right answer. We needed a rule of thumb, and at least in the case of Group A this was provided for us by David Shadbolt, who started from the proposition that each academic year comprised approximately 1000 hours, of which roughly half would be timetabled in some way and half consist of private study. On this basis two years of course time would amount to about 2000 hours, and we could expect to find about 1000 of these accounted for as lectures or seminars.

This formula was obviously not a precise gauge but it gave us a base from which to work, and if the number of hours of contact time in subject study fell significantly below either half of the identifiable total or the thousand level we had grounds for further enquiry. In the early years of CATE's work an inadequate proportion of subject study within courses was among the commonest reasons for their having to be referred back for another look in a year's time, and sometimes we had the impression that the required balance was quite difficult to achieve, both for practical reasons and because of the kind of philosophical resistance described in the previous chapter. In general the problem became less pronounced as our term advanced since institutions grew more aware that CATE had no flexibility in implementing this criterion and they had more time to adjust course structures to comply with it.

Curiously, however, the most blatant failure to achieve what was required came to our notice during our final year and resulted at our very last meeting in the most drastic negative recommendation that CATE made. In September 1989 Group C brought forward two proposals in respect of Derbyshire CHE. One of these drew attention to serious deficiencies in their primary BEd, which patently did not meet the subject studies criterion. We were told that the institution, with the backing of its local committee, professed a philosophy of producing generalist primary teachers and believed that its degree course was a sound basis for that purpose. Some change had been introduced, but not enough. Even if all the curriculum work were added to subject studies this accounted for only about 23 per cent of the course and there was little evidence of progression. The Chairman asked whether we should not be recommending withdrawal of approval without further delay. Members of the Group considered that the institution must be given a chance to restructure but in December we were told that Group C were still not satisfied. They had considered taking the easy way out and referring a decision to our successor body after a further period's grace, but in the end they had decided that this would merely be prevarication. What they had encountered was not only an apparent inability to meet the Criteria but an unwillingness to do so. The institution disagreed with the subject studies requirement and was not prepared to adapt radically. Accordingly the Council agreed to recommend that approval be withdrawn from the BEd and from a two-year version of it which was similarly considered to provide an inadequate skills base.

It was also near the end of CATE's term that Group A encountered a major difficulty about the amount of contact time within the subject studies element of a course. After a meeting with representatives of Wolverhampton Polytechnic in July 1989 we had asked for more details of the hours devoted to subject studies in the primary BEd. This produced a 'clarification' of subject time, which the institution took to include not only lecture and seminar time but what they termed generated or structured time, which might or might not be supervised but was monitored and assessed. In some subjects also there was no supervised generated time and a ratio of 7:3 or even higher of non-supervised generated time to lecture/seminar time. In some cases the timetabled hours amounted to about 500 or less. We thought that this was inadequate and that the only hope of the institution being able to pass muster would be if they could satisfy us more convincingly on the nature of generated time. When a further written exchange failed to give us what we needed we decided to invite the representatives to another meeting in an attempt to resolve the problem before the end of the year. A fairly constructive discussion took place at the beginning of December. We decided at the end of it that we could now propose that the reconstituted Council should reconsider it in the autumn of 1990 in the light of developments which we had been told would be implemented from February of that year. This was agreed at the final Council meeting.

Academic Association

In May 1986 the Secretary of State asked five small colleges (Bishop Grosseteste, Charlotte Mason, North Riding, Rolle and Westminster) to enter into 'close academic association' with nearby universities, and two others (Bretton Hall and La Sainte Union) were asked to examine links with other institutions. Like other government requests this one was hard to refuse, since it was clear that the continued survival of the colleges was at stake. The first courses resulting from these arrangements came to Council in November 1987, when there were proposals for North Riding College and Bretton Hall; both institutions had entered into academic association with the University of Leeds. The others came before us over the following two years and in no case did academic association as such present any problems.

It so happened that Group A dealt with four out of the seven institutions named and the questions we asked related to the ways in which integration and coherence had been sought and achieved. A common though not universal pattern was for students to spend the second year of their BEd out of the college taking classes in subject studies at the associated university, and clearly it was pertinent to enquire how this was prepared for and followed up, the level of study before and during the university year, and how the subject applications were related. In general, however, it appeared that these potential problems had been carefully addressed, and the colleges spoke highly of the harmonious and cooperative spirit in which the arrangements had been made. In most cases we were talking about forms of academic association which were still about to be implemented or had only just got under way; no doubt their progress would be a matter for our successor body to pursue.

Subject Clusters

At a fairly early stage in the Council's consideration of submissions from institutions the question arose how to respond if presented with a seemingly incoherent grouping of subjects for study. The guidance offered in Catenote 3 about 'a wide area of the curriculum' (see chapter 11) could be read as implying that there should not be more than three subjects, but larger groupings were occasionally encountered — for example, drama, music, movement and literature at Bangor Normal College; art and design, PE, theatre arts, drama and music comprising expressive arts at Polytechnic South West. Derek Mortimer argued that it was up to institutions to demonstrate that there was coherence in such instances, and that was the line which we followed.

While subject studies in concurrent courses for intending secondary teachers were to be pursued only in one or in two subjects, clusters occasionally appeared in PGCEs. For example, the secondary PGCE at Queen's University, Belfast, offered main and second subject study specialisms, one of which was in social sciences. Introducing Group A's proposal about this course to Council in February 1989, I explained that here 'social sciences' meant politics, economics and sociology. Though these were not subject studies as such, Mary Hallaway observed that if this cluster were taken with another subject students would actually be studying the methodology of four subjects — could this be done? We had not really looked at this, and though the DENI Inspector who was present explained that in practice it would not happen that way it was agreed to include a note in the Secretary's letter to the institution. In principle the point was a valid one.

By the end of our final year we knew that the new criteria would restrict subject studies in primary phase undergraduate courses to not more than three subjects. We therefore warned institutions if any courses which we encountered at that time appeared likely to infringe the new rules.

Chapter 13

When is a Subject not a Subject?

As we proceeded with consideration of the courses submitted to us it soon became apparent that there were two aspects to the requirement that subject studies should be relevant to the school curriculum. Both were touched upon in the Chairman's paper and ensuing debate described in chapter 11, but in practice a distinction could be made between them. One was to determine whether the content of a subject offered in initial training, whatever its title, was adequately related to what was actually taught in schools; the other was to distinguish subjects that appear in school timetables from forms of professional skill which some or all teachers need to possess but which do not constitute part of the school curriculum. Both discriminations could be difficult to make and both led to considerable unhappiness on the part of institutions when CATE's decision went against them.

The first case which brought the second issue into sharp focus arose from Nottingham UDE, and did so on a substantial scale. The prospectus for the UDE's secondary PGCE offered fourteen 'second area studies' which the UDE itself placed in two groups. The eight courses in the first group were clearly timetable school subjects. The six in the second group were community studies and education, media studies, personal and social education (PSE), remedial education, special needs education, and youth and community studies. Reporting Group B brought the PGCE course to the Council for the first time in July 1986 and attention was drawn to the group of second subjects which were not curricular. There was a general view that several of them were not 'subjects' in terms of the Criteria, yet that they were worthy elements in a course of initial train-ing. CI Pauline Perry sought to reassure us by pointing out that new areas of the curriculum are not dependent on people being trained to teach them: she instanced American studies, European studies and third world studies, all of which had grown up because historians, geo-graphers, or whoever had been prepared to teach them. PSE should be done in every school, but it was not a specialist subject in teacher training. Derek Mortimer offered a distinction between pupil-based skills, which are subjects in the curriculum, and teacher-based skills, which are things teachers need to be knowledgeable about. The outcome of that day's discussion was to delete from the proposal for a positive recommendation to the Secretary of State all of the second group of second subject method specialisms except media studies, which appeared unproblematic, and to ask Group B to look at the other five again. Branch also undertook to give further consideration to 'community studies' as a subject specialism.

Group B brought the Nottingham courses back to Council in October 1986. They now proposed to allow PSE but not to recommend approval for the other four, none of which was seen as being a timetable subject; they lacked curricular content and methodology. They were to be commended for their pedagogic value but should be elements in professional studies. Some members considered that they related to skills which were best developed through in-service education after some years of teaching. It was indeed Government policy that all specialist training for special needs should be provided on an in-service basis after normal teacher qualification and experience in ordinary schools; and we were told that a similar view was taken of youth and community studies provision. The Council's recommendations were not immediately conveyed to the Secretary of State since the total proposal in respect of the Nottingham PGCE was conditional on progress being made in staff development. In the usual way, however, the institution was made aware informally of what the Council had provisionally agreed, and the University then wrote to the Council Secretary questioning the decision not to approve the four excluded subject method specialisms. In support of their case they cited two DES Circulars which had been issued in 1983. This was reported to the Council in December 1986. But investigation had revealed that institutions were misinterpreting the list of subject specialisms which accompanied these Circulars if they regarded it as defining those subjects approved for QTS. The purpose of the Circulars — or Judd letters, as they were sometimes referred to, after their signatory — was consultative; they had constituted a report to ACSET on the range of secondary subjects which were then on offer. The inclusion of subjects in this list, some of which were described as being actually rather bizarre, did not constitute a blessing on the part of the Department, and no further list had been issued. In this particular case Council agreed that it was not our responsibility to define the curriculum (a question discussed in greater detail in chapter 11) and it was for the Department to clarify the status of the Judd letters. This view was upheld on appeal from the local committee.

Early in 1988 the Nottingham courses came back to Group B on second review. During discussion of the outstanding issue of staff development (on which the Group was now satisfied that the condition had been met) the Branch Assessor queried the inclusion of PSE in the intended proposal. The Group therefore looked at it very carefully once more to see if it was indeed a 'taught' subject in school with consequent methodology. They now came to the conclusion that it did not meet that criterion, for this particular course was essentially concerned with class management: it was a practical introduction to developing interpersonal relationships in the classroom and to understanding group dynamics. With this information before it in June 1988 Council approved with little further discussion the revised proposal to exclude PSE, in addition to the four from which approval had already been withheld, as a second subject method specialism.

However, the ultimate rejection of PSE at Nottingham did not mean that a course with that title would always be inadmissible. Indeed this point was illustrated by another course brought to Council by the same Group and also initially in July 1986. In this case PSE was a second subject method specialism in the primary PGCE at Sheffield Polytechnic and in the interests of consistency it was also referred back for further consideration. In October 1986 Group B reported that they had reconsidered this specialism and still wished to include it among the recommended second subjects. The topics studied in the course included elements of self-assessment, decision-making and option choices, careers education, personal relationships, life at work and in the community and health education. Though it was essentially practical in nature the course rested on a body of theory and research, teaching practice was provided in schools where some aspects of PSE were established and HMI spoke highly of 'this pioneering work' on the part of the institution. Council endorsed the proposal and the course was duly recognized by the Secretary of State as a second subject.

A similar conclusion was reached in respect of an application from Cambridge UDE to include a second choice subject methods course in PSE in the two-subject version of its secondary PGCE, and since this case was dealt with by Group A I was aware of the arguments which arose in discussion. The accompanying documentation suggested that this additional methods course had enabled the two-subject programme for teachers of RE to improve its recruitment of suitably qualified graduates and would also help to satisfy a need in secondary schools, where PSE had developed as a subject and was frequently the concern of teachers of RE. The issue as we saw it was whether preparation for PSE was properly part of subject studies rather than professional studies. Bill Wright raised the question what students on this course would be doing in the corresponding parts of professional studies: would there not be an overlap? Tony Becher took the view that PSE was not curricular: it was what senior staff in a school were required to do. Against this I drew attention to the UDE's statement of course aims, which included enabling students to consider the principles involved in constructing a PSE syllabus and helping them to construct lesson plans and schemes of work. Some months later the secretariat obtained further information from the UDE. This confirmed that all the students who took PSE as their second option along with main subject RE were placed for teaching practice in schools which agreed to give them a timetable in both subjects and where there were staff competent to act as supervisors. Against this background Group A had little difficulty in reaching the conclusion in January 1989 that a positive proposal could be made to Council.

Another institution where comparable issues arose and with which it fell to Group A's lot to deal was St Martin's CHE, Lancaster. In December 1986 we had proposed to omit from the Council's recommendation the community and youth studies course which constituted the institution's only secondary BEd, and from its secondary PGCE to omit a second subject method course in special needs education. As already indicated, it was known to be Government policy that provision for both specialisms within ITT should be discontinued. We also proposed to omit, on the grounds that they were non-curricular, second subject specialisms in the primary BEd in 'social ethics (introduction to special education)' and 'social ethics (the handicapped and disadvantaged person in society)'. However, in December 1987 the Principal wrote to say that the College was very disappointed by the exclusion of the social ethics options. All previous indications had been that the course was thoroughly suitable — and indeed it was true that HMI had commended it in their report. In asking for the Council's decision to be reviewed he stated that the College had a national reputation for its work in religious and moral education and that its students were unusual, because of the College's determined match between academic and professional competence, in being trained in the disciplines of ethical analysis and the art of making moral judgments. Group A considered this appeal in January 1988 and Ernie Grogan told us that he had also received a query from the Branch Assessor why we had not proposed the social ethics courses for approval and why, in our positive proposal for the institution's secondary PGCE, we had included a second specialism in 'social education'. We rehearsed our thinking about the social ethics courses, which was that we had nothing against them, indeed we hoped that the College would continue to run them, but they were part of professional studies rather than subject studies. So far as the social education strand in the PGCE was concerned, we had not given it a great deal of attention in our original discussions but Bill Wright's notes of our meeting with the College representatives indicated that they had confirmed that they provided teaching practice in it. This implied that it was a curricular subject, and that was our answer to Branch.

We reported to the Council on the College's appeal, and our decision to stand by our original judgment was endorsed. I suppose we all thought that the matter was then closed but more than a year later the Branch

Assessor wrote to Gillian Murton to ask for it to be reconsidered. What had happened in the interim was that the College had been invited to submit any further evidence or comments before the Secretary of State took a decision on CATE's negative recommendation. There had been a meeting with Branch and the Inspectorate as a result of which the College had agreed to change the title of the second subject specialism from social ethics to moral education, reflecting the fact that the College's progamme had always been seen as the academic counterpart of professional work in this area; it would have classroom applications. The supporting papers sought to relate this to the Education Reform Act's stated aim of promoting spiritual and moral development, gave an outline of academic course content and also supplied some detailed and rather fascinating examples of related activities for primary school children. It appeared that the Inspectorate had suggested to the institution how the course might be redesigned in this way. Group A was now persuaded on balance that the new moral education was a 'subject'. There was a feeling that its path through Council and past the Secretary of State might be easier if the course were simply called religious education, but we agreed to make a positive proposal for the inclusion of the revised course in the College's primary BEd. The Chairman, who had made some rather sceptical comments about the previous course titles, was with us on the morning of the September 1989 Council as we considered the form of our proposals. He asked if there were any precedents for a course with the new title. No one could remember any but in the afternoon it had a fairly easy ride at the Council. The DES Assessor who had asked us to reconsider the course spoke in support and I was able to explain that the academic side now drew in content from RE, PSE and moral philosophy; we had satisfied ourselves about its application. The Chairman pointed out that St Martin's was a Church college with a strong tradition in this field, and so at last the course was recommended to the Secretary of State.

Few other courses caused as much heart-searching as this one, but occasional problems of the same nature arose. In May 1987 a proposal from Group B which incorporated second subject method specialisms in careers education and guidance and in social and life skills at Worcester CHE was approved without discussion. But three months later the Group explained to Council that they had had to look at the latter again since Branch had queried its inclusion. The Group had worked from the principles they had had to establish with Nottingham UDE: if a course was on something which appeared in the curriculum and therefore had a methodological aspect it was all right. Their original decision in this case had been a conscious one which they reaffirmed, and Council supported them. Later that year the same Group brought forward positive proposals in respect of second subject specialisms in special educational needs in the secondary BEd and PGCE at Brighton Polytechnic. The Group felt able to propose them positively because the label was misleading: the courses really consisted of English and mathematics.

South Glamorgan IHE included as a second subject specialism in its secondary PGCE 'developing language skills for the less able pupil'. When Group C brought to the Council in March 1988 a proposal which encompassed this course the question arose whether it was equivalent to special educational needs. The Group said no — the course was related to the curriculum and to working in schools; the emphasis was on the 'language' rather than on the 'less able'. This specialism was withdrawn for further consideration but after some hesitation, and with the encouragement of HMI, the Group proposed the course again and it was included in the conditional decision to recommend the PGCE to the Secretary of State for approval.

An unusual variation on the theme arose from Leeds UDE. In December 1988 Group B brought to the Council a redesigned secondary PGCE which would permit some students to follow only one teaching subject method and instead of a second subject to take additional modular provision in TVEI, humanities, health education, special needs or TESL/ TEFL. These modules would not appear on the QTS letter and success would be reflected in students' references. The DES Assessor raised the familiar point about special needs, whether it was not really a professional issue. The Chairman gave what in this situation was the fundamental answer: the Criteria were a minimum, and if they were satisfied we need not be concerned about what an institution might offer as an extra.

It was Group C which brought forward the last two proposals to be affected by this problem. In July 1989 it was agreed to recommend that approval be withdrawn from a second subject method specialism in remedial education in the secondary PGCE at Crewe and Alsager CHE. And in November 1989 Council agreed to exclude from the recommendations in respect of the University of East Anglia a second methods course within the PGCE on 'school-industry and the new curriculum' on the grounds that it too was non-curricular. (Marian Giles Jones reported that UEA referred to it as SINC, which prompted the Chairman to ask if it drew teachers from the PIT.) At our final meeting in December we were told of a letter from the UDE objecting strongly to our decision. Council's position was, of course, that we had no objection to this option — indeed Group C thought it commendable — but that it did not count as subject studies. We had no difficulty in agreeing to stand by the decision and to point out to the institution a misconception in their letter, which referred to a recommendation to withdraw the course; on the contrary, we hoped they would go on with it.

In summary, therefore, while there were practical difficulties in maintaining consistency in this area, the principles which we sought to apply were clear. To be admissible as subject studies in ITT, and therefore to appear on a successful student's letter confirming QTS, a subject must be curricular in school; to be curricular there must be associated methodology, and the firmest evidence of this was that specific teaching practice should be provided.

Chapter 14

When is a Subject not in the Primary Curriculum?

At the beginning of chapter 13 I distinguished two aspects of the requirement that subject studies courses in ITT should be relevant to the school curriculum. I went on to deal with one of these — the case of subjects in training which were to do with professional skills required by some or all teachers but not actually taught in schools. The other issue was in connection with subjects in training which were undoubtedly academic subjects but were not adequately related to the school curriculum. This arose in its most acute form in courses for intending primary teachers, not only because the primary curriculum is more restricted than that of secondary schools but because, as noted in chapter 11, CATE interpreted the Criteria as meaning that students training for primary teaching should be prepared to assume a leadership or consultancy role within their school in some area of the curriculum. Circular 3/84 stated that the Criteria were based in part on the requirements of the White Paper, *Teaching Quality*, and paragraph 31 of that document had read:

> There is a strong tradition that one teacher should be responsible for each primary class. The Government recognizes the merits of this tradition, particularly in relation to the early years, and believes that all primary teachers should be equipped to teach across a broad range of the curriculum. But teachers are rarely able to deal satisfactorily with all aspects of the curriculum from their own knowledge. In some cases help from a member of staff with specialist expertise may be sufficient; in others, especially with older children, it is desirable for classes or other groups of children to be taught for particular topics by teachers with specialist expertise. (White Paper, 1983)

The point was developed in Catenote 3, which recorded that 'many [primary] schools are using teachers with such expertise as subject leaders or consultants' (CATE, 1985c); and it cited the more recent White Paper,

Better Schools, published after CATE was established, as emphasizing the need for intending primary teachers to have 'the ability and enthusiasm not only to undertake the role of class teacher, but also to share specialist knowledge with fellow teachers as well as with their pupils'. From these references, therefore, a critical test for subject studies in primary BEd courses was established: if the content was not sufficiently closely related to the primary school curriculum to enable students to play a leadership role on a school staff in some subject or area of that curriculum it did not satisfy the Criteria. In this chapter I describe how the Council wrestled with the problem of applying this principle in a variety of difficult cases.

Psychology

At the Council meeting in March 1986 Group C raised the question of the acceptability of psychology for main subject study in a primary BEd. It was agreed that this was a problem on which the Council needed more background information and at the following meeting Group C's proposals in connection with primary BEd courses at Liverpool IHE were deferred until the question about psychology had been decided in principle. For the May 1986 meeting the Chairman wrote the paper referred to in chapter 11 on 'non-curricular' subjects. In this he noted that among such subjects psychology occupied a special place, mainly but not entirely because of the way in which training for educational psychologists was accredited by the British Psychological Society. The BPS was willing to recognize suitable BEd courses with a specialism in psychology as satisfying two of the requirements for qualification as an educational psychologist — an honours degree in the subject and a teaching qualification; but from the point of view of the Criteria, though a BEd student specializing in psychology was provided with knowledge and skills that were valuable for making a strong contribution to the work of a primary school in the analysis of learning difficulties, remedial education, pastoral care and counselling and in meeting special educational needs, the student also sacrificed the opportunity to obtain understanding in depth of a subject or subjects in the primary curriculum. There were elements in courses in psychology that were relevant to the development of a teacher's curricular knowledge and skills — the paper instanced quantitative and computational methods, experimental design and statistics, biological approaches to the study of behaviour and the psychology of language — but psychology as a subject study in ITT was not a means of acquiring knowledge directly relevant to the content of the primary curriculum.

The Chairman's paper suggested that, nevertheless, there were three considerations which might persuade the Council in principle to consider BEd courses in psychology for accreditation — the apparent value of this route into the profession of educational psychology, the way in which they satisfied two of the main purposes of the subject studies criterion (ability to make a specialist contribution in the primary school and the benefit of pursuing study of a subject in depth in a manner appropriate to higher education) and the small number of such courses then on offer. He suggested, however, that before coming to a decision the Council might wish to know the views of HMI and the Department on current and likely future supply and demand in the school psychological service, on whether there was evidence of institutions other than those of which we were then aware being interested in developing such courses at the possible expense of the supply of primary teachers with a curriculum specialism, and on the question of precedent in relation to other non-curricular subjects. The point was made in discussion that it was not within the Council's remit to determine that subjects should be accepted for reasons other than their meeting the Criteria, but Group C's proposals about Liverpool IHE were deferred until the issue could be more fully resolved.

At the Council's next meeting, in July 1986, it was reported that the Department had taken soundings from the BPS among others and had concluded that there would be no adverse reaction if approval was not given to 'pure' psychology courses. In other words, there was no serious problem about the supply of educational psychologists. But courses in psychology could be approved on their merits if they contained enough of other subjects to satisfy the Council that the content contributed to knowledge of a specific curriculum subject or area. The question was raised whether this needed to be promulgated to the system. Another question to arise was whether degrees in psychology were appropriate for admission to PGCE courses: this, however, was seen as being a decision for institutions, whereas the subject content of BEd courses needed to be accredited by CATE. If that was an anomaly it was intrinsic in the Council's remit. To avoid unnecessary delay Group C now amended their proposal in respect of the primary BEd at Liverpool IHE by deleting the inclusion of the psychology subject specialism, and the remaining subjects in the degree were duly accredited.

When the Council next met, in September 1986, it had before it the paper from Andrew Collier, also referred to in chapter 11, in which he argued that the Council should consider seeking clarification of the subject studies criteria in relation to the curriculum. The Council's decision not to endorse psychology as a suitable subject for the primary BEd at Liverpool IHE seemed to him to have embodied a narrow view of the curriculum. On a broader view it could be argued that a teacher trained in psychology would bring valuable skills to bear on pupils with special needs, especially slow learners and pupils with behaviour problems. In discussion the Chairman adhered to the distinction between subjects which appeared on school timetables and those which did not. There was some support from other members for the relevance of psychology to the primary school curriculum, but the minute, which has already been quoted, did not refer explicitly to psychology.

The psychology specialism in the primary BEd at Liverpool IHE came back to Council in January 1987, when Group C proposed to reconsider it in a year's time. They believed it to be an excellent course produced for a valid purpose, but that purpose was a professional one and outside the subject studies criterion; the Council had to be consistent and look at actual course content as it was doing in other problematic instances, and here the argument was based on supply, a justification in terms of producing educational psychologists. The DES Assessor queried the proposal for a year's deferment: since the Criteria were not going to change would it not be more appropriate to make no recommendation? Andrew Collier said he accepted the judgment on this course, but it was an important decision for the system as a whole; he would regard it as profoundly unsatisfactory if no more educational psychologists were to be produced through the BEd and he thought that the attention of the Secretary of State should be drawn to this effectual outcome so that he should have the opportunity to change to Criteria if he did not like the implications. The DES man asked why this should arise. He could see two arguments. One was that a background in psychology can be helpful in teaching: this was agreed, but in training it can be part of professional studies. The other was the supply argument, but what was so special about the BEd route? Andrew replied by pointing out that in a BEd course where psychology was the main subject the student could not spend on it more than the equivalent of two of his four years, whereas a student who had spent three years acquiring an undergraduate degree in psychology could acceptably become a teacher with only one consecutive year of professional training. Renford Bambrough, however, said that this argument was simplistic since a degree in psychology would in practice include other things.

The Chairman was anxious that we should avoid that headline, 'CATE condemns psychology'. The actual proposal which Group C had put to the Council was 'that because the course does not at present meet the Criteria in ensuring that the student may expect to make a special contribution to a particular subject or area of the curriculum, the Council make no recommendation to the Secretary of State regarding its Schedule 5 approval, but reconsider it in one year'. It was now agreed to delete the last phrase, but to draw the attention of the Secretary of State to the fact that while the recommendation was specific to this particular course it might prove to be generally impossible to formulate a psychology course that met both the Criteria and the requirements of the BPS. In this event BEd courses would no longer be capable of providing a route to careers in educational psychology.

The Secretary of State accepted the Council's recommendation on this course, and approval for the psychology specialism in the primary

BEd at Liverpool IHE was withdrawn. The *THES* noted in October 1987 that this was the first time that CATE's recommendations had resulted in a course closure. (The headline — 'CATE rings death knell for Liverpool psychology BEd' — was only a little less dramatic than the Chairman had imagined.) The report added that this decision might have major implications for other institutions whose courses offered psychology as a main subject specialism; it claimed that there were fourteen such courses at six institutions. Interestingly, however, this report prompted a letter in the *THES* a week or two later from the Executive Secretary of the British Psychological Society. The BPS had written to the Secretary of State seeking reassurances about the position of psychology in ITT courses and Mr Baker had replied quoting the following advice from the Chairman of CATE:

> the Council do not take the view that a psychology subject specialism within an initial teacher training course for primary teachers is necessarily incapable of meeting the criteria. Although psychology as such is not a subject that features in the primary school curriculum, we should be ready in principle to accept that a psychology specialism met the criteria if in a particular case we were satisfied that the studies involved embodied sufficient elements directly relevant to that curriculum. (Newman, 1987)

The fact was, however, that from this time few subject specialisms in psychology were submitted to CATE as part of concurrent degrees for intending primary teachers, and none was ever approved. In the middle of December 1987 Group A were due to meet representatives of Nene College. Shortly beforehand Ernie Grogan sent us a copy of a letter from the College. They believed that it was possible to provide a psychology-related subject study which would not only meet the Criteria and be of great professional relevance but would also help attract good entrants to the early years sector. In the light of the Chairman's clarification they now submitted a draft proposal for a subject study in psychology of early childhood education for students specializing in the 3–8 years age phase. It would aim to provide students with a sympathetic understanding of psychological theories and concepts underpinning the early years curriculum through the key themes of development, learning and individual differences. We all agreed that as presented this would not do: it lacked curricular relevance. That was explained to the Nene representatives at the end of our meeting, and though no doubt disappointed to find that this horse was not a runner they expressed appreciation for the clear guidance given.

An institution which did offer psychology as a main subject specialism in a primary BEd was Trinity and All Saints' College, Leeds. In June 1988 Group B reported to Council that the institution had sought to justify the course mainly by links which 'informed' English, but the Group had not been convinced that its relevance to the needs of primary school children had been established. HMI had commented of the version running at the time of their inspection that 'it did not enable graduates to fulfil the responsibility of subject leadership in a primary school'. Council endorsed the Group's proposal to make no recommendation in respect of this course. Group A's experience with the modular degree which included psychology at Oxford Polytechnic is described separately.

An interesting instance of a primary PGCE for honours graduates in psychology was encountered by Group A when we were looking at the courses offered by Stranmillis College, Belfast. It was adapted for intending educational psychologists who wished to proceed to an MSc course at Queen's University, and entry was therefore conditional on candidates being acceptable to the University Department of Psychology. At Stranmillis the graduates studied the professional role of the educational psychologist and received an enhancement to the professional training given to other PGCE students in terms, for example, of the reading curriculum and the development of children's mathematical understanding. No conflict was seen here with the Criteria, and the course was approved by Council in May 1987.

Sociology

This was a subject which appeared to require especially careful handling because it was known to be regarded by some in education as a particularly relevant discipline for teaching, whereas the Secretary of State responsible for establishing CATE, Sir Keith Joseph, had made no secret of his hostility to it. Accordingly, in October 1986, when Group B proposed a positive recommendation in favour of the BEd primary course at St Mary's College, Twickenham, they drew Council's attention to main and second subject specialisms in sociology. We were told that they covered subjects like the family, the school, work and the workplace, the state, the media and other societies, all of which the Group saw as relevant to the primary school curriculum. Peter Scott said he was worried by a reference which had been made to Durkheim: he would rather the course were about 'our street'. The HMI Assessor pointed out that Council had accepted a degree in sociology as admissible for entry to a PGCE course; she felt that a trained sociologist on the staff of a primary school might help to give some bite to a topic like 'our street'. The DES Assessor, however, indicated that it was the opinion of the Secretary of State that sociology should be part of professional studies rather than a main subject. The Chairman said we had to recognize that sociology had acquired a symbolic character because of Sir Keith Joseph's known views. Our recommendation might be interpreted by the press in this light, so we must make it easy for the Department. He suggested that we ask the institution for more information.

In January 1987 Group B reported that they had carefully considered a further submission from the College. They were satisfied that sociology was an academically rigorous and coherent course option and that it was appropriate for intending primary teachers in that it added a significant dimension to a number of important areas of the primary curriculum such as RE, maths (through statistics) and social studies. A note to the Council from the Group also pointed out that the course could be justified in terms of the Criteria by helping students to become more effective when dealing with multicultural issues, the relationship between schools and the outside world and the values of a free society and its economic and other foundations (see Chapter 22). The Chairman said he agreed with the Group's proposal, but again drew attention to the 'symbolic' nature of this decision. The DES Assessor said he also agreed, but he thought it important to be clear why we were approving this course: its content was relevant to history, geography, the background of administrative structure — but we should not necessarily approve other courses called 'sociology'. In that spirit the proposal to recommend accreditation of the course at St Mary's was duly approved.

A primary BEd main subject specialism in sociology which was not recommended for approval was that at Trinity and All Saints College, Leeds. It was again Group B to whose lot it had fallen to review it, and they reported to Council in June 1988. The justification given by the institution had not been in terms of direct subject content but of the course's ability to inform history and geography. The Group were not satisfied that its relevance to the needs of primary school children had been established, and proposed that no recommendation in respect of it be made to the Secretary of State; this was endorsed by the Council.

A rather similar conclusion was reached in July 1989 concerning courses at Hatfield Polytechnic. Here sociology was both a main and a second subject specialism in the primary BEd. Group C proposed not to allow it as a main subject on the grounds that the course was concerned with process and skills rather than content; Branch, however, thought it acceptable as a minor subject where there was a stress on media work and availability was restricted to taking it in combination with one of only four specified main subjects. Both aspects of the proposal were accepted without discussion.

The Council's consideration of sociology in this context came full circle in September 1989 when we found ourselves dealing again with St Mary's College, Strawberry Hill. The College had developed a new BA (Hons) course with QTS for intending primary teachers and sociology was again offered as a main subject. This time, however, Group B had reached a different conclusion. Though the College argued that sociology was a strong subject in its own right, had links with other curricular areas and was a good background for project work, the Group had concluded that the St Mary's course was inadequate in terms of appropriate content, while its application was unsatisfactorily mediated through geography. It was also deemed to be insufficiently related to the National Curriculum, which had by now been promulgated. Council agreed that this course should therefore be excluded from its positive proposal in respect of the new degree.

French in Primary Schools

While modern European language courses for secondary teachers were neither unusual nor in principle problematic, two difficulties occurred with courses in French for intending primary teachers. One was the scarcity of schools where teaching practice could be experienced and the other, which towards the end of our term compounded the first, was the non-inclusion of a modern foreign language as a foundation subject for primary school children in the National Curriculum. (The place of the Welsh language in the school curriculum in Wales was recognized in Government policy, and there were no corresponding difficulties with the courses in Welsh provided by institutions in the Principality.)

The problem about school experience arose with the first such course which the Council encountered, in July 1986. This was at Liverpool IHE, and in separating the French specialism from the remainder of the primary BEd Group C proposed to attach to the former the condition that within a year substantial further progress should have been made in ensuring adequate attention to its methodology. Mary Hallaway explained that the Institute had not been able to find enough primary schools teaching the subject. If that difficulty could not be overcome the Group considered that this strand of the BEd would have to go. This was agreed, and the condition made rather more explicit.

It was for the Council's next meeting that Andrew Collier produced his paper on *CATE and the Curriculum*. He was not of course arguing against the approval of courses in primary French, but he made the point in discussion that only one LEA out of seventeen in the north-west had French in its primary schools at that time. In spite of this the Chairman denied that there was any inconsistency between CATE's attitude to French in principle and its caution concerning certain other courses since French did appear as such on some primary school timetables. That there was indeed no problem in principle about a French course for intending primary teachers appeared to be established in December 1986, when Council accepted a provisional proposal from Group A for the primary BEd at St Martin's CHE, which included French among its second subject specialisms.

The French subject specialism in Liverpool IHE's primary BEd returned to the Council in July 1987. Group C reported that the condition imposed a year before had not been met, they were not satisfied that students were adequately prepared for teaching French language in the primary school and they therefore proposed that no recommendation be made to the Secretary of State. This proposal was endorsed by the Council, and thereafter facilities for teaching practice were always carefully explored; when any proposal which involved French as a subject of study in a degree for intending primary teachers came before Council Marian Giles Jones in particular made a point of ensuring that the question was not overlooked.

Another aspect of French for intending primary teachers emerged from Group A's consideration of the BEd at Westminster College. There were two versions of this degree, one for the age-range 7–13 and one for 5–9. The choice of spans had been influenced by the existence of a middle school system in Oxfordshire, and the College made the interesting point that with the advent of the National Curriculum French would cease to be an optional subject in middle schools and demand for teachers of French would increase. When we queried its relevance for the younger range the College stressed the purpose of the course as the understanding of language; they argued that it was in the teaching of language that students would be able to provide curriculum leadership. However, we were not persuaded that French was a suitable subject for language consultancy work in primary schools. We therefore asked Council in November 1988 to recommend that approval of French as a main subject in the primary BEd should be restricted to the 7–13 age-range and this was agreed. Having thus been alerted to this point, Council made similar distinctions according to age-phase in approving the inclusion of French in several other primary courses.

In describing below our engagement with the modular degree at Oxford Polytechnic I refer to a discussion of French in primary schools in relation to the National Curriculum. Another aspect of the impact of the new legislation arose at the Council in April 1989 when I was introducing on behalf of Group A our proposals in respect of the University of Ulster, which included French and Irish as main subjects in the primary BA. Marian Giles Jones enquired whether it would be possible to continue with French after the introduction of what in Northern Ireland was to be known as the Common Curriculum and the consequent likely reduction in the number of primary schools teaching it. The DENI Assessor and I accepted that it might not, but it was agreed that speculation about the future was no reason not to accredit a course now running satisfactorily.

Classical Studies

In November 1988 Group C brought to Council proposals for additional main subjects in the primary BA at the University of Durham. One of these was Greek and Roman 'civilization, which was said by Marian Giles Jones to involve many things relevant to the primary curriculum — literature, history, myth and legends, philosophy, etymology and several aspects of art. Doubts were expressed about the ability of the course to provide curriculum leadership. Renford Bambrough said he thought it would be unfair to penalize it for having a wide range; the content had many connections with the curriculum. In classical times knowledge was not perceived as departmentalized into subjects, and this was why classical studies were a sound educational foundation. Council was moved in favour of a positive recommendation by the structure of the Durham degree; the course would be taken in combination with others. The Chairman observed that important questions underlay the discussion — the precise relationship between a subject in an initial training degree and the 'same' subject in the school curriculum. CATE had not assumed complete symmetry between what a student would be teaching and what he had been taught, but rather a general competence in a particular area.

However, a different conclusion was reached in September 1989 when Group B brought forward proposals for courses at St Mary's College, Twickenham, which included classical studies as a main subject in the primary BA. It was the Group's view that this subject should be excluded from a positive recommendation in respect of the degree as a whole. They had found the content to be too narrow to be justified as a sub-set of history and judged that it would not serve a primary teacher in training well. This aspect of the proposal was accepted, and classical studies at St Mary's did not receive CATE's approval.

Communication

On a number of occasions courses came before the Council which included the word 'communication' in their title, and this was felt to need some investigation. The first instance arose in December 1986, when Group C proposed conditional approval for a main subject specialism called simply communication in a primary BEd which Bangor Normal College wished to introduce. The proposed condition related to curricular leadership but when the Group brought the course back to the Council in July 1987 they considered that they had received satisfactory assurances from the College: the course was essentially English literature with some language element included. On that basis a positive recommendation was made. Another such instance was similarly resolved in January 1988 when Group C brought to the Council a number of proposals relating to Liverpool Polytechnic. Among the main subjects in the primary BEd was literature and communications. The Group were asked whether this meant in effect language and literature, and replied that this was more or less so, with a visual element as well. The Chairman remarked on the difficulty which sometimes arose in discerning a course's underlying rationale from its title, and the Council agreed to recommend this one.

A more difficult case arose at Trinity and All Saints College, Leeds. Its primary BEd included as a subject specialism communication and cultural studies. Introducing Group B's proposals to the Council in June 1988, Derek Mortimer confessed that there were slightly differing views about this course among members of the Group. Bernice Martin told us she had been swayed against wishing to see it approved by the apparent willingness of the College representatives whom they had met to take bits out or in without regard to the integrity of the course as an academic discipline. David Winkley on the other hand thought there were aspects of the primary school curriculum to which it could make a direct contribution. Peter Griffin wondered what favour was being done to students by mounting a course with this kind of title and diffuse content when what heads wanted in making appointments were teachers with precise knowledge. It was in the end agreed to defer a decision until the following Council meeting, in preparation for which we should all be sent full details of the course. The papers which were duly circulated included various documents from the College and comments from HMI. The inspection report had suggested that course content needed careful consideration 'if it is to have more than limited relevance for the future primary teacher'. Group B's HMI Assessor had been more forthright in suggesting that students who took such a course might find their career prospects stunted. The case submitted by the College argued that there was indeed relevance to the primary curriculum, and cited the aesthetic and creative area of learning and experience, the linguistic and literary areas, social studies, moral issues and the history of communication and culture, with methodological links to practical maths, science and technology. Representatives of the College when they met Group B had drawn attention to the widely recognized importance of the media and of students understanding how meanings are produced and circulated. They related many aspects of language in the course to the recently published Kingman Report.

When the Council met in July 1988 with these papers before us Derek Mortimer stressed that the level and academic rigour of the course were not in question. But not every member of the Group could accept the assertion that media studies had a place of their own in the primary classroom, even though this course had some interesting cross-curricular applications which might be of potential use to a primary school teacher. Other members of the Group again contributed their own somewhat conflicting views. Andrew Collier, for example, admitted to finding the course difficult to assess. In principle he thought it might just creep past criticism; his problem was that if he were designing a course on these lines he would start from a curricular focus and then broaden out, whereas this course started to the side of the curriculum and then an attempt was made to apply it. Renford Bambrough, speaking from outside the Group, declared that the course could not satisfy the Criteria as it was deeply and deplorably misconceived. It could not yield the right kind of relevance. The primary curriculum must have particularity, it must start from where children are, and that was not in discussion over coffee-tables! Having established that the institution would be unwilling to modify the course, the Council moved quickly from this point to a decision not to recommend approval.

Subject studies in language and communication in the primary BEd at Hatfield Polytechnic, proposed by Group C, were accepted by Council without discussion in July 1989.

Some Unusual Subjects

In introducing proposals concerning the primary BA at the University of Durham in July 1987, Group C drew attention to three main subjects which they had discussed at length. These were archaeology, anthropology and social policy. Their eventual conclusion was that the first two were allowable but that the course in social policy was extremely general and rather confused. It lacked relevance to the primary curriculum and the Group's proposal, which was endorsed, was not to include it in the recommendation to the Secretary of State. In November 1988 the Group brought to the Council three further subject specialisms which Durham wished to add to their already accredited primary BA. One of these was unproblematic; one was Greek and Roman civilization, which has already been described; the third was Islamic studies. The Group's proposal was to include all of them, and we were told that Islamic studies was not just about religion but was also relevant to history and geography. In the structure of the degree it would be taken along with subject studies in history, geography or theology. This was approved. In February 1989 Durham's primary BA figured on the Council's agenda once more. In response to CATE's earlier recommendation the Secretary of State had provisionally decided not to approve social policy as a main subject but had invited the UDE to make representations. After a meeting with DES officials and HMI the University had submitted details of a revised course and Group C had had to decide whether this differed significantly from the one that had been submitted before and if it did whether the Council would now be justified in offering different advice to the Secretary of State. The case was that the course drew on history and geography but the Group had concluded that it still failed to enable a student to make a special contribution to the primary curriculum and consequently their proposal was unchanged. Council agreed to confirm its rejection of the specialism.

In June 1989 Group B brought forward proposals for courses at the

Polytechnic of North London and Jews' College. There were five main subjects in their primary BEd — health, physical education and recreation studies; Jewish studies; language, literature and media studies; mathematics, computing and technology; and work and the urban environment. Bernice Martin observed that these titles might suggest that the courses were not calculated to produce curriculum leadership, but they had in fact been designed recently for what the institution supposed was in the Secretary of State's mind and it was ready to adapt them to the requirements of the National Curriculum. Each encompassed a cluster of subjects relevant to the curriculum and the Group had been ready to allow the first simply as PE, the third as language, and the last as history and geography; the fourth was self-explanatory. So far as Jewish studies were concerned, this had proved, contrary to the Group's expectations, not to be RE but a course for students going to teach in voluntary-aided Jewish schools, or schools with many Jewish pupils, to equip the students for curricular leadership in the humanities, especially language, literature, and history, in that context.

The Chairman at once identified that as a sensitive issue where a positive recommendation by CATE could be used as a base by other groups in society — for example, for courses in Muslim studies. Jews and Muslims already had a right to their own RE: did we want them to have their own curriculum as well? The DES Assessor pointed out that students emerging from this course would have QTS and could in principle teach in any school; he therefore thought that their ability to contribute to teaching the humanities should extend beyond the context of Jewish studies. He sought to draw a parallel with Steiner schools, though the Chairman suggested that Steiner education consists in process rather than in content. After some desultory discussion it was agreed to defer a decision and ask the Group to look at the course again. They were also asked to have another look at work and the urban environment, since the title seemed a little dubious for a primary course, and at health, physical education and recreation studies. Because of some other concerns which arose this submission did not reappear on the agenda until our final meeting in December 1989. It was still not possible to wrap it up completely and it was referred to the reconstituted Council. However, Group B had reached a firm decision not to recommend work and the urban environment. Further scrutiny had suggested that it contained no history and little geography, being mainly social sciences, and therefore provided an inadequate base for curriculum leadership within the National Curriculum.

Environmental and Social Studies at Nene College

In spite of the comment from the Secretary of State recorded in chapter 11, subject courses designated environmental studies or some variant of that phrase, which were not uncommon, did not present any difficulty in principle for CATE as they usually had a clear curricular relationship with history and geography and occasionally with other school subjects such as science or RE. Group A, however, encountered one course which caused us prolonged debate and heart-searching and which illustrated some of the problems of applying the subject studies criteria. This was a main and second subject specialism entitled environmental and social studies in the primary BEd at Nene College. We met representatives of this institution in December 1987 and resolved to our satisfaction most of the issues in their submission which we had identified in advance. It was in our discussion after the meeting that attention began to focus on this particular subject. The course relied heavily on the study of certain environmental and social issues — for example, natural resources, housing, unemployment, class and equality, race relations, the north-south divide, migration and immigration — and our principal anxieties related to the relevance of these topics to the primary curriculum and how far the course could prepare students for curricular leadership in history or geography, particularly the former. The tutor-in-charge, who was a historian, quoted a survey of primary schools in one part of the country which had revealed that only 14 per cent had 'history' as such on their timetable, and said this corresponded with her own experience. The implication obviously was that the Criteria, or our interpretation of them, were pushing the clock back to a subject-centred approach which did not reflect what was happening in the schools. But Bill Wright, also a history graduate, was looking for some kind of 'historical framework'. Over a period of several months we obtained a considerable amount of further detail about course content, but this did not allay our doubts. Few of the topics, for example, appeared to be history-led; there was very little history prior to the twentieth century to give a sense of chronology. The College's documentation used phrases such as 'a reflective, discussion-based mode of learning', which also rang some alarm-bells.

Another strand of doubt related to the structure of the course. The emphasis on issues, without a solid base of subject study, seemed to point to a lack of coherence and conceptual development. We were unclear about a basis for student choice which would avoid overlap and ensure progression. We could not see adequate bridges between the topics and their application in the primary classroom. The advice we received from HMI confirmed our reservations: the course was considered 'disappointing' in the sense that the institution was capable of providing a better one; it was sociologically based, whereas students would need a grounding in history and geography in order to make sense of it. We eventually decided that we should need to meet representatives of the College again, and did so in September 1988. They defended their position with conviction. The aim of the course was to develop competences; they were concerned less with subject content than with equipping their students methodologically, and the students did not have a free choice among the topics which they studied.

Doubts on the part of some members of the Group were not allayed, and we went back to the institution yet again, obtaining a written assurance that students would 'acquire a body of knowledge and set of capabilities in concert'. We eventually concluded that we must give the institution the benefit of the doubt, though when I had explained our concerns to Council in some detail in November 1988 and made it clear that our positive proposal was 'nem con' the Chairman looked as if he thought we were being generous perhaps to a fault. Derek Mortimer asked a rather complex question which I understood as seeking to establish whether the interdisciplinarity of the course was its form of delivery to the students or whether it equipped them to teach only in a topic-centred way. He professed himself reassured when I said I thought the former, and the proposal was then duly endorsed.

'The Individual, Society and Culture' at Kingston Polytechnic

A course which had also caused Group A difficulties, though of a rather different making, was a main subject in the primary BEd at Kingston Polytechnic entitled 'The individual, society and culture'. We concluded that it was insufficiently related to the primary curriculum to satisfy the Criteria and in July 1986 Council accepted our proposal that it should be excluded from our recommendation to accredit the degree. The institution was shocked and surprised by this decision and asked for more details of CATE's objections. Our SI agreed to go and talk to them and this resulted a few months later in a revised submission bearing the sub-title 'Studies in society, religion and health'. Now, for example, the theme of the individual and society was to be pursued in the second year through the study of drug use and abuse on the one hand and of religion in contemporary British society on the other. HMI considered the new form of the course to be promising though there were still questions about what its students would actually teach. We also wondered a bit about the applicability of some parts of the health education element to the primary curriculum, but when we met again with the institution's representatives in June 1987 we found them thoughtful and persuasive, and having satisfied ourselves on all the points which we or HMI had identified we made a positive proposal which was duly endorsed by Council.

However, at Group A's last meeting before Christmas 1987 the Council's senior DES Assessor joined us to disclose that officials and HMI had visited the Polytechnic and there were further problems about the course. The institution had admitted an error which gave rise to discrepancies in the documentation about the amount of course time. Moreover, our understanding of the content of the course — that in subject terms it comprised health education and RE — was not the way it had been presented to them, which was 'very sociological'. The institution had not got its act together on coherence, progression and structure. The Chairman was also present to assist us in handling this new development. He said he thought this was the first occasion on which there had been a visit to an institution after a CATE recommendation had been made on it, and he asked about the formal position: was the course being referred back to us? The DES man asked in turn whether what he had just said constituted new material for us or was it just a difference of perception? There followed a lengthy discussion which was continued at our first meeting in 1988. Some of our concern was procedural: Reporting Groups were going to be placed in a very difficult position if all the relevant views and information about a course were not made available to them before a decision was reached. Then there were the questions whether we had in fact been given any new information to justify us in changing our view and whether that view had been correct in the first place. Finally there was the political dimension: if the Secretary of State acted on Branch advice he would be seen to be rejecting a recommendation from CATE and this would be certain to attract attention; on the other hand it could be even more damaging to our standing and independence if we seemed to be, in the Chairman's phrase, a paper tiger, ready to change our minds at his behest.

By the time we met on the second occasion members of the Group had had an opportunity to consult our notes and reflect further and it soon became clear that none of us saw any reason to alter our decision. We had asked all the pertinent questions and received satisfactory answers. The Chairman, with us again as it was a pre-Council meeting, accepted that if we had no new information we should be entering a labyrinth by changing our recommendation now. This course had all the triggers that would set the Carlton Club alight — religion, Buddhism, sex, drugs; but let us stand firm, and let it be on the Secretary of State's head to turn it down. Ernie Grogan suggested that we ought nevertheless to inform the Council of what had happened, and the Chairman did so as one of his report items later in the day. Renford Bambrough seemed at first disposed to argue that we should be prepared to think again, but in the end Group A's position was unanimously supported.

Oxford Polytechnic — A Diverse Modular Menu

The BEd at Oxford Polytechnic for the age-range 3–13 was difficult to come to grips with because it was a modular course with a complex structure of unit credits. The subject modules or 'fields' were taken along with students who were not training to be teachers and were taught by specialist staff who had little contact with schools. The staff of the School of Education were concerned only with applied education — the linkage courses designed to 'translate' the academic subjects into their application in the primary curriculum. HMI had drawn attention in their report to the danger of too much choice leading to lack of coherence. However, when Group A met representatives of the institution in July 1987 we were satisfied that this danger was well understood and there were forms of counselling and direction which prevented personal timetables from becoming arbitrary or ill-advised. Nevertheless, we had two serious difficulties about the course. One was that it did not appear to provide adequately for study of the application in the classroom of the subjects which students might select for specialist study. The other related to these subjects themselves. A few were orthodox, some might be expected to have a reasonable proportion of relevant content but others bore little apparent relation to the primary curriculum (food science and nutrition, publishing, German language and literature, law). To the last category the institution had indicated that they were about to add another course — tourism.

There could be little doubt that we had encountered here a conscious philosophical challenge. The HMI Report had noted that some fields within the modular course were not part of the existing primary curriculum. In its formal response the institution had rejoined: 'We would argue that the study of any subject, at degree level, is relevant because it provides an opportunity to develop the fundamental skills of analysis, problem-solving and autonomous learning which is vital for any student aspiring to introduce those same skills to primary children.' They went on to argue that all subject fields had relevance either to the context of primary schools or indirectly to humanities topics. This approach was clearly at variance with the Criteria and appeared to be deliberately so. Group A decided that it had no alternative but to recommend non-acceptance and explain the situation fully to the Council. We had thought of specifying to the institution the subjects about which we had the gravest doubts and possibly indicating others which seemed 'all right', but after careful consideration we decided it would be best to place the onus on the institution to demonstrate the relevance of each subject to the curriculum. The Group's proposal to reconsider the course in a year's time was taken to Council in July 1987. The Chairman immediately commented in rather hard-line style: the Criteria had been published in

1984 and presaged some time before that — if an institution chose deliberately to flout them on a central point was there not a case for simply recommending to the Secretary of State that the course be not approved? To offer tourism at this stage was a bit much. As Peter Ward put it, a snook was being cocked. Nevertheless there were sensitivities in the situation, one of which was that the Polytechnic had a national reputation for its modular structures. The Chairman therefore proposed to offer the institution a further meeting at which he himself would clarify the Council's position.

Early in 1988 the Director of the Polytechnic sent to Ernie Grogan proposals which included a 'major restructuring' of the BEd course and which they believed took account of our suggestions and met the Criteria. They had in particular omitted ('with some regret') several of the subjects previously studied by BEd students. We found that these were accounting and finance, German language and literature, German language and contemporary studies, tourism, law and publishing. They drew special attention to a field designated politics, saying that they would wish to discuss further with the Council the arguments for and against retaining it. It was May 1988 before we were able to consider this fresh submission and we found that on one or two grounds our SI remained a bit suspicious: she thought we ought to explore further the subjects which they were still proposing to leave in this modular structure, such as psychology and sociology. And French, she observed, was not in the National Curriculum for primary schools, then on its way through Parliament. Bill Wright questioned how far that argument was relevant since the National Curriculum did not yet formally exist. I made the further point that even if the National Curriculum were enacted it would not be exclusive: the fact that something was not designated as a foundation subject would not mean that a school was not permitted to teach it. The SI conceded that this was so but argued that the prospective National Curriculum was still a measure of what would be appropriate for teachers in future. Bill Wright had implied that academic studies should not touch on subjects that were also in professional studies: if they did what were the students doing in professional studies? Tony Becher, however, referred to what he described as the reputable and established notion of 'the spiral curriculum', meaning approaches to a particular topic from several different angles. For instance, if sociology did not include a topic like race, which bears on multicultural education, it would lack credibility as subject study. In response to the institution's query about politics there were some jocular suggestions that it would have to go on 'political' grounds. Perhaps the institution had offered it as one that we were likely to axe in the hope that they would then get away with retaining the rest. Michael Dixon suggested that we might ask them to tether out another goat.

More seriously, we concluded that to make a judgment about politics we should have to ask for a full syllabus and we also decided that we should have to meet representatives of the Polytechnic again. The points we had to establish seemed fairly clear. Were the courses about which we still had anxieties of direct relevance to the primary curriculum? Did they equip students for some form of curriculum leadership? Was there adequate opportunity for the application of the subjects in methodology courses and in school experience? And was there a significant amount of overlap with professional studies which either unduly diluted their status as subject studies or raised questions about what the students were doing when they covered these topics again in another context? Our meeting at the end of June 1988 lasted for some two-and-a-quarter hours and in discussion our visitors were coherent and consistent. In particular they stressed that in reviewing their courses after their previous meeting with us they had looked carefully at all the relevant official papers they could find — from HMI and the DES, Schools Council and APU — in order to obtain objective measures and they were satisfied that they could justify in these terms all that they were now proposing to do. When the Group was able to resume consideration a week or two later Tony Becher began with the general observation that he did not consider their method of argument from externally proposed objectives to be valid. They relied on asserting that elements in the respective courses contributed to achieving some of these objectives but almost any area of study could be said, for example, to contribute to the acquisition of skill in rational discussion. Our concern must be with curricular relevance. With this injunction in mind we commenced to look at the individual courses, and we did not have too much difficulty in deciding that we could not make a positive proposal in respect of sociology or advise them to proceed with the inclusion of politics.

So difficult were several of the other fields that our discussion of them stretched over four meetings, and in one or two cases we had to go back to the Polytechnic for still further information. In summary, our eventual conclusions were as follows.

Psychology — The bias of the course was strongly towards the experimental aspects of the subject and the basis of the argument by the institution was that the course was a valid preparation for teaching science. However, our SI said she had asked a science subject specialist colleague for the bottom line for content in an adequate course for teaching science and his answer had included aspects which were not covered here. On balance we agreed that the course did not meet the subject studies criteria.

Computer studies — We reached the same conclusion. Michael Dixon alone seemed prepared to regard the course sympathetically, on the grounds that children had to be prepared for an increasingly computerized future.

But Anne Cattoor, while agreeing that the expertise of a teacher who had taken this course would be useful in a primary school, considered that it would be in terms of its application; computer science as such would not be on the timetable. Tony Becher could also see that it would be helpful, but our concern was not with relevance to pedagogy or pastoral care or management or anything else that went on in schools, but with the curriculum and the ability of a newly-trained teacher to make a contribution to it. Secondary skills should be added by in-service development.

Food science and nutrition — Having looked carefully at the content of this field we decided that it was acceptable as a foundation for science.

French — We considered that we could recommend the course on French language and literature since there clearly were primary schools where French was taught. I suggested a distinction between this and the separate course in *French language and contemporary studies*; however, in spite of continuing rearguard action on the part of our SI, who had strong reservations about the place of French in primary schools, we agreed to let both courses go.

Anthropology — Tony Becher and I were at first prepared to give this one the benefit of the doubt, but our DES Assessor at once remarked that if we put this course through Council the Secretary of State would certainly query it and we should need to be clear why we were recommending approval for anthropology but not for sociology. We were prompted by this to obtain more detail of course content and it then became clear to us that it did not satisfy the Criteria.

History of Art was another dubious subject in terms of curricular relevance, though we thought *visual studies* acceptable. Bill Wright put the point that in reviewing primary PGCE courses we must on several occasions have accepted an institution's submission that it was reasonable to admit a student whose first degree had been in art history; what, then, was the justification for excluding it as a main subject in a BEd? We rehearsed, not for the first time, the formal difference between the two cases: for a postgraduate course it was for the institution to determine candidates' suitability, taking account of the subject of their first degrees and other aspects of their experience, whereas CATE must judge the relatedness of subject study in a BEd to a subject or area of the school curriculum. This particular course had clearly been devised without intending teachers specifically in mind and only by straining ingenuity could it be seen as leading directly to expertise in an area of curricular relevance to the primary school.

Thus we had achieved a thorough review of the institution's offerings and at last reached conclusions which we could place with some confidence before the Council in December 1988. We were prepared to recommend approval of fifteen of their revised list of subject fields. There were five which we would recommend should not be approved (anthropology, computer studies, history of art, psychology and sociology); and we would also advise the institution that politics would not be acceptable. I introduced our proposal to Council with as much of the background as I felt necessary. As often happened at this stage the point that was picked up was not one which we had foreseen, or in this case for which I was well prepared. CI Alan Marshall expressed mild surprise that although we were proposing to exclude computer studies as a main subject we were allowing microelectronic systems. It was difficult in these circumstances to turn up a definitive reference at once, and Bill Wright defended the course, perhaps a little lamely, in terms of preparation for teaching science and information technology. The DES Assessor pointed out that IT was an area which all students were expected to encounter as a professional issue; but the point was not pursued. I checked afterwards that a reasonably convincing case had in fact been made to us in terms of physics and chemistry, technology and mathematics; but again, as Gillian observed to me later, we might have expected that such a detailed point could have been raised at an earlier stage. However, it was with no little relief that in mid-December 1988 we were able to strike Oxford Polytechnic off our pending list.

Miscellaneous

It would be possible from CATE's files to compile a list of all the course titles in use in training institutions 1984–89. The list would be very long, though most of the titles that did not coincide with school timetable subjects were recognizably related to them. To this category, for example, would belong expressive arts and creative arts. PE appears to be an area which is particularly prone to varieties of description; in the primary phase alone we came across dance (Middlesex Polytechnic), movement studies (St Mary's College, Strawberry Hill and Thames Polytechnic), physical and adventure education (Bangor Normal College), sport and physical activity in contemporary society (St Martin's College) and human movement studies (Derbyshire CHE and College of Ripon and St John). Worcester CHE designated most of the main subjects in its primary BEd as 'studies' — for example, English studies, studies in history and society. Group B had no worries about these particular courses, but the designation was queried by the Chairman: 'classical studies' usually meant no Latin or Greek! Westminster College offered a second specialism in third world studies in its primary BEd but withdrew it in face of some sceptical questioning from Group A.

When the Council was considering Kingston Polytechnic's 'The individual, society and culture' an SI observed that it might be a good idea for institutions running courses with titles like that to put the curriculum subjects in brackets afterwards — as, in this case, '(health education and RE)'. This, she suggested, might be philosophically distasteful but politically wise. It would certainly have been helpful in such other cases as people and society (University of Ulster), home and community studies (Bath CHE) or time, place and society (Kingston Polytechnic). Other unusual titles encountered were design-related activities (Liverpool Polytechnic) and writing (Crewe and Alsager CHE). The last of these, we were assured by Group C, meant creative writing and not orthography. It was claimed to have application and methodology in relation to all subjects, and dealt with the interaction between reading and writing; it was not seen as problematic. As always, CATE's concern was with the reality behind the title.

Chapter 15

Coverage of the Primary Curriculum

The Criteria prescribed that:

> The professional studies of intending primary teachers should
> ...prepare them for their wider role of class teacher. It follows
> that, particularly in the case of those intending to teach children
> in the early years, all relevant areas of the curriculum including
> religious education should be included in both the students'
> study and teaching practice. (DES 1984a)

In general the application of this clause did not give rise to many problems. It embodied an established aim of initial training for primary teaching and CATE was not required to enforce any quantitative measures other than those applying to language and maths which are discussed below. It was normally a matter more or less of routine to satisfy ourselves that some attention was paid to all aspects of the primary curriculum. Sometimes the number of hours devoted to a particular subject was evidently small, but any inclination to judge it inadequate had to be tempered by our awareness of the many other components which had to be squeezed into the course. Only rarely did a Reporting Group feel it necessary to make a positive proposal conditional upon progress being made towards more adequate coverage of the primary curriculum because some subject such as geography or RE seemed to be almost entirely missing.

However, problems could arise in assessing the comprehensiveness of curricular coverage when courses relied heavily on process models or topic work. An early case in point was the primary PGCE at Birmingham Polytechnic. HMI had commented that:

> the professional knowledge base acquired by students is difficult
> to assess. Nevertheless, it is clearly patchy and in many cases
> quite inadequate, notably in art, music and science, and it is

barely adequate in mathematics and language. The course tutors
need to consider whether the underlying philosophy of the course
would be seriously undermined by more specific, structured support in major areas of the curriculum...much is subsumed in
work on the topics.

Although the institution had rebutted this criticism on the grounds that it
was based on observation of the first intake of a newly-validated course,
its documentation for CATE claimed that the preparation of students to
teach all areas of a balanced primary curriculum was done by means of a
topic process which aimed to encourage child-centred teaching. Group A
concluded after meeting with representatives of the Polytechnic in June
1985 and subsequent clarification that a positive proposal was warranted.

However, this was the primary PGCE referred to in chapter 6 about
which we were told, after our proposals had been endorsed by Council,
of serious reservations on the part of HMI. The view of the Inspectors
was that the time and attention given to each element of the curriculum
was likely to be insufficient. Too much was left to chance and to school
experience as a means of covering curricular gaps. The claims that the
course was child-centred, process-oriented, and so forth, represented 'a
1960s Plowden view of the primary curriculum and does not prepare
students for the kind of curriculum they will find in schools today'.
Further information obtained from the institution purported to show the
subject area outcomes which the topic approach was intended to produce
and described how subjects were distributed and how tutors monitored
subject coverage. But HMI's reservations were not removed: they considered that what we were being offered was a model which responded to
individual needs, but suppose these needs did not arise? Trenchant comments were also made about some of the 'outcomes' such as those for
environmental studies, 'to have enabled students to create an awareness in
children of the world around them'. Our SI asked us, 'What the hell does
that mean?'

Clearly we had to go back to the institution again. The Secretary
wrote to say that the Council wished

to be further assured that students on the course acquire, in
adequate depth and breadth, those concepts and skills in each
primary curriculum subject which are required of the primary
school teacher. They would therefore be grateful for a more
precise statement of the concepts and skills which, in each curriculum area, the course is designed to impart.

The institution's response gave further details, including specific reference
to skills and concepts; these were listed for each area in tabular form

under the headings: outcomes; experience, activity; skills; concepts. Group A saw this as an improvement, though we noted that there was no account of measures by which to judge how far the outcomes had been achieved and some relevant concepts appeared to be missing. The situation incorporated a number of familiar CATE dilemmas: how could we know the extent to which what actually happened corresponded to the words with which we were presented? Given that it was not our job to dictate a syllabus, how far could or should we go beyond requiring minimal compliance with the Criteria into the realm of curriculum development? To Bill Wright the course appeared to belong to 'the wishy-washy school of primary education' but on balance we were sufficiently satisfied to recommend approval and this was endorsed by Council in January 1987.

In November of that year Group C reported a somewhat similar problem which they had encountered with the primary BEd and PGCE courses at Bedford CHE because the institution placed so much stress on topic work. The Group had difficulty in satisfying themselves how standards could be assured across the curriculum. Mary Hallaway gave as an example her anxiety about the RE content of a topic on desert islands — unless, she suggested mischievously, it consisted in 'My God, how do I get out of here?' In March 1988 we were told that HMI had been asked to investigate the topic approach and had confirmed that there was a danger of areas of the curriculum being omitted. The Chairman commented that this illustrated what had been known since the time of Plowden, that a topic-based approach in fact needs more care and resource than a straight disciplinary one. The sequel, however, was satisfactory. In June 1988 Group C felt able to make a positive proposal in respect of the BEd, and in November 1989 they reported that they had met the institution again and the PGCE had been redesigned to achieve the necessary curricular coverage; HMI considered the approach to have been strengthened. Both proposals were endorsed.

The requirements of the Criteria about teaching language and maths were more specific than those which applied to the primary curriculum as a whole. A minimum of about 100 hours was to be devoted to the study of each of these and to the understanding of their significance across the curriculum. This coverage might be achieved through a combination of taught time, structured school experience and private study. There were occasional difficulties in grasping what was actually happening in particular courses, but in principle this was a relatively straightforward criterion to check, and CATE was two-thirds of the way through its term before a question of interpretation surfaced. In making a positive proposal in April 1988 in respect of the primary PGCE course at King Alfred's College, Group B explained that the course had been held over pending demonstration of adequate coverage of language and maths; they further explained that they had adopted seventy-five as a reasonable number of hours in the prescribed 100 which should involve tutorial contact. Members of Group A glanced at each other, for we had adopted no such rule of thumb. A short discussion ensued. From Group B Andrew Collier said he had heard seventy-five hours' contact referred to by a local committee chairman as a CATE rule, though Derek Mortimer agreed that there was a variety of behaviours intermediate between direct teaching and private study, and that some of these might take place in a school. According to a slightly complacent minute, 'it was agreed that the Council's present practices were both reasonable and defensible'.

The subject received another airing in July 1988 when Group B withdrew a proposal in respect of the primary PGCE at Trent (now Nottingham) Polytechnic because they were not yet satisfied about the language and maths requirement. The total time in the course for each was well above 100 hours, but it was sub-divided into five components. The institution argued that four of these were contact time, but the Group could accept only two, and on that reading the contact hours were under half. In this course the problem proved to be presentational rather than substantive but the Chairman pointed out that the Kingman Committee, whose report into the teaching of English language had been published in March of that year, had found that some courses of initial training for primary teachers offered only twenty hours of 'taught time' and had thought this unacceptable. Group C reported that at an early stage they had consulted HMI and had been advised to look for about two-thirds contact time. The SI who was at the Council that day said she would consider 60 per cent a minimum. Alerted by these discussions, Group A subsequently took issue with the University of London Institute of Education, where we found timetabled sessions for English and maths in the primary PGCE to be forty and fifty-two hours respectively, and asked them to increase these to about sixty hours each.

We had similar concerns about the early years PGCE at St Martin's College. Here students worked in periods of fifty minutes, which meant a minimum requirement of seventy-two periods in order to achieve sixty hours, and they scraped home on paper by raising both to seventy-three. But these included twenty periods of 'school-based contact time' which the College claimed to be 'countable as contact time, since students will be required to plan, carry out and evaluate specific activities with groups of children'. It was not stated that a tutor would be present throughout, and we assumed that this could not be the case. Further enquiries from the institution produced only a defence dependent on acceptance of their definition of contact time to include 'that time in which directed and structured activities are carried out under the direction and supervision of the course teams'. Group A found itself in something of a dilemma in arbitrating on this. Though the figure of sixty hours had emerged from discussion at Council as an attempt to ensure consistency among the Reporting Groups there had been a lack of clarity about what should count towards this minimum requirement, and in any case the Criteria themselves gave no support to the view that there was any minimum number of contact hours within the prescribed 100. Admittedly the new criteria, by now in draft, did refer to 'a minimum of sixty hours contact time', but we could not anticipate that ruling. Eventually I suggested that we propose a recommendation for approval, but with a rider encouraging the institution to increase the number of (indisputably) contact hours. In introducing this proposal to Council in October 1989 I explained how we had come to the conclusion that what the College was providing was just acceptable unless either of the other Groups felt that it was grossly out of line with what they would have allowed. Both indicated that it was not, though Peter Scott reminded us that Group B had pulled back from a harder line in deference to the consensus. We had proposed to ask specifically for a report on the provision of contact hours to the reconstituted Council by the end of April 1990, and this was agreed.

The last institution to present us with problems on this score, and in a fairly substantial way, was Wolverhampton Polytechnic. In the primary PGCE the hourage on language and maths was clearly deficient, even on their own figures, and in the BEd it depended on whether school experience could be counted — without it there were only about thirty-five hours of lecture time. I have referred in chapter 12, to difficulties about contact time in subject studies generally in this institution's primary BEd which resulted in our seeing its representatives again less than a fortnight before CATE's final meeting. In the light of a fairly constructive discussion and changes which were to be introduced we were able then to propose a positive recommendation for the PGCE, though a decision concerning the BEd had to be left over for our successors.

The new criteria were to be firmer in specifying minimum hourage, but it could be expected that questions of definition would still from time to time arise.

Chapter 16

Problems with Subjects in Secondary Courses

Technology

At the beginning of CATE's work technology was not a common subject specialism in the courses which came before us and was often presented in combination with craft and design (CDT) or with design only. (Design and technology, a DES Assessor suggested to us in the spring of 1988, was more up-market than CDT!) The first institution at which a technology course presented difficulties for CATE was the University of Bath, which informed the Council during 1986 that it had been asked to extend its concurrent secondary BSc/Certificate in Education, for which CATE had already recommended approval, to include this subject. The new course was to be a concurrent sandwich degree in engineering with the certificate in design and technology. Group A, which had dealt with Bath's original submission, regarded this supplement as a comparative formality and put forward a positive proposal to Council in October 1987. However, at the end of November CI Alan Marshall attended a Group meeting personally to inform us that there were 'a lot of HMI worries' both locally and centrally about the situation. These related to student numbers, accommodation, resources, staffing and the manner in which approval had been obtained from the Local Committee. Not all of these matters were the direct concern of CATE and we were assured that there were no doubts about the quality of the University's engineering courses, but we had to take seriously the doubts expressed concerning the way the institution had set about preparing for this course in terms of staffing and methodology and concerning inadequate attention to health and safety. There were procedural and political concerns here too, as there had been at Kingston Polytechnic (see chapter 14), and these occupied a good deal of our time and attention. It also became apparent, as Alan Marshall was unwilling to let us meet directly with the Subject Inspector (Subject Inspectors, he said, tended to be John the Baptist for their subjects), that we had become involved in a difference of view within the Inspectorate. After a good deal of agonizing about how to handle the situation it was agreed that the Chairman and Secretary of CATE should meet the Head of the Bath UDE, and the outcome of this was that the UDE would consult the local Inspector.

However, because of its assured place in the National Curriculum, technology in general was now becoming a subject with a higher and more controversial profile. In preparation for a meeting of Group Convenors in November 1988 Gillian Murton had prepared this note:

> Submissions are now being received which include engineering and technology subjects. HMI and the Department have some misgivings about this development against a background of continuing debate on the nature of technology and the realistic attainability of engineering in the school curriculum. The problem for CATE is how to approach consideration of these courses. It has been suggested by HMI that any courses described as engineering or technology — to be recommendable for accreditation — should be strongly rooted in CDT. It has also been suggested that CATE might consider giving guidance to institutions on courses in these fields. I doubt whether CATE could or should attempt such guidance — particularly at a time of unresolved debate — but clearly we need to ensure internally a CATE line on this issue.

As usual at Convenors' meetings there was little time for discussion, and this question was referred to as a minefield.

A revised submission came forward from Bath UDE early in 1989 for what was now to be a 'technology: science' course; this meant that technology would be the main subject and science a subsidiary. It soon became apparent from our HMI Assessor that there were continuing concerns within the Inspectorate. These related largely to course content: what amount of CDT was included and what skills did it impart? what was the significance of 'design' being dropped from the course title? We decided to ask for another meeting with the institution at which they could give us a presentation of the course, and this took place in April 1989. HMI supplied us with a battery of questions which we 'might wish to explore', and we had a very thorough discussion. We confirmed from our visitors what HMI had hinted to us, that the course had not recruited well: in fact there was only one student! Nevertheless we concluded that considerable thought had gone into the planning of the course, which took advantage of the technological expertise and facilities of the University and the well-founded professional components of the PGCE programme. In other words we saw no obstacle to preparing a positive proposal.

However, shortly before our meeting with Bath discussion at the

April 1989 Council meeting had arisen from a proposal put forward by Group B in relation to King's College, London. This institution had secondary BSc courses plus certificates in engineering, mathematics and physics, each with education; it also included in its secondary PGCE a specialism which it called technology with science and which Peter Scott said was essentially a course in problem-solving. Alan Marshall queried this, pointing out that so far there was only an interim report on technology within the National Curriculum and no formal definition of what technology actually was. The outcome of this discussion was to defer for the time being decisions on both the BSc plus Certificate in Engineering with Education and the technology with science specialism in the PGCE pending progress in consideration of similar courses by other Reporting Groups, while Alan Marshall undertook to provide a note on current issues affecting technology in ITT. As Group A moved to a decision on Bath, therefore, we were not surprised by indications from our Branch Assessor that the CI was not ready to give HMI approval because the Working Group under Lady Parkes had yet to produce its final report. We considered, however, that this was no reason why we should not put forward our proposal to the Council, especially if we added the suggestion that the letter conveying the decision to the institution should indicate our expectation that the University would take into account the findings of the National Curriculum Working Group and make such adjustments to the course as might be necessary. When I presented this to the Council in June 1989 (in the absence, as it happened that day, of Alan Marshall) there seemed to be general agreement that technology courses should not be held up because the Working Party had not pronounced. Indeed the next proposal on the agenda was a resubmission by Group B of the two courses at King's College, London, and a recommendation for their approval was also agreed subject to the same advisory comment. On the PGCE specialism in 'technology with science' the Chairman remarked that this again raised the question what technology was: he didn't see how you could have technology *without* science. In this particular case, however, the point was that the course included an integrated science component.

In the meantime Group A had acquired another submission in this area — one for a secondary PGCE in technology put up jointly, at the instigation of the DENI, by the two Belfast Colleges, St Mary's and Stranmillis. It had been validated by Queen's University, and there was agreement that candidates should normally have an engineering degree. However, our DENI Assessor told us that the Northern Ireland Inspectorate had concerns about it on the grounds that it was too science-based and needed to be more practical and creative. We shared the regret expressed by the Inspector that the first joint venture by the colleges respectively serving the two religious communities in Northern Ireland should appear so disappointing, but in the face of the criticisms expressed we had no option but to defer further consideration until more detailed comments were available. For some months we continued to hear that the Inspectorate were trying to get it knocked into a shape in which we could look at it again with greater hope of a satisfactory outcome.

Against all this rather confusing background it was with some interest that in June 1989 we received the Secretary of State's proposals for design and technology for ages 5–16 based on the final report of the National Curriculum Working Group. In her covering letter Lady Parkes stated that their approach to design and technology was intended to be challenging and new. The aim of their proposals was to prepare pupils to meet the needs of the twenty-first century: 'to stimulate originality, enterprise, practical capability in designing and making and the adaptability needed to cope with a rapidly changing society'. The attainment targets and programmes of study which the group had constructed were intended to assist and encourage the coordination of the knowledge, skills and values necessary for design and technological activities and currently to be found in art and design, business studies, CDT, home economics and IT. Teachers of these subjects would need to collaborate on the delivery and assessment of the new programmes.

The document was on the Council's agenda in July 1989, when it was briefly introduced by George Hicks, who had been the HMI 'observer' on the Working Group. He explained the Group's view that design and technology capability should be developed through the 5–16 age-range in relation to artefacts, systems and environments. The report identified two kinds of knowledge — skills and values essential to the acts of designing and making, and processes which were context-related. It stressed the importance of undertaking design and technology activity in a variety of contexts such as home, school, recreation, community, business and industry. IT was seen as a separate strand, with the underlying premiss that it should be used as a tool in all subjects and not treated as a special element in the curriculum. The Chairman referred to the variety of course titles which Reporting Groups had encountered and said that it was now a question of interpretation of what 'technology' courses should be. What were the main points for delivery by institutions and for scrutiny by CATE? Alan Marshall suggested that there were three. The first, for PGCE courses, was the problem of match of first degrees, which he considered might be in engineering or business studies or product design. The criterion for student selection should be a reasonable element of designing and making in the first degree. Secondly, the 'recent and relevant' experience for appropriate staff (see chapter 24) now needed to be in designing and making subjects. And thirdly the same consideration must apply to students' experience in teaching practice: it must be provided in schools where this was happening in a range of contexts.

Group A was very willing to have another look at the joint submission from the Belfast colleges and a revised version came before us in November 1989. However, it appeared that there were still worries within the Northern Ireland Inspectorate. These now turned mainly on health and safety aspects, which were not regarded as adequately permeating the course. We agreed to defer a decision until our final Group meeting in December, and though some reservations were still reported to us we were conscious that safety was not an aspect which had figured prominently with CATE before and we decided to go ahead with a positive proposal supported by a rider encouraging further attention to this. It turned out to be the very last proposal to come before Council at its final meeting, and in view of its ecumenical significance it was accepted with general satisfaction. A monitoring report was to be sought in the summer of 1991, after a year of operation.

English as a Second or Foreign Language

During the summer of 1985 Group A was reviewing courses at Birmingham Polytechnic. Subjects offered in the secondary PGCE included as a main subject specialism the teaching of English as a foreign language (TEFL) and as a second subject the teaching of English as a second language (TESL). Insofar as there was consistency in the common usage of the two expressions, TESL seemed usually to apply to giving help with the mastery of English to children in Britain who came from homes where another language was normally spoken, whereas TEFL would be used to refer to teaching English overseas or to providing courses in the UK for foreign students who would usually be adults. On these definitions TESL appeared in principle to be acceptable as a curricular subject but TEFL not so. In the case of the courses at Birmingham Polytechnic the latter was withdrawn from our proposal for further consideration.

Shortly after this, Group A reviewed the courses at Leicester UDE, where the first and second method courses in the secondary PGCE included 'English as a second or other language' (TESOL). Examples were given in the prospectus of a variety of possible contexts for practitioners of TESOL: secondary education in Britain, adult education abroad, industrial English in Britain, English for science, technology and commerce overseas. As well as producing competent practitioners the course aimed to improve student teachers' knowledge and understanding of English language structure and the societal contexts in which ESOL operates and to consider theories of language learning. The imprecision with which terminology was used in this area was illustrated by the fact that in completing their Cateform the institution referred to this subject as EFL. Nevertheless, in the terms in which it was described, and bearing in mind the large ethnic minority population in Leicester from the point of view of teaching practice, we did not regard it as problematic, and a positive recommendation was made by the Council in March 1986.

Another example both of the submission of such a course and of the problem of labelling arose with Sheffield UDE, which again fell to Group A to review. The subjects in its secondary PGCE included one described as 'TEFL/TESL'. However, we satisfied ourselves when we met representatives of the institution that the course was indeed targeted at the school age-range, and it was included in the positive proposal endorsed by Council in July 1986. The same test was subsequently applied to such courses running at a number of other institutions.

In the early summer of 1988 Group A began consideration of the submission from the University of Manchester, where the qualifications on offer included a Diploma in the Teaching of English Overseas, described as a one-year course for the age-range 5–18. The graduate entrants were required to have a minimum of two years' teaching of English as a foreign language, and at the time of the HMI visit most of the students had other work experience as well. The Inspectors' report spoke highly of the staff and of the reputation of the qualification, though it noted that the amount of teaching practice was not adequate for training to teach in Britain. But by conferring QTS the course had the potential to make a valuable contribution to education in city areas where problems of bilingualism and the teaching of children whose first language was not English could be alleviated by the presence of teachers who had taken it. In spite of these favourable comments we felt that there were a number of issues in relation to the Criteria which we had to clarify when we met representatives of the UDE at the end of September 1988. Our most basic concern was to establish whether the course justified recognition for QTS, and the UDE acknowledged that in this connection the course title was probably unhelpful: they emphasized their commitment to the UK and maintained that the course was designed as much to prepare students for supporting language work in this country, a role which they said was increasing in the early years area, as for teaching overseas. Teaching practice in British schools had now been extended to six weeks, and during overseas practice, normally carried out in secondary schools in Portugal, students were supervised by two tutors from the UDE.

Since we had asked for supplementary information about others of Manchester's courses it was some time before we resumed discussion of their DipTEO and in the meantime we began consideration of the submission from the University of London Institute of Education. Among the main subjects offered in its secondary PGCE was 'English for speakers of other languages'. When Gillian Murton arranged a meeting of Reporting Group Convenors in November 1988 she placed the question of TEFL/TESL courses on the agenda. Pointing out that CATE had recommended, and the Secretary of State had approved, the inclusion of this subject in some courses recognized for QTS purposes and that other courses were under active consideration by Reporting Groups, she said she understood that the Department was considering a change of policy whereby at least TEFL would cease to be a subject for QTS. A paper was likely to be before Ministers at the end of the year and we should need to consider the implications for current CATE reviews and for submissions already received. At this stage there was not much more to be said; I observed that if a distinction were to be enforced between courses preparing for teaching abroad and those preparing for teaching in schools in this country it should not be on the basis of course titles, since we had found little consistency about this.

Group A met with representatives of the University of London Institute early in December 1988 and in respect of the TESOL course our enquiries focussed mainly on teaching practice. The specific concern was that for some students the course structure entailed their final teaching practice being in Spain. However, we were assured that they were supervised on the spot by Institute staff; and after some further loose ends concerning London had been tied up a proposal including the main subject specialism in TESOL was endorsed by the Council at the beginning of June 1989. To the same Council meeting Group B brought proposals in respect of the University College of North Wales, Bangor, which included a conditional recommendation for a secondary PGCE in 'TES/FL'. This was again a course for British graduates with some teaching experience, usually abroad. Part of the teaching practice was provided in Madrid, so that students were prepared for teaching both overseas and in Britain, and a second method option in a modern language or English was being introduced. The DES Assessor said that Branch was still struggling with the concept of TEFL and TESL; courses did not come in any standard form and it seemed necessary to take them case by case. The proposal for conditional approval at Bangor was endorsed. At the following Council meeting, in July 1989, the DipTEO at the University of Manchester was also approved by the Council, subject to a division of the age-range, after we had obtained written reassurances about the UDE's arrangements for teaching practice.

In the middle of September 1989 Gillian told me that the Secretary of State had not confirmed CATE's recommendations for the accreditation of either the TESOL course at the London Institute or the DipTEO at Manchester. He had written to the Chairman to say that he had decided to continue the existing approvals of the courses at these UDEs with the exception of the TEFL/TESL specialisms and that his officials would be writing to the heads of the institutions. These letters simply said that he had deferred a decision while he gave closer consideration to the suitability of the courses for ITT; existing approvals stood for the forthcoming academic year until a final decision was made. Gillian felt that the position needed clarification and she proposed to raise it a meeting of Convenors which was to follow Council in about a week's time. Nothing more had been heard of the DES paper which we had been given to understand would appear before the end of 1988, and in respect of courses which had come before us in the meantime she felt that guidance had had to be dragged from the DES rather than being volunteered and was usually in the form that individual courses would be considered on their merits. If this was what was happening in the cases of the London and Manchester courses that was one thing, but if the delay in deciding about them was a disguised indication that the DES did not like such courses in principle then CATE needed clear advice.

At the September 1989 Council, prior to the meeting of Group Convenors, another TEFL/TESL course appeared on the agenda. This time it was in a proposal from Group C in respect of the secondary PGCE at the University College of Wales, Aberystwyth, where it was offered as a second method course. It aimed to prepare prospective teachers for the teaching of English as a second language to immigrant pupils in the UK or to pupils or students in overseas schools and institutions, for the use of English as a medium of education for pupils or students who knew little or no English on school entry, and for the use of English in bilingual education programmes. HMI had commented after their inspection three years previously that most of the students aspired to careers overseas. The DES Assessor now repeated that the Department's line was to consider such courses on their merits in relation to the provision of teaching practice (which in the case of Aberystwyth was where possible in multiracial schools or in centres admitting learners of English) and to their relevance to the school curriculum in this country. This course was recommended for approval without further discussion.

In her agenda note for the Convenors' meeting Gillian referred to a departmental minute indicating that concern surrounding courses in ESL was not solely with its suitability as a subject in ITT but with whether the Criteria were being met in respect of students' first degrees being appropriately related to the work of schools and in respect of the breadth of subject study achieved in course content. I could see a basis for the first of these points, since we had observed that quite a number of the first degrees were in non-linguistic subjects, and indeed this had been defended on the grounds that a formal grammatical approach was not what was wanted in teaching English as a second language. But Marian Giles Jones said she did not understand what the second point meant since all PGCE courses are in methodology and not subject study. As usual at a Convenors' meeting held after Council there was little time for discussion and the DES Assessor seemed to have said all he had to say on the subject already that afternoon in connection with Aberystwyth.

Even in the absence of clear guidance the Council's work had to go on, and in our attempt to clear our pending tray before the end of the year Group A now went back to the TEFL course at Birmingham Polytechnic which had been put to one side in September 1985. In preparation for a meeting with the institution we were told that students did not necessarily have a language background or pre-course experience; the course was described as practical and classroom-oriented. All the students taking TEFL as a main subject method in the PGCE also took TESL as a subsidiary, so that they became qualified in two fields; over the years there had in fact been an equal division in students' destinations between TEFL abroad and TESL in Britain. The three successive experiences of teaching practice were respectively in an inner-ring school in Birmingham, an FE centre in Birmingham and a secondary school in Barcelona, where there were comprehensive arrangements for supervision. Our discussion of the course gave us no reason to dispute the Polytechnic's conviction that it was a valuable one both socially and linguistically, but at our meeting with the Polytechnic's representatives I did not disguise my view that our conclusion was bound to be a negative one in the sense that the course was not school-related. By their own definition of TEFL it was for FE in the UK or for school teaching abroad. Our visitors did not seem unduly dismayed and indicated that if the Secretary of State was recommended to withdraw approval from the course in terms of QTS they would be sorry but would probably continue to run it because of its intrinsic value and popularity. Group A duly put a negative proposal to Council in October 1989 on the grounds that TEFL was a subject inappropriate to the secondary curriculum. The DES Assessor repeated the familiar formula about looking at each course on its merits and asked only if we were being consistent. One or two recent cases were mentioned and Gillian confirmed that they were all different. Our negative proposal about this particular one was then endorsed.

When we came to our final meeting in December 1989 there were still several instances of second language courses pending. The DES Assessor was able to tell us only that it had been decided to grant approval to all courses so far recommended by CATE but to refer the principle of TEFL/TESL courses to the new Council. Applying the tests which had been developed elsewhere we confirmed our positive recommendations for the second subject specialism in TES/FL at UCNW, Bangor and recommended approval for one in ESL at Reading UDE. We decided not to recommend one at the University of East Anglia which had first been submitted as TEFL and then retitled TESL; Group C had concluded that their teaching practice arrangements were not an adequate preparation for teaching school-age pupils. Thus although the future of this subject for QTS remained unresolved at the end of our term, the criteria which we developed had been applied consistently and could be defended in principle.

Community Languages

At the end of October 1987 the Dean of the Faculty of Education at Birmingham Polytechnic wrote to the Council Secretary about a community languages option which had just been validated and launched within their already approved secondary PGCE modern languages course. The course team, in partnership with Birmingham Community Languages Unit, had written a course for teachers of Punjabi and Urdu which could be taught within the framework of the modern languages route. There were elements of the latter which were generic to all language students, so that parts of the new course could be jointly taught with other modern language students; other areas of methodology were specific to community languages. A supporting paper presented the rationale. The course had been developed in association with Birmingham LEA in response to local and national educational needs — firstly to exploit fully the linguistic resources of bilingual children in the schools and secondly to increase the supply of ethnic minority teachers. It was hoped that the course would also help promote the study and status of Punjabi and Urdu within the school curriculum.

It was February 1988 before this supplementary submission came before Group A. The point on which discussion focussed was student selection. Applicants could be expected to be native speakers of the languages concerned but they might not be graduates in these languages, and native speakers do not necessarily have a strong background in the literature or culture of the language they speak. GCSE examinations were on offer in community languages, so there was a case for teaching them, and the object of this course was to produce teachers of these languages in school rather than teachers of other subjects through these languages. We decided we needed to know more about the professed aim of exploiting the linguistic resources of bilingual children and about the requirements for entry. The Polytechnic's response on the first point was that bilingual children personified a linguistic phenomenon which was an important and permanent aspect of British life; the gift of bilingualism was both a strength for the individual and a gain for society. It was the right of bilingual children to see that their mother tongue skills were valued and recognized in schools and that at the secondary level they should be given the opportunity to study the language, literature and culture of their home as a school subject. Students would be encouraged to draw on the experiences of ESL teachers in terms of methodology and materials. So far as selection was concerned, the Faculty would not necessarily exclude any literate and fluent speaker of Punjabi or Urdu, though fluency would not be enough in itself. An Urdu-speaking physicist might in principle be an acceptable applicant but they would be looking in addition for experience of working with children in a language-teaching situation, or evidence of sensitivity to language issues. We decided to ask the institution for a list of the people they had accepted for the course, showing their qualifications, together with an assurance that students must be graduates and that their degrees should contain a linguistic element.

Before we were able to resume our consideration of the Birmingham course the Council received, in September 1988, a proposal from Group B for a positive recommendation in respect of an additional main and second subject method specialism in community languages in the second-ary PGCE at Sheffield Polytechnic. Here the language in question was Urdu and in introducing the proposal Andrew Collier said they had looked carefully at selection and other aspects of the course and had asked all the appropriate questions. Admission was restricted to native speakers of the language who had studied it for a minimum of two years in higher education; the Chairman remarked that it was surprising there were enough people around who satisfied these conditions. It was recognized that though this was not strictly our problem the course might present a question for the DES since the Secretary of State had recently indicated that he would prescribe approved languages to be taught under the National Curriculum; on the other hand, even if languages from the Indian sub-continent were not included in the approved list they could still in principle be taught in the discretionary area of the timetable. Andrew said there might be another problem in regarding Urdu as a foreign language, for while it was foreign to him it would not be foreign to most of those to whom it was taught. The DES Assessor, however, did not see any difficulty about this, and it was agreed to endorse the Group's proposal for approval of the new specialism.

It was September 1989 before Group A considered the information which Birmingham Polytechnic had supplied about the community lan-guages course there. Though entrants had been few, all were graduates, some of universities in the sub-continent, and all were experienced in language teaching, though the Dean pointed out that every student brought different skills and experience to the course. We were to meet representatives of the institution again in October, and we agreed that we should have to probe the linguistic and cultural background of the stu-dents and how it was assessed. It transpired at the meeting that for 1989/90 there had been no entrants at all but the Faculty still wanted approval to run the course. They admitted that there were problems about checking overseas degrees — they used the rule of thumb that a Master's degree in the sub-continent was equivalent to a first degree here — but the DES left the decision to the institution. In answer to my query about the ability of any native speaker to teach culture they said they looked at applicants' background in literature and culture. Teaching prac-tice was no problem: there were plenty schools teaching community languages, though when they got into schools these teachers tended to be used to teach other subjects through the language. On this basis we felt able to take a positive proposal to the next Council meeting, where there seemed no disposition to query it. David Winkley asked if only the two languages were to be offered. I was able to report that Bengali had been considered, but Punjabi and Urdu appeared to be where demand mainly lay. The proposal was endorsed.

Psychology at the University of Hull

The status of psychology as a subject specialism for intending secondary teachers might not have been thought to present the same intrinsic difficulty as it did on primary courses since the subject is taught in a few secondary schools. However, some problems arose for Group A from a course at Hull UDE. This was an integrated Honours BSc and Graduate Certificate in Education with psychology as one of the main subject study specialisms. HMI had noted that it was difficult to provide adequately for its methodology since it did not appear widely on school timetables. But the course was designed to prepare students to cater for the needs of older children with learning difficulties, and representatives of the University told us that students would actually do their teaching practice in English or maths, in which they must have an 'A' level, and would be able to offer one of these subjects to pupils up to age 16. This was a curious situation, as it meant in effect that a second subject in training became the students' main subject in teaching. We concluded that this was not acceptable and in July 1987 the Council agreed to exclude the psychology main subject from its recommendation for approval of the course as a whole.

In spite of this the Hull submission lingered on Group A's agenda for more than a year, during which time we had some complex discussions with the UDE about possible alternatives. We had at first been inclined to think that a resubmission of psychology as a *second* subject specialism might be successful, since the requirement for school experience would then be reduced by two-thirds. But the institution offered no other second subjects and had no established pattern for such provision. The revised proposal which they produced was for a course in maths and psychology which did not seem to us capable of doing justice to either subject; and although they sent us a list of seventeen schools and colleges in their catchment area which entered candidates for external examinations in psychology and which could therefore be used for teaching practice, it transpired that not all of these offered it below age 16, and none of the teaching practice was with pupils of compulsory school age. The Chairman of course took no part in these discussions and left the room when anything to do with his own University came to Council. Thus in November 1988 I found myself not only explaining in detail to CATE the position at which Group A had arrived but chairing the meeting at the same time. It was accepted that Hull's second submission must also fail, but since it was for a course neither running nor in firm planning we concluded that no further recommendation to the Secretary of State was required; the UDE had simply to be given a clear response.

Miscellaneous

Science was not of course in principle a problematic area of subject study but like some others it came before us in a variety of guises. Apart from standard offerings of chemistry, physics and biology, courses described as 'combined', or more frequently 'integrated', were not unusual and became more common towards the end of CATE's life. In September 1989 it was observed that the secondary PGCE at the University College of Wales, Aberystwyth included a second method specialism in 'balanced science'. The Chairman asked somewhat incredulously if this was actually what was going down on the QTS letter. It appeared that 'general' and 'integrated' were both now *démodé*, and Alan Marshall confessed that HMI were encouraging 'balanced'. The Chairman shrugged defeat as David Shadbolt whispered to me that there might be a case for reverting to 'natural philosophy'. I suggested aloud that we might resume the debate when an institution submitted a course in unbalanced science, but this jest was capped later in the meeting when Keele UDE was found to offer 'broad balanced science'. So, it later emerged, did Loughborough UDE. It was approved as a second subject at Trent (now Nottingham) Polytechnic and St Mary's College.

In September 1987, when games appeared before the Council as a second subject specialism in the secondary PGCE at the University of Leeds, it was thought to be the first time we had encountered a course with this title. But HMI had commented favourably on it and it was a timetable subject in schools, so it was considered acceptable. Group A later came across games coaching as a second specialism in the secondary PGCE at Westminster College, and we discussed this with the institution when we met them in September 1988. Our concern had been with the relevance for the course of students' qualifications but we were assured that students were required to have good experience of at least two major sports in which they were knowledgeable and proficient at representative level. A working knowledge of a range of other sports was also required since the course was designed to equip students to teach games lessons and share in coaching work in support of PE specialists. It was planned, taught and evaluated in conjunction with a local comprehensive school. When we proposed the course to Council in January 1989 there was some discussion as to whether it was properly a teaching subject as opposed to specific coaching qualifications. However, when I quoted the institution's stated aims concerning pupils' health and safety, methodology and the development of sensitivity to the differing needs of learners our proposal was accepted, albeit somewhat unenthusiastically.

In January 1989 Group C proposed a positive recommendation for the secondary PGCE at Roehampton Institute with the exception of a second method specialism in peripatetic music. This was available only to those taking music as a main subject but the Group had concluded that it was not a second subject in the ordinary sense. The Chairman said it seemed an odd title — a bit like 'mobile library' — but discussion suggested that it really meant instrumental teaching on a basis other than class work, and as Bill Wright pointed out, that might have been expected to be covered in methodology anyway. Its exclusion was agreed. Six months later we were asked to consider a two-year part-time PGCE at the same institution in music 'for teachers of music'. One question to arise about this was whether the graduate-equivalent qualification possessed by entrants could be one for performers rather than for teachers; if so, it might contain inadequate theory. However, this anxiety was resolved, and the course was approved in September 1989.

Also encountered and approved as subjects for intending secondary teachers were fashion and textiles (Bath CHE), technical graphics (King Alfred's College), outdoor activities (University of Leeds and University College of North Wales), sports studies (Roehampton Institute) and health-based PE (Worcester CHE). The last of these came up from Group B at our final meeting; it had been devised with an eye to health education as a cross-curricular theme in the National Curriculum.

Chapter 17

The National Curriculum

A number of references has already been made to CATE's awareness during the latter part of its term of the impending impact of the National Curriculum. Although the Great Education Reform Bill, popularly known during its time of passage as the Gerbil, was not published until November 1987 its contents had been foreshadowed in the consultative document which preceded it in July of that year. In October, when the Minister of State visited the Council, Mrs Rumbold referred to the effects of the Government's proposals on the school curriculum; ITT would be expected to pay greater attention to preparation for science teaching in primary schools. The Chairman said he proposed to make the National Curriculum an agenda item for our next meeting. He had already discussed its implications with Branch and it seemed to him that the criteria to which CATE was working would be necessary but not sufficient for the new dispensation.

In November there was in fact no extensive debate. The Chairman drew attention to three paragraphs in the consultative document which appeared to have a special bearing on our work — those respectively which placed science as well as English and mathematics among the core subjects, which excluded foreign languages from the foundation subjects in the primary school, and which referred to the need for teachers to be trained for assessment. He said we could not wait until our term expired before preparation for the National Curriculum should begin. A variety of points were made by members, but Tony Becher was clear that we had no authority to make demands of the training institutions not warranted by the current criteria, for example in relation to primary science: 'they haven't been told to do it, and we haven't been told to make them do it'.

In July 1988 the Gerbil became law, and with our agenda for the September Council we were sent the first few pages of the Education Reform Act, which covered the curriculum. The reports of the first two subject working groups — those on mathematics and science respectively

— had just been published, and much of the debate which ensued was concerned with the implications for in-service education and how these needs should be met. However, the Chairman did express the view that the National Curriculum reinforced the need for subject study. Critics of the Criteria might claim support from the fact that the National Curriculum pointed to an interdisciplinary approach but there was a real danger of teachers who lacked understanding of individual subjects trying to teach in an interdisciplinary mode which they thought was inventive and imaginative but was actually vapid and empty and just plain wrong.

He was concerned about the final year of the Council's work. We must not be seen to be dying. The National Curriculum must influence our proceedings, and what we did must be consistent with foreseeable developments. Marian Giles Jones observed that people were already saying that the CATE criteria were out of date; she had heard frustration and disquiet expressed about this at conferences as long ago as April. The Chairman asked if an awareness exercise was needed; should we take any specific action such as producing a Catenote 6 on the relationship between the Criteria and the National Curriculum? But DES advice appeared to be against this, and we were reminded that our 1984 criteria referred to the curriculum 'as it may be expected to develop in the foreseeable future'. So it was argeed that we should make no public statement but should take such opportunities as offered at conferences and so forth to make it clear that the National Curriculum did not render Circular 3/84 obsolete: we were already concerned with the emergent curriculum as well as the curriculum as it was then.

In December 1988 the afternoon of the Council meeting was given over to a further debate on the National Curriculum. For this occasion we had with us the Chairman of the National Curriculum Council, Duncan Graham, and its Vice-Chairman, Professor Paul Black. Mr Graham told us they were pleased by how far some institutions had already gone in thinking about the needs of those students who would be leaving in 1989. In the longer term he thought ITT would need re-examination, especially for primary schools. Would everybody have to be an expert, and was this feasible right across the curriculum as well as in a specialist area? How could schools develop team collaborative teaching, become a thinking community rather than people locked in boxes? We had to consider not just the mechanics of this but its context in terms of parents and the political arena. How far was specific training required for the National Curriculum? He thought there were specific areas, such as assessment. Was there a need for a national curriculum for teacher training? He thought so, provided it meant a commonality and not an arid greyness. How could the colleges be apprised of the National Curriculum and kept up to date on the changing scene? What types of teachers were needed, especially for secondary schools? How were the cross-curricular themes for 14–16-year-olds to be handled? Professor Black added a few further points, including a comment on the levels of adherence becoming apparent from schools in relation to the guidelines already published: these ranged from following them line by line to having just bought a set of new science books and not going to throw them away.

The debate which followed was not very productive. It became apparent that the Chairman had structured it in advance by asking selected members to prepare an input from some particular point of view, with the result that little advantage was taken of our visitors' presence to ask them questions or indeed to address the questions which they had themselves raised; word came back that they had found it rather a waste of time. Andrew Collier seemed to me to make one of the more valuable contributions in pointing out that nowhere did the Criteria ask whether a course produced good teachers, and that it might be better to look for levels of competence, to establish output measures, and work back from there. David Winkley argued that it was critical to get the aims of the National Curriculum into the minds of teachers in the classroom, to get them thinking about the whole curriculum, something they had been bad at in the past. It was also interesting to hear the Senior Chief Inspector, who had joined us for the afternoon, refer to the Education Reform Act as radical because attainment targets could liberate schools from subject domination. We should not be aiming at the total expertise of every teacher but of every primary school staff. There must be differentiated teaching in primary schools because we knew that when teachers feel insecure they can shut down an area of study. We were moving into a period of shortage: there must be an emphasis on quality and more flexible ways into teaching.

We concluded with mutual expressions of desire to keep closely in touch, and CATE's next engagement with the subject came in February 1989, when we welcomed Philip Halsey, Chairman of the Schools Examinations and Assessment Council. He referred to this body's strong commitment to the notion that assessment should be continuous and seen as part of the teaching and learning process. Outlining the Council's timetable for the ensuing few years, he said he thought the necessary in-service training should come from the ITT institutions so as to facilitate transfer of skills. Anne Cattoor stressed the magnitude of this task for primary schools: new teachers might have the skills but would lack experience, while mature teachers would lack training. The Chairman asked for our impression of the attention paid to assessment in the courses we had reviewed. 'Very thin', said Michael Pipes, and others agreed: courses were directed at delivery rather than evaluation. As the Chairman pointed out, assessment tended now to be covered as a professional issue and to be 'owned' by the Education staff; the need now, our HMI Assessor suggested, was for a shift to curricular studies and to applications specific to each subject. Mary Hallaway thought things were moving in many institutions, but CATE was not as yet asking much about this. When Gillian Murton and I both raised the question of whether and how our stance should alter, the Chairman reminded us that the Criteria already referred to students gaining 'experience of the purpose and practice of the assessment of pupil performance and a knowledge of the appropriate levels of performance to be expected from children of differing ages, abilities and aptitudes'. In short it was all there, and it was up to us from now on to give this area more prominence in our enquiries about the courses submitted to us.

Although we were now less than a year from the end of our life my observation was that the Council did during that period pay more attention to how institutions were handling the question of assessment and indeed to how courses were being generally adapted to meet the needs of the National Curriculum. We could not change the rules under which we were operating, but no one queried our right to be interested in the significant developments which were by now affecting the whole of education, and similarly it became not uncommon for institutions to justify to us the new and revised courses which they submitted for accreditation in terms of their relevance to the National Curriculum. The discussions recorded in this chapter also served to focus CATE's own thinking about the changes we thought necessary or desirable in the criteria which it would be the responsibility of our successors to enforce.

Part Three

Other Aspects of the Criteria

Chapter 18

Selection and Admissions

'The Government are also concerned that the training institutions should improve the selection of students for training': thus the 1983 White Paper, *Teaching Quality*. It pointed out that at that time some 20 per cent of those entering training courses failed to complete them satisfactorily. In March 1985, when the Chairman reported to the Council on a meeting with the Secretary of State, levels of entry qualifications for BEd courses were mentioned as one of Sir Keith Joseph's particular concerns. And indeed it was no doubt significant that the Annex to Circular No. 3/84 in which the Criteria were set out devoted five of its seventeen paragraphs to selection and admission to initial training courses. The section began by following the White Paper closely in stating that institutions should have adequate procedures for assessing whether or not candidates display-ed the personal and intellectual qualities suitable for teaching and showed evidence of professional potential. Special arrangements for exceptional entry by mature applicants are dealt with in the next chapter but specific points concerning normal entry could be itemized thus:

1   The procedures should in all cases involve a personal or group interview with each candidate.

2   Experienced practising schoolteachers should be involved at this or some stage of the selection process.

3   Institutions should ensure that selection procedures at all stages provide equal opportunities for all applicants, irrespective of race or sex.

4   In assessing the personal qualities of candidates, institutions should look in particular for a sense of responsibility, a robust but balanced outlook, awareness, sensitivity, enthusiasm and facility in communication.

5 Previous employment or self-employment, or experience of work with children or adolescents in a school, youth club or otherwise, should normally count in a candidate's favour.

6 All entrants must have attained a grade C or above in the GCE 'O' level examinations (or equivalent) in mathematics and English.

7 Entrants to postgraduate courses must hold a degree of a British university or the CNAA or a recognized equivalent qualification.

8 Entrants to undergraduate courses should fulfil the normal academic requirements for admission to first degree studies.

9 Undergraduate students intending to teach secondary pupils should normally hold an 'A' level pass (or equivalent) appropriate to the disciplines intended to be their main teaching subject(s).

10 For students intending to teach primary pupils a broad base of studies at 'O' and 'A' level is particularly important.

11 Institutions should satisfy themselves that all entrants to courses of initial teacher training are able to communicate effectively in spoken and written English and, where appropriate, in Welsh.

12 All entrants should have a satisfactory health record.

At the end of 1985, when considering a draft version of Catenote 4 about links between institutions and schools, the Council decided not to include detailed guidance on the involvement of teachers in student selection but to make this the subject of a separate Catenote, and a working party was set up to prepare such a document. The initial membership was Peter Ward as Chairman, Angus Clark, Michael Dixon, Peter Griffin and Peter Scott. It was significant that the first three of these were the Council's non-educationists, for it was in this area that the members from industry or commerce were expected to have the greatest contribution to make. It was September 1986 before a draft Catenote appeared on our agenda, and even then Ernie Grogan explained that it had been produced by the secretariat and not actually seen by the working group in its present form. Peter Griffin immediately expressed serious reservations about one paragraph which committed the Council to recognizing that local circumstances might make it impossible to engage teachers in the interviewing of every candidate. The Chairman was prompted by this to observe that we should not underestimate the political content of the whole issue.

The draft followed the pattern of the already published Catenotes in beginning with a summary of the requirements of the Criteria and the procedures which institutions would need to follow in order to comply with them, and then went on to discuss these in more detail. One paragraph observed optimistically:

> Institutions will be aware of much of the considerable body of research which has been conducted into ways of assessing the predictive value of formal academic qualifications, of identifying personal qualities, and of determining the value and relevance of these to particular vocations. The Council hopes that institutions' selection procedures will take full advantage of this research.

Someone suggested that we ought to append a bibliography. In general, however, the draft did not appear to be saying a great deal and Mary Hallaway expressed the fear that the final section (on interviewing procedures) would be greeted with derision in the system as an exercise in teaching grandmothers to suck eggs. We took our lunch break in the middle of this item, and Renford Bambrough asked me if I thought anything would be lost if we abandoned this Catenote altogether. Clearly he did not. However, discussion resumed in the afternoon, and it was agreed that the secretariat would prepare a revised version for consideration by the working party.

A second draft came to Council in February 1987 but again it transpired that this was the work of the secretariat since the working party had not been able to meet. Points of both detail and principle were made by Council members and the paper had a fairly rough ride. There was a general feeling that exposition of the Criteria did not sit happily with illustrations of good practice — prescription and commendation became blurred — and a minority remained unconvinced that a Catenote on these lines was worth producing. Stressing the need for care in what we said, someone suggested that this Catenote might still be being read in 1991; Ernie Grogan rejoined, 'We may still be discussing it'. The discussion also brought out the strong view of the non-educationists on CATE that selection processes for teacher education were incredibly amateurish compared to what happened in industry. The Chairman responded that it was possible to entertain high wastage rates as a price worth paying and to take comfort from the supposition that something rubs off on everyone. As time began to press he sought to wind up the debate and it was agreed that another draft was needed. 'The ship is flawed and holed and starting from the wrong port', he concluded, 'but still worth designing'.

For some time thereafter we were told regularly at Council meetings that the putative Catenote 5 was not yet ready; then even this ceased. When Peter Ward resigned from the Council in the autumn of 1987 I assumed that the project had now sunk without trace but this did not prove to be the case; a revised version appeared among our agenda papers for a Council meeting at the beginning of March 1988. Renford Bambrough at once repeated his doubts about the value of telling people very largely what they already knew but the Chairman took a straw vote and most members thought the paper worth proceeding with. We were invited to put detailed comments in writing and this resulted in yet another draft in April. Most of my own and evidently some other suggestions had been incorporated; I could, for example, claim credit for the final sentence of the paragraph on equality of treatment for candidates, since my knowledge of fair employment practice in Northern Ireland had prompted me to propose forms of affirmative action rather than mere avoidance of bias. The general view, which the Chairman said was shared by HMI, was that this version of the Catenote was a considerable improvement on its predecessors. The only remaining ground for hesitation in the minds of most members was that the document was appearing so late in CATE's life; Derek Mortimer suggested that a reference at the beginning to its being 'the fifth in a series of Catenotes designed to help training institutions secure accreditation for their courses' might appear somewhat cynical at this stage and it was agreed to refer instead to amplification of a particular aspect of the Criteria. With this and a few other minor changes the document was at last approved and Catenote 5 was published in June 1988. In September the Chairman reported that there had been many requests for copies.

On the issue of the involvement of practising teachers in the selection process the Catenote attempted to take a balanced view. Having recognized 'active participation in the interviewing stage' as the ideal form of contribution, it went on to accept that 'local conditions' might make this impossible for every candidate. There were other ways in which teachers could make a contribution, such as assessment based on observation of applicants' conduct and relationships in schools, or the design and review of selection procedures. There was no doubt that of the various aspects of the Criteria relating to admissions this was the one which had to be probed most carefully, and which occasionally prevented unconditional recommendations from being made. Reporting Groups looked for convincing evidence that there was a structured teacher influence in each institution's selection procedures. We were often told that it was resource constraints, both in the institutions and in the schools, which prevented the physical participation of teachers in interviews from being more widespread, though occasionally we felt that institutions created unnecessary burdens for themselves by the high proportions of applicants selected for interview.

As with one or two other of the Criteria it was surprisingly late in CATE's life that what might have been thought a fairly fundamental point of interpretation arose at Council. In July 1988 Group B mentioned in introducing proposals for Newman and Westhill Colleges that in only about 60 per cent of cases were teachers involved in selection. This passed without further comment but in October I raised within Group A the acceptability of what we had been told was only a 15–20 per cent involvement of serving teachers in BEd selection at Westminster College. My colleagues on Group A did not see this as a significant cause for concern but I felt that an issue of consistency was beginning to emerge. It came to the fore in April 1989 when Group B introduced a conditional proposal for courses at King's College, London. Explaining one of the Group's reservations, Bernice Martin said that although teachers were involved in determining the criteria for selection the actual strike rate for teacher participation in interview was only 20–25 per cent. Bill Wright and I queried whether the Criteria warranted any specific expectation of teacher presence, and Marian Giles Jones said that similarly Group C, while looking carefully at how teachers were involved in devising criteria and maintaining standards, had not been insisting on any given rate of actual participation. The DES Assessor and CI Alan Marshall also agreed that teacher participation was not specifically in the Criteria and there was no warrant for a harder line. It was agreed at the end of the discussion to downgrade Group B's proposed condition to an advisory comment. It so happened that at the very next meeting, in June 1989, Group B found themselves proposing a similar condition in respect of PGCE courses at the University College of North Wales. Bernice said they had been careful about this in view of the recent discovery that Group B had been taking a harder line on the issue than the other two Groups but all this institution appeared to do was show application forms to teachers in advance of interviews; there was no systematic procedure. In this instance the requirement for progress on teacher involvement in selection was accepted by Council. (The courses were eventually approved.)

Other aspects of the admissions criteria were relatively unproblematic. The necessity for students to possess 'O' level English and mathematics prior to entry was established by Group A in relation to Manchester UDE, which ran a part-time PGCE to meet the needs of ethnic minorities. It had been the practice to allow those not qualified in maths to complete the course within a year but our SI told us firmly in October 1988 that this was not an acceptable procedure: an institution had no authority to admit a student without 'O' level maths. We did not, however, find any problem with an arrangement at London University Institute of Education, which was prepared in some circumstances to provide its own examination in English and maths for applicants to their PGCE course such as mature students who might lack these qualifications and be too late to enter for GCSE. The part-time PGCE at Manchester presented another difficulty which occasionally arose — that of establishing the standard of overseas degrees. Manchester UDE took advantage of having the Joint Matriculation Board virtually on campus and drew on their expertise in assessing equivalence; all non-standard qualifications were scrutinized by a Senate Sub-committee. Tony Becher was anxious to defend the right of the UDE to determine its own admissions, saying that no other position was possible.

We rarely made much enquiry into the personal qualities for which institutions looked in their applicants but these were sometimes mentioned in their written submissions. In a critical article about the Criteria in the *TES* in July 1986 Professor Jean Ruddock of the University of Sheffield pointed to a lack of research evidence in this area. A writer whom she cited had queried the desirability of 'a robust but balanced outlook', suggesting that 'a critical and reformist attitude' might be no less relevant. A long list could in fact be produced of qualities other then those quoted in the Criteria for which institutions said they looked. Some which I noted were a sense of humour, imagination and resourcefulness, a lively mind, reliability, adaptability, stamina, tenacity, resilience, the developing ability to reflect on experience gained, potential as an autonomous learner, self-knowledge, open-mindedness, social composure, healthy self-confidence, friendliness, warmth of personality, an outgoing personality, the ability to think quickly on one's feet, the ability to articulate ideas about education, breadth of cultural and general interests, realistic anticipation of all the implications of a career in teaching. Candidates possessing all these attributes, one occasionally reflected, might even have become members of CATE.

Chapter 19

Exceptional Entry

There was another aspect to admissions policy and this proved rather more controversial. It also proved to be the one element in the Criteria which was changed during the life of CATE. Paragraph 16 of the Criteria related to what became known as 'exceptional' entry to initial training.

> Mature applicants for undergraduate courses who lack the conventional entry qualifications for first degree studies may be admitted as special entrants if they have suitable personal qualities and appropriate experience of adult and working life. The admitting institution and its validating body must, however, be satisfied as to the relevance of that experience, the intellectual capacity of the student to complete a degree course successfully and his or her competence in the use and understanding of mathematics and the English language. Institutions should be able to demonstrate that they have carefully considered the basis on which any special entrants are admitted, that the standards of courses will not be compromised in order to accommodate such students, and that end-of-course qualifications will be awarded only to those who have attained the professional and academic standards required of all prospective teachers. In any event, at least 75 per cent of the students entering any one course should possess the normal qualifications for entry to a first degree course. (DES, 1984a)

Cateform 1 called for a statement of the number of students admitted to each undergraduate course for the two most recent intakes with normal entry qualifications, with equivalent qualifications, and 'exceptionally'; and a note explained that 'exceptional admissions means students without the normal "A" level or equivalent qualifications'. From these returns it was possible to see at a glance whether the 'exceptional' admissions, if any, exceeded 25 per cent of the total intake to any course.

Council noted in March 1985 that although this limit was firm as a criterion for accreditation it could apply to course intakes only since the issue of Circular 3/84.

At the end of October 1985 the Secretary of State wrote to the Chairman to record his special interest in two particular aspects of the Criteria. One of these related to what the Swann Report had had to say about the recruitment of ethnic minority teachers. A DES consultation paper of July 1985 had referred to a number of special access courses which had been developed: —

> in order to allow adults who successfully complete them to gain entry to higher education courses (including teacher training) without the normal minimum entry requirements. These courses certainly have a role to play in increasing the number of people from the ethnic minorities who obtain professional qualifications including teaching qualifications. It should be noted, however, that the criteria for the approval of initial teacher training courses require that at least 75 per cent of the students entering any one course should possess the normal qualifications for entry to a first degree course, in order to ensure that the standards of the course are not compromised so as to accommodate a higher proportion of non-conventional entrants. As the vast majority of special access courses do not lead to any recognised qualification, and as most such courses are not certificated, they will normally be regarded as non-standard entry. (DES, 1985)

The linkage made explicit in this passage between exceptional admission through such means as special access courses and the recruitment to teaching of people from the ethnic minorities indicated that the subject was one of some sensitivity. At the end of the Council's last meeting in 1986 the Chairman mentioned it as one of a number of tricky issues to be faced in the following year. He added, and the DES Assessor made it clear that he agreed, that the equivalence of courses to 'A' level was an issue for the Department and not for CATE and that we must avoid getting involved in a 'race' issue. In February 1987 Derek Mortimer said there was no doubt the 25 per cent issue was being politicized: he had heard it stated that CATE had set its face against exceeding this figure. The DES Assessor suggested on this occasion that the question should be seen in the setting of access to higher education as a whole; there was a move through the CNAA to give access courses wider currency than mere recognition by their own institutions. The Chairman thought this a helpful contextualizing comment: what we must try to avoid was a big cloud of smoke obfuscating the main work we were trying to do. In May he reported correspondence on the subject with Sir Peter Newsam, Chairman of the Commission for Racial Equality.

During the latter part of 1987 Group A began to deal with courses at institutions in which there was a substantial number of special entrants. They were, as it happened, institutions that were either associated (West Midlands CHE and Wolverhampton Polytechnic) or merged (Bradford and Ilkley Community College), and in both cases there was a conscious mission to extend opportunity through recruitment by exceptional entry. Though HMI had found the performance of access students in the BEd at West Midlands College to be below that of the normal-entry students in some areas of study, the institution believed that 'exceptional' students did not perform significantly worse by the end of the course, and this was also the view of Bradford and Ilkley, which was in a position to be quite selective among applicants for exceptional entry. It also emerged when we met representatives of Bradford and Ilkley that most of these applicants were white; their coloured applicants tended to be fully qualified. Nevertheless, the limit imposed on exceptional entry by the Criteria was unequivocal, and in the case of West Midlands/Wolverhampton we had an additional concern in that they were seeking 'to ensure a balance of intakes across courses which more accurately reflects the community which the institutions serve'; this appeared to imply a strategy of positive discrimination and we decided that we needed advice from Legal Branch.

At our Group session before the November 1987 Council the Chairman disclosed that the Secretary of State had withdrawn the 25 per cent limit. He said we now had to consider how to check that the floodgates did not open — 'not that they would do that', he added quickly. The Secretary of State had made his announcement in the House of Commons in reply to a Parliamentary Question and at the Council meeting we had before us the full text of his reply and a 'Dear Bill' covering letter to the Chairman from Clive Saville, Assistant Secretary in the Further and Higher Education Branch. The Government, we were told, was committed to the recruitment of additional trainee teachers from the ethnic minorities and it would be regrettable if rigid application of the 25 per cent criterion were to diminish the recruitment of suitable candidates for teaching from such groups. The Secretary of State did not wish to undertake piecemeal amendment of the Criteria but he would now be prepared to consider recommendations from the Council for the approval of courses which did not comply with the 25 per cent criterion where the Council was satisfied that the course in question was nevertheless of the high quality required. Institutions would still have to satisfy themselves about the relevant personal and intellectual qualities of their recruits and to monitor their progress, and the Council would be expected to satisfy itself that the institutions had suitable procedures for this purpose. Institutions whose courses had already been approved should be given the opportunity to make a further submission if they expected their pattern of admissions to change. We also received confirmation that the DES had written to the CNAA asking them to develop in consultation with the universities a suitable network for standardizing access courses.

Some discussion ensued about how we should monitor the new policy and in particular ensure that we knew about any cases where an institution now decided to permit exceptional entry of more than 25 per cent to a course which had already been approved under the previous rule. It was agreed that the Chairman and the DES Assessor would work out a way of communicating with the field, and at the next Council meeting, in January 1988, we were told that a letter was going to the institutions from the Chairman. It enclosed a copy of the DES letter from Saville and drew attention to its terms and to CATE's continuing responsibilities. Institutions which envisaged increasing beyond 25 per cent the proportion of exceptional admissions to a course already approved were asked to give the Council 'the earliest possible notice of that likelihood'. Subsequently the Council's increased discretion in the matter of special entry was set out in the text of Catenote 5, to which reference was made in chapter 18.

Soon afterwards Group A received approaches from both Bradford and Ilkley Community College and from Essex IHE about raising their proportion of exceptional entry under the new dispensation above 25 per cent. We noted that whereas the former envisaged a specific ratio of 60:40 (standard:non-standard) the Essex proposal was open-ended. We agreed that the Council had been given no warrant to impose a limit, though clearly if exceptional entries became dominant they would alter the character of a course. Tony Becher observed that there was a built-in check in that no institution had an inducement to recruit students who were below par and thus give itself extra work in preventing them from failing. So far as monitoring was concerned, Essex had replied to an enquiry from Ernie Grogan to the effect that the BEd course team, like all its course teams, was required to monitor and evaluate the course, including admissions and outcomes. As part of the monitoring procedure the course leader systematically reviewed the dropout and failure rate among special-entry students. The conclusion in recent years had been that they were well represented among the best students, the average students and the below average students; they were underrepresented among the poorest students. The Institute had established a group of admissions tutors who would help to monitor its policy towards access and exceptional admissions students. We had to consider whether we regarded these arrangements as adequate. David Shadbolt suggested that we might ask for an annual report from any institution which deliberately exceeded the 25 per cent ratio.

When we brought the issue to the Council in July 1988 in the context of presenting the submission from Essex IHE the Chairman suggested that local committees (see Chapter 25) might be asked to assume a monitoring function in a case of this kind — after all, they were looking for a continuing role. This was generally considered to be a good idea. We were conscious of a difficulty in asking for annual reports in view of the limited assured life of the Council, and Tony Becher pointed out that it would be at least four years before even one intake above the 25 per cent level had made its way through an institution; on the other hand, the Chairman observed that a body like CATE had to behave as if it were going to live forever and let others deal with the consequences of its demise. It also emerged that HMI were to look at higher exceptional entries on a sampling basis and institutions would be asked for reports to the Secretary of State on intake proportions and on student progress. It was minuted that the Council agreed to the Group's proposal for continuing approval of the BEd course at Essex subject to calling for a report on the quality of the intake from the local committee in six months' time.

In September 1988 Group A received further details from Bradford and Ilkley; the courses to which they wished to increase the recruitment of ethnic minority students were their primary BEd and their secondary BEd in Home Economics. They had established admissions procedures designed to maintain standards and a research programme to reinforce monitoring of student performance. These appeared to us to be satisfactory, though for the sake of consistency we attached the same condition as for Essex IHE. This was done in the case of a number of other submissions which came forward and were generally seen by Reporting Groups as commendable initiatives on the part of the institutions concerned.

In March 1989 Group A received a revised submission in respect of Wolverhampton Polytechnic, which had now formally merged with West Midlands CHE. The number of exceptional entrants for all its courses exceeded 25 per cent, the highest proportion being for the primary BEd. In its supporting documentation the Polytechnic referred to a particular commitment to making provision for local mature students, especially those from ethnic minority groups. It recognized the access courses offered by almost all colleges of further education in the West Midlands and carefully monitored the progress of access students. Some time previous to this we had received an indication from the DES Legal Branch that what the institution had been doing was probably all right from their point of view but when we discussed this new submission we had some concern about whether the access courses could provide an adequate foundation for subject studies in the BEd. Gillian Murton asked the Polytechnic for more information on the selection of exceptional-entry students and on how support was subsequently given to ensure that individual and group standards were maintained. She did raise the question of 'positive discrimination' and the Polytechnic responded by sending its detailed statement on equal opportunities. We were also given details of a careful process of selection which began while potential students were on their access course, and representatives of the institution assured us when we met them in July that much importance was attached to counselling students in the most appropriate choice of subject studies. Transition from access courses to the BEd was 'challenging but not problematic' for most students, and national monitoring indicated that access course students achieved results comparable with other polytechnic and college students in higher education and dropped out in fewer numbers. By this we felt fairly well satisfied. There were other reasons why we were not able to make a positive proposal for this institution's courses before the end of CATE's term, but the high proportion of non-standard entrants would not by itself have been an obstacle.

During the summer of 1989 Bradford and Ilkley Community College also reappeared on our agenda through responding to the Council's call for a monitoring report. The local committee had established a working group to explore the situation in some detail and it had looked carefully at the quality of the non-standard entrants and the College's plans for monitoring progress. These arrangements appeared to us to be on the right lines. Since this was the first such report we had received we considered how it should be handled procedurally and concluded that we should inform Council of its receipt and of our satisfaction with it. This we did in September 1989.

Thereafter such reports became standard practice. In October Group C raised the general question of what CATE should regard as satisfactory in the monitoring of exceptional entries. Gillian Murton pointed out that Group A had been the first to encounter this problem, and I said we had taken the view that the duty laid upon CATE by the Secretary of State was not to do the monitoring ourselves but to ensure that institutions had adequate monitoring arrangements. This was accepted. It was also noted that after our term was complete, monitoring would become more important both for local committees and for the reconstituted Council.

Although the submission of monitoring reports on an annual basis had been mentioned during our initial discussion of the subject I raised it again on behalf of Group A at the November 1989 Council meeting. The Chairman turned up the Clive Saville letter of November 1987 and read out, as if in support of the proposition that we should be looking for annual reports, a sentence which said that the Secretary of State would 'expect the Council to continue to satisfy itself that institutions have suitable procedures for assessing the potential of candidates for admission to their courses'. It seemed to me that this statement gave the support he assumed only if 'continue to satisfy itself that institutions have suitable procedures' meant 'take a continuous interest in the procedures of each institution', whereas the more straightforward interpretation in the context was 'go on satisfying itself about institutions' procedures even after the issue of this letter'. However, it seemed perfectly proper for us to make the process of satisfying ourselves an ongoing one, so I did not quibble. The decision was in effect a memo to our successors, and it was thought that they would need to consider the kind of evidence required from institutions.

At the Council's final meeting, in December 1989, Group B reported a variation on the theme which no one had come across before. The Polytechnic of North London and Jews' College provided a primary BEd to which not only was there a high level of exceptional entry but some students were granted accelerated entry. Admission to the second year usually applied to students who held an NNEB Certificate and had at least five years' experience as nursery nurses provided that this was deemed the equivalent of what would be covered in the first year of the course — in other words, those awarded advanced standing in respect of the first year of the course could themselves be non-standard entrants. The institution accepted that for the course to pass muster all the Criteria must then be satisfied in years 2–4, and although the Group felt very uneasy at this unusual arrangement they had not been able to find any criterion-related reason for turning the course down. In her introduction Bernice Martin virtually invited other members of Council to try where they had failed, and lengthy discussion ensued: what, for example, was going on in the first year if all the Criteria were satisfied subsequently? There was also the question of the status of the NNEB and the need for DES guidance; we were told that Branch would be issuing a Circular about this. In the end we felt that there were too many unresolved issues here for us to make a decision at our very last meeting, and the proposal was withdrawn. The principle of the acceptability of non-standard entry to non-standard courses would need to be explored with Branch and the validating bodies.

Chapter 20

Links with Schools and Teaching Practice

As presaged in *Teaching Quality*, an important aspect of the Criteria was a requirement for constructive links between training institutions and schools, and an agenda item at CATE's first meeting was a paper on the subject prepared by HMI with a view to its being issued for guidance. However, it was decided after some discussion not to publish it at that stage and a revised version did not come back to Council until September 1985. A further process of discussion and redrafting (devoted in the main to improvements in clarity and syntax rather than to issues of principle) resulted in the publication in January 1986 of Catenote 4, *Links between Initial Teacher Training Institutions and Schools*. Like its two immediate predecessors the paper began by quoting the relevant passages from the Criteria. These related to the need for links in connection respectively with school experience for students, with renewal of teaching experience on the part of tutors, with the involvement of practising teachers in student selection and with teacher representation on local committees.

Of these topics there was no need in Catenote 4 to deal with local committees, which had been the subject of Catenote 2 (see chapter 25), and it was decided not to include detailed guidance on two other matters — school experience in PGCE courses and the involvement of teachers in the selection of students — since it was envisaged that they would be the subject of separate papers. In fact it was only on the latter topic that a subsequent Catenote eventuated, as has been described in chapter 18. But the result was that the contents of Catenote 4 were confined in effect to three issues — students' school experience, with particular reference to concurrent courses, the involvement of schoolteachers in students' training, and teaching opportunities for tutors. So far as the present account is concerned, the last of these is deferred until chapter 24.

Before embarking on the substance of its advice Catenote 4 included a historical paragraph with references extending from the James Report of 1972 to ACSET in 1983 to demonstrate that in this respect the Criteria reflected 'a long standing concern for the close involvement of teachers in the training process'. It stressed the importance of classroom experience in this process and gave as one example of a collaborative model for its provision the DES/Open University IT(Initial Training)/INSET project established in 1977 and subsequently developed at Leicester UDE. The only occasion in the life of CATE when members received a presentation on an aspect of teacher training had occurred in September 1985 when Dr Pat Ashton and two of her colleagues from Leicester had explained the principles and practice of IT/INSET. Attention was also drawn in the Catenote to the need for careful co-operative planning of teaching practice and school experience — two expressions, incidentally, between which CATE never attempted to distinguish. Examples were given of ways in which experienced teachers could be engaged in the preparation of entrants to the profession, such as the associate tutor system, conferences between institutions and schools about teaching practice arrangements and the inclusion of teachers in planning groups for new courses. The objective in all this should be 'a spirit of partnership' in pursuit of 'a shared professional objective'.

These were general principles, but the role of CATE in enforcing the Criteria with regard specifically to school experience was relatively straightforward.

> Initial teacher training courses should be so planned as to allow
> for a substantial element of school experience and teaching prac-
> tice which, taken together, should be not less than fifteen weeks
> in a postgraduate course, and not less than twenty weeks in a
> four-year BEd. (DES, 1984a)

The nature of this requirement led to a somewhat mechanistic approach. We had simply to satisfy ourselves that each course provided the appropriate number of weeks in school. In practice this was not always as easy as it might sound, for many BEd courses had rather complex structures of school experience — short and long blocks, a day or a group of days here and there, a term or part of a term when students were in school for perhaps a day per week. Such patterns obliged us to resort to arithmetical exercises, with pencilled annotations against the information supplied to us by the institution in order to be sure that the requisite seventy-five or 100 days were accounted for. Occasionally clarification might have to be sought from the institution's representatives when we met them, but since the basic requirement was no less clear to them than it was to us the issue rarely caused serious difficulty. Criteria concerning the participation of teachers in the planning, supervision and support of students' school experience and in its assessment, and the linking of educational and professional studies with this experience, tended also to be checked at meetings with the institutions, and at least as far as Group A was concerned without probing in any great depth.

One aspect of school experience which occasionally gave rise to some problem of interpretation or definition was the common practice of requiring PGCE students to undergo a short period of school observation, usually one or two weeks, before the start of the course proper. This arose in March 1985, when Council gave preliminary consideration to the first group of institutions to be reviewed. The issue related to an aspect of the Criteria to which I have given little attention in this account since in general it presented no problems for CATE, though it was of considerable significance for the institutions. This was the requirement that PGCE courses should have a minimum duration of thirty-six weeks. It was accepted that CATE had no power to relax this stipulation, and whether a preliminary period of school observation could be reckoned as part of the course for that purpose would have to be decided in individual cases. The essential point was that as a general rule it should count, in the words of the minute, 'only when it was a compulsory, planned, supervised and integrated part of the course'.

The issue was one about which David Shadbolt had strong feelings and in one instance they brought Group A as close as we ever came to a significant difference of view. This arose after we had met representatives fo Sheffield UDE in July 1986. We had discussed with them the two initial weeks of primary school experience in their secondary PGCE and I thought they had given a persuasive account of how both the students and the receiving schools were issued with written briefings about what was expected from the experience. But David was unconvinced that it was sufficiently integrated with the course as a whole. There were only four of us present that day, and though Peter Ward seemed sympathetic to David's view, Tony Becher indicated that he would not be prepared to make this an obstacle to a positive proposal. Ernie Grogan was left to draft a proposal for us to put to the Council, and his solution was to make it positive but with this footnote:

> The Group also propose that the University be invited to consider whether the experience acquired by students during their initial two weeks in primary schools could be more directly exploited during later parts of the course. This would not, however, be a condition of the recommendation for the Secretary of State's approval.

At the Council meeting David introduced the proposal in this form and it led to lengthy discussion. He had to answer several questions on the UDE's exact procedures. The critical issue for him was that while all students had to produce a written assignment based on their two weeks' preliminary observation, only in some cases did this count towards assessment. The Chairman was anxious to ensure a uniform approach to the question and invited the other groups to say how they responded to similar arrangements. Both had looked carefully at structures of this kind but cases tended to differ in detail. Some members thought we should be exceeding our brief in seeking to dictate a particular kind of arrangement. The Chairman, on the other hand, pointed to the danger of a message going out to the system to the effect that this issue did not really matter too much since Sheffield had got away with a mere comment from CATE. This led to inconclusive attempts to strengthen the wording, and we decided to return to the problem in the afternoon. Over lunch I remarked jocularly to David Shadbolt that it was a pity Group A had made so much trouble for itself since none of us had really felt so very strongly about it. 'I did', he responded; 'I think it's absolutely crucial.' In the end, influenced in part by a decision made about another institution, the Council accepted a proposal from Tony Becher not to add a rider at all. In September 1986 Group B brought to Council's attention a similar query about two weeks of 'pre-course directed school experience' in the PGCE at Newcastle UDE. The Chairman pointed out that inclusion of two weeks' preliminary teaching practice could be seen as an easy way to extend a course; he was concerned to 'avoid slippage'. The Newcastle courses were recommended for approval but the secretariat were asked to prepare a paper giving an overall picture of pre-course school experience in PGCEs so far considered by the Council and drawing attention to good practice. However, this paper never materialized, and the issue was laid to rest.

Another question arose in April 1987 when Group B asked for the Council's guidance on points which had arisen in their consideration of courses at Worcester CHE. One was that while the College did include fifteen weeks of school experience in its secondary PGCE, assessment was completed after twelve weeks, leaving the last three, in the third term, for 'professional development: involvement in a selected aspect of the curriculum related to the teaching interest and intentions of each individual student'. These optional professional courses had been commented on favourably by HMI, but Group B also wished to draw attention to the fact that the placement could be in FE. The DES Assessor said that Branch had no objection to this in principle; an FE establishment would be acceptable if the practice was with the 16–19 age-group and in connection with a curriculum similar to that of a secondary school. Discussion extended to other options offered for these final three weeks, concerning which the Assessor merely commented that the kinds of schools used for teaching practice must be relevant to future employment. Michael Pipes queried the validity of experience in an independent school on the grounds that probation must be completed in an LEA school. But the Assessor did not accept that this followed, since it is with service in LEA schools that probation is concerned. The DENI Inspector reverted to the point about assessment after twelve weeks, and said he would be concerned about how the last three weeks were perceived both by the students and by the institution; there would be a temptation to regard them as not mattering so much. However, at the following meeting the Council endorsed a proposal from Group B to recommend approval of the Worcester courses.

A recurrent problem about partnership in respect of school experience was essentially one of communication. A comment in the HMI report on North Riding College of Education expressed this well.

> There is a clear set of aims and objectives for each teaching practice and these are given in the documentation provided for tutors, students and schools. Although students are aware of the differing requirements of each successive practice, this information appears to be less well understood by teachers. Some attention should be given to detailing the changes in role expected of teachers on the various practices.

When Group A considered this in September 1987 and recognized it as a familiar difficulty our SI remarked that responsibility was often given to 'the school' and not to individual teachers. In its documentation the College had referred to practising teachers being 'regarded as equal tutors during block practice'. Bill Wright was rather tetchy about this: if it were true, how could the teachers be unsure of their role? He wanted to know whether the schools had any say in assessment; did they have any muscle? When we met representatives of the institution in November 1987 they told us that the College obtained assessments of teaching practice both from the supervising tutor and from the head of the receiving school, and the Principal said that on occasion he had to adjudicate between them. My impression was that that was a fairly common arrangement, and in this particular case we did not make any more of it. (Early in August 1989 the *TES* reported a survey conducted by a research team at the University of London Institute of Education which suggested that teachers often failed to give advice or assistance to students on teaching practice (Swanwick and Chitty, 1989)).

Towards the end of our term a new dimension to school experience became apparent through the development of more school-based courses. A notable example was the 'internship scheme' pioneered by Oxford UDE in its secondary PGCE, which Group A considered early in 1989. The essence of the scheme so far as school experience was concerned was that, as the HMI report put it:

> After their preliminary placements in a primary and a secondary school, those learning to teach are each involved in the work of one school, and one subject department within it, throughout their training year. Continuous experience of this sort is seen as the best way for interns to acquire a full understanding of the

realities of teaching and to develop as reflective learners who can contribute to their schools as well as gain from them.

This Oxford scheme had attracted a good deal of favourable attention by the time we came to consider it, and it obviously had much to recommend it. The close partnership between school teachers and University tutors which, as HMI observed, was evident in its planning, execution and monitoring, appeared to be an exemplary instance of strong links between training institutions and schools.

We did wonder, however, whether confining the experience of each student to one school might restrict opportunities for encountering pupils from the full range of ability, and we raised this anxiety with representatives of the UDE when we met them in March 1989. Their answer was that all the participating schools were fully comprehensive and care was taken to ensure that students had experience across the range. They were conscious that in schools in the more rural areas there might be little exposure to multiethnic situations, but they were attempting to remedy this by taking students from such schools for a day in Brent. We were sufficiently reassured by this and other points to bring a positive proposal to the Council at the beginning of June, though in introducing it I mentioned our initial concern. Mary Hallaway expressed disquiet about the restricted nature of the school experience, and asked whether my reference to a day in Brent meant a day a week, a day a term? We had to concede that it meant in fact one day, and there was clearly a feeling round the table that the value of such an outing was dubious; it smacked, as the Chairman put it, of 'educational tourism'. Mary pursued her point by suggesting that more could be done closer at hand — for example, in Slough. On the general issue of students' experience being predominantly in one school I could only repeat that this was an intrinsic part of the scheme: we had to take it or reject it. There was in fact another worry about the course, which is described in chapter 24, and near the close of our debate Mary Hallaway asked pointedly whether we should have allowed it if it had come from Teesside Polytechnic. 'I hope Group A is not being accused of social discrimination', I responded, to some laughter.

In the end our proposal for approval of the course was accepted, though with the rider, as expressed in Gillian's minute, 'that certain ramifications of the University's "Internship" approach would be pursued in writing with the Secretary of State'. The terms in which this was to be done were left rather vague. (Michael Dixon, sitting beside me, had jotted down the opening of a Betjemanesque address: 'Come Oxford Ude, intern in Slough.') When the Council met again in July the Chairman explained that in spite of several drafting attempts he had not pursued his undertaking to write to the Secretary of State about the limitations of single school experience lest what he said appeared to relate to the DES initiative about articled teachers, which had been announced towards the end of June.

However, the issues raised by this type of course remained significant ones. At Group A's first meeting after the 1989 summer break we had before us a request from Leicester UDE for our views on a proposed change in their secondary PGCE, which had first been Cated in March 1986. They wished during the academic year 1989/90 to run a pilot scheme with some students which would involve extending the IT/INSET component, increasing the time spent in schools and 'transferring the location of aspects of our Professional Course (concerned with whole-school issues) from University to school'. The details of the scheme bore an obvious similarity to the Oxford model. But as we discussed the Leicester proposal questions began to arise in our minds, prompted to some extent by HMI, about the ability of the schools to deliver the course components for which they were to become at least in part responsible. What was expected from them, as opposed to what they might choose to offer? Gillian Murton detected a trend among institutions to move towards a more school-based approach because they thought this was what they were being encouraged to do; this kind of question was going to arise more frequently, and indeed Group C had a similar submission before them. This proved to be from the University of Durham.

We looked at the Leicester submission again later in September 1989 in the light of further information supplied by the UDE. Delivery of professional elements of the course would, it appeared, be wholly the responsibility of their tutors, even for students participating in the scheme, and the model of working in the schools would be based on IT/INSET principles and would focus on classroom observation and evaluation. It was evident that some doubts remained but I drew attention to the fact that it was a pilot scheme we were being asked to approve; this implied formal evaluation, and indeed Leicester had told us how this was going to be done. We therefore agreed to propose the scheme to Council for temporary approval, it being understood that our successor body would consider its extension in the light of the evaluation.

I duly explained all this to the September Council, pointing out that the scheme added only eight days to the time which participating students would spend in schools. The point which Group C wished to discuss about Durham was that that UDE also wished to introduce a pilot scheme, which in their case was to be based on two days a week in school for thirty-six students on their secondary PGCE taking English, physics and geography. The Chairman elaborated on the issue which had caused both groups to hesitate about these submissions. The aspect of the Criteria relating to staff development was a response to concern whether college tutors had enough experience of schools to train teachers effectively; now there was reason to ask whether schoolteachers had a sufficient base for undertaking the role of trainers. On the other hand it was pointed out that neither of the submissions before us that day went so far in the direction of school-based training as Sussex UDE, whose PGCEs, with their unique approach in integrating its own staff with serving teachers, had been recommended for approval without demur on this score in April 1988. Group C indicated that they did not wish to stand in the way of the University's doing what it wished and Group A's position was very similar with regard to Leicester. Council decided to take the view that both pilot projects for more school-based delivery would be covered by existing course approvals, so that no formal recommendation to the Secretary of State was actually required. Any extension to the schemes would be considered by our successor body in the light of evaluation of the pilots.

Immediately after this meeting of the Council there was a brief get-together of the Group Convenors with the Chairman and Secretary. Gillian had placed on the agenda an item on developments in teacher education, suggesting in her note that there were cases where dangers might be more apparent to CATE than to the institutions. She instanced deepening school experience, sometimes in substantial 'pilot' schemes, where Reporting Groups might fear that an institution was sacrificing breadth of experience and the full range of professional elements. There was general agreement that the trend towards school-based work was the most obvious development at that time, but discussion became side-tracked into output measures and competences. There was no reference to Gillian's specific suggestion that CATE might consider issuing further guidance to institutions even at this late stage or, perhaps more realistically, noting such major changes for the information of the new Council. Whatever we said or did not say, however, it was clear that that body would have to come to terms with the rapidly changing scene.

Chapter 21

Age Differentiation and Early Years Courses

A further requirement of the Criteria, and one which had also been foreshadowed in *Teaching Quality*, was:

> The approach to teaching method should differentiate according to the age group which the student intends to teach, whether primary (with special emphasis on age-ranges such as 3–8, 5–8 or 7–12 years) or secondary (11/12–18), while giving due emphasis to the differences between children in the rates at which they develop and learn. (DES, 1984a)

It occasionally happened that course submissions to CATE did not indicate the kind of differentiation which this clause prescribed. Early examples were both the primary PGCE and the primary BEd at the University of Durham, which Group C brought to the Council in July 1986 as for 4–11. CI Pauline Perry pulled us up by drawing attention to this and saying she assumed it was divided into the usual 4–8 and 7–11 streams and that it should be approved on that basis. This was agreed, and on several subsequent occasions institutions were asked either to break a primary course in this way or, if they were already doing so, to ensure that their documentation reflected that fact. The most apparently startling case encountered by Group A was the University of London Institute of Education, which submitted a 5–19 PGCE: it transpired, however, that in reality there were the normal sub-divisions. The Institute had some reservations about the possibly restrictive effect of separate primary categories, since their policy was that students trained to teach the whole primary age-range though with a bias towards either 3–8 or 7–11, but after some negotiation the PGCE was recommended for approval in three streams. The advent of the National Curriculum and the concept of key stages in children's education gave added point to age differentiation in ITT.

Later during CATE's term it became not uncommon for institutions to wish to extend primary courses downwards in terms of age. One of the first to make a formal request was West London IHE; they sought to change their primary BEd options from 4–8 and 8–12 to 3–7, 5–8 and 8–12. Group A saw this as unproblematic, and in July 1988 proposed approval to the Council, which regarded it as a welcome development; reference was made to the growing number of under-5s in ordinary schools. It was at this stage that Lesley Abbott and Anne Cattoor joined Group A, and as a result of their interest and expertise in early years education our approach became rather more rigorous. When Leicester UDE came forward with a proposal to change the lower span of their primary PGCE from 5–8 to 3–8 we decided in October 1988 to ask some questions about what was being added to course content, the location of school experience and the qualifications of their staff. A positive proposal was made and endorsed when these matters had been satisfactorily clarified.

In the autumn of 1989 we had to look again at early years provision at West London IHE, partly because they now wished also to extend their primary PGCE, which had been approved for the age-range 5–11, to 4–12. In response to a request for further information the institution reported that school experience with rising 5s was not mandatory on the course but could be made so if we required it. Lesley Abbott thought that their use of the phrase 'rising 5s' in this context showed they had a wrong attitude, and that it was essential for there to be experience with 4-year-olds not only in infant or first schools but also in nursery schools. But the institution's rationale for wishing to change the course was that the admissions policy of many LEAs now meant that students on teaching practice were encountering children newly turned 4 in reception classes, and Bill Wright did not think there was warrant in the Criteria for us to insist on nursery experience. Gillian Murton was left to explore with them what arrangements they could make, and the upshot was that they withdrew the submission to lower the approved age range. We conveyed our hope that the Institute's commendable intention to do so could be further developed.

By now the establishment of early years courses had become so much the expected thing that in September 1989, when Group C reported to the Council on a PGCE at Derbyshire CHE for 5–8 and 7–12, whereas the same institution's primary BEd was for 3–8 and 7–12, someone asked why the PGCE did not also cover the lower age-range. In October Marian Giles Jones said she regretted having agreed to ask this question since it had no warrant in the Criteria; the institution's answer had in fact been that they had enough to do in thirty-six weeks without bringing in the lower end of the age-range as well. Prompted perhaps by this incident Lesley Abbott raised a general issue later in that meeting. She thought that in view of current policy on school admissions all lower primary courses should start not older than age 4. Andrew Collier had made the same point in the context of the draft new criteria, but of course the reality was that 5 remained the statutory school starting age. Michael Pipes observed that it was better for institutions not to mislead by describing courses as dealing with the early years if they could not actually deliver that specialism.

Chapter 22

Professional Issues

As well as calling upon training institutions to 'provide students with adequate mastery of the basic professional skills, on which to build in their teaching careers', the Criteria included a number of specific requirements which CATE came to refer to as the professional issues. Cateform 2 identified these as follows.

(a) Students should experience a wide range of teaching and learning methods and be given ample opportunity to discuss and assess them.

(b) Students should experience and understand the contribution of new technologies to all aspects of children's learning.

(c) Students should be prepared for the diversity of ability, behaviour, social background and ethnic and cultural origins encountered in ordinary schools; and in how to respond to that diversity and guard against preconceptions based on race or sex.

(d) Students should be prepared to recognize, understand and cope with different levels of performance, including special needs and gifts.

(e) Students should be prepared for the pastoral and administrative responsibilities of teaching, and be made aware of the teacher's relationships with colleagues, parents and the community.

(f) Students should acquire an appreciation of the structure and administration of the education service and be able to see their role as a teacher within the broader context of educational purposes.

(g) Students should understand the nature, values and economic foundations of contemporary society and the relationship between the school curriculum and the adult world.

These issues were not made the subject of guidance in a Catenote and on the whole they did not present CATE with significant theoretical or practical problems. Such difficulties as did arise over the professional issues were in the main of two kinds. One was that some of these topics were occasionally found to be covered in optional modules, so that a particular student could complete the course without meeting all of them. It was necessary in these cases for us to insist that each issue must be part of the programme of study for every student. Another aspect of this was the subject of comment in an HMI review of ITT in universities which was published by the DES in the spring of 1988. At a meeting of Group A I drew attention to this passage:

> The general policy of optional attendance at lectures, which is adopted by some universities, is applied to initial teacher training courses also. In a professional training course, in which some elements are considered essential for all students, this is a cause for concern. In one lecture, for example, only just over half the PGCE students attended, even though this was a major element of the short course on special educational needs...There were several examples of students attending follow-up seminars on, for instance, multicultural education or learning difficulties when they had not been present at the lead lecture. This is clearly unsatisfactory. (DES, 1988a)

I pointed out that we had never really enquired into this. Bill Wright recalled that while he was in Group C they had discussed it long and earnestly — indeed philosophically, for issues of freedom and responsibility had been raised. Tony Becher was a little defensive about the matter. In his experience students were usually fairly apologetic if they missed lectures, and it would show up in their work files. Nevertheless, I said, a student could in theory opt out completely from, say, special needs; it was a gap in the system. Tony supposed that medical students could opt out of public health, but they didn't. I mentioned the point again at the June 1988 Council, when the HMI document was on the agenda, and most members seemed to recognize optional attendance as more of a danger than Tony had been prepared to acknowledge. There was some suggestion that we might probe the point but I cannot recall that at least Group A ever raised the matter in discussion with UDEs.

The other general difficulty quite frequently encountered by Reporting Groups arose when institutions indicated that some or all of the professional issues did not constitute specific elements in a course but that they permeated the course as a whole. One could see the point of this: the question of special needs, for example, could well occur contextually in subject applications, in educational studies and in school practice. At the same time there was an evident risk that if this was all that happened coverage would be fragmentary and incomplete and leave students without a confident conceptual or practical grasp. In these circumstances we would try to satisfy ourselves that the institution had addressed this problem, and where the permeation model had been adopted had developed some system of monitoring the experience of individual students.

At the end of October 1985, as noted in chapter 19, the Secretary of State wrote to the Chairman to register his interest in two particular aspects of the Criteria. The first of these was the inclusion within ITT of elements concerned with special educational needs, which the letter traced back to a 1984 recommendation of ACSET. Although it was now Government policy to phase out pre-service specialist training and redirect resources to the in-service training mode, institutions would need to review their courses and their arrangements for staff development to ensure that they could satisfy the requirement to provide all their students with an introduction to the subject of special needs.

The other concern of the Secretary of State arose from two of the recommendations of the recently published Swann Report concerning the response to ethnic diversity in ITT. These were that CATE should be asked to pay particular attention to the need to incorporate in ITT courses an understanding of the cultural and racial mix of society and that efforts should be made by all ITT institutions to ensure that their students would have an opportunity of gaining some experience in a multiracial school. It was recognized that it might not always be possible for every institution to arrange such experience for all of its students, but in that case it was all the more important that other elements of the course should provide opportunities for students to gain a basic understanding of the multiethnic basis of our society. The last point was commented upon when the letter came before Council; institutions in Wales and Northern Ireland in particular would have difficulty with this Swann recommendation. In general, however, it was considered that institutions were aware of the issues involved through their work with schools, and there was some evidence that progress along the lines desired was being encouraged externally, for example by local committees.

In February 1987 Council was told about attention having been drawn at a conference to a students' rag magazine at an ITT institution in which the humour was heavily racist; the question had been asked, 'What is CATE doing about this?' The Chairman said he believed CATE had a clear conscience in having checked compliance with the multicultural criterion but there were some who would wish to make it a very major, important emphasized element in the curriculum. He thought we might include treatment of it among the examples of good practice which at that stage we were still proposing to collect. Andrew Collier said he hoped we would not be too nervous about bringing something out in this area, and the attendant SI suggested that we could do so in the context of curricular issues like special needs. David Shadbolt observed that another approach was through representation of ethnic groups on local committees, and Ernie Grogan added that there had been some correspondence from these groups.

I referred in chapter 20 to students from Oxford UDE visiting Brent, and such arrangements were not uncommon on the part of institutions in regions where students were unlikely to encounter many children from ethnic minorities on teaching practice. Thus for example Charlotte Mason College in the Lake District used a base for multicultural education in Preston and its students were given two weeks' school experience in London. In their report on this institution, however, HMI made a comment which interestingly expressed a different perspective.

> Many students indicated an interest in multiethnic education, although in a considerable number of cases their experience, knowledge and understanding were limited. In particular some students equated the issue with inner-city areas inhabited by members of ethnic minority communities. They appeared unaware of its relevance in the education of all pupils, including those living in all-white, especially rural areas such as that in which the college is situated.

It was an aspect of professional studies which had many nuances. When Bill Wright pointed out to Group A in June 1988 that Manchester UDE was offering 'anti-racist studies' as well as multicultural ones, and that these were not the same thing, Tony Becher responded that this option was additional to what was prescribed to meet the Criteria and it was not our job to censor extra elements.

Information Technology (IT) was clearly another important professional issue. Michael Dixon unofficially became Group A's lead interrogator on the subject, and at our meetings with representatives of institutions we usually explored fairly thoroughly how they ensured that all students received a reasonable grounding. In June 1988 the Council received an HMI survey of IT within ITT to which the Secretary of State had asked for a CATE response. CI Alan Marshall explained that it was largely the work of one SI who had done some moonlighting on the subject, and he had thought that it might be published, as such surveys often were, largely as a guide to good practice. However, Secretary of State Kenneth Baker, who had at one time been Minister for IT, had expressed some concern about its findings and had reaffirmed his belief that all students in ITT should be properly educated in the effective use of IT; a working group on the subject was to be set up. Alan suggested that the message of the HMI report was: 'Permeation — how do you know?' This, as I have indicated, was a pertinent question regarding any of the professional issues.

In November 1988 the Council was told that CATE had been invited to give evidence to the IT working group, which had now been established under the chairmanship of Miss Janet Trotter, the Principal of the College of St Paul and St Mary. Michael Pipes thought this was an area in which the Criteria might have to become more specific, though the Chairman pointed to the danger of adhockery overloading the curriculum. No one seemed to have any very clear ideas about what we might or could say to the working group but Bernice Martin thought it would look bad if we did not contribute and the Secretary was asked to produce a response in consultation with interested members. Miss Trotter's group must have worked hard, for she was able to send her report to the Secretary of State before the end of March 1989, and it came to CATE in published form in July. In a covering letter Miss Trotter told the Secretary of State:

> In the course of our work we were greatly disturbed by the patchiness evident in all dimensions of IT provision: namely in the general capability of staff, in staff development opportunities, in the generosity of resources provided, in institutional awareness of the issues and, above all, in the sparse and sporadic distribution of good practice. (Information Technology in Initial Teacher Training Expert Group, 1989)

This certainly made it appear that whatever impact the Criteria had had there was still a long way to go. However, Council's brief discussion focussed on the constructive aspect of the report. The Chairman drew attention to its specification of the capability in IT which all students should possess by the time they completed training; this was reflected in the draft new criteria which had just been published. His own view was that IT was rather like happiness — if you aimed for it directly you would not find it; it came as a by-product of other things. He asked whether it was our impression that institutions were applying it, and the answer was an emphatic yes. Alan Marshall said there were massive resource problems; what CATE must satisfy itself about was that students were being equipped for IT across the curriculum. The point was repeated in October 1989 when the Council received a short HMI paper on the implications of the Trotter Report. As Alan put it then, the nub of HMI comment was that an essential aim must be the encouragement of the pervasive use of IT; basic courses on IT should have parity of status with other aspects of training. There was a feeling among members that understanding of computing among young people in higher education was not as great as might have been hoped or expected, and David Winkley reminded us that for schools it was still very much a resource problem. According to him and to Peter Scott schools that were in the best position, and able to replace obsolescent equipment, tended to be those with well-to-do parents.

Another issue to which attention was drawn by a report published during CATE's term was school discipline. This was subsumed in the Criteria only under the general rubric of 'class management and control', but in March 1988, in response to concern about the problems facing the teaching profession, the Secretary of State set up a committee of enquiry under the chairmanship of Lord Elton. The Elton Report recommended that when the Secretary of State was reviewing the Criteria he should incorporate a number of relevant requirements, including the need for all ITT courses to 'contain compulsory and clearly identifiable elements dealing in specific and practical terms with group management skills'. In April 1989 the Council received a copy of a letter from the Secretary of State to the Chairman in which he drew attention to this recommendation and asked that even in anticipation of a revision of the Criteria CATE should pay particular attention to this aspect of courses. The letter actually referred to 'separate, compulsory elements of practical training', and the Chairman indicated, to the Council's approval, that in his response he had politely reverted to the language of the report and substituted 'clearly identifiable' for 'separate'. There was no further discussion of the matter, and the Report came too late in our term to have any significant influence in the way we scrutinized courses; we did not in practice make much of this specific area of training.

The same might be said about gender issues, though the Criteria enjoined institutions to show students how to guard against preconceptions based on sex as well as those based on race. In September 1989 the Council received a summary of a report recently published by the Equal Opportunities Commission on the extent to which INSET work on gender issues was being matched in ITT. Their investigation had revealed 'an unsatisfactory situation of benign apathy towards equal opportunities'; the approach of most institutions was found to be reactive and incoherent. The Council did not make time to discuss the report, and the Commission's recommendations arising from it were referred to the Secretary of State. Again this came near the end of CATE's term, but I think the general view might have been that we had to consider so many other issues that were perceived as more central to teacher training that there was just not enough time to pay much regard to this one. (It would, however, be true to add that Group A did on a number of occasions draw polite attention to the all-male character of most of the deputations which came to meet us from the institutions. It appeared to me that when women were included they were often the ones with the firmest grasp of how courses were actually delivered; no doubt this was because they held less senior positions!)

Chapter 23

Further Education

The role of CATE was to advise the Secretary of State whether courses were suitable for the professional preparation of teachers and hence for the conferment of QTS. It followed that CATE was not concerned with courses of preparation to teach in Further Education (FE), and issues relating to FE impinged only tangentially on our deliberations. I have already referred to one of these in chapter 20: arrangements at Worcester CHE for teaching practice established that this could acceptably take place in an FE establishment provided that it was with the 16–19 age-group and in relation to aspects of the curriculum which might also occur in secondary schools.

However, the length of time spent by some Worcester students in FE was only three weeks; the answer was not so clear if a longer period were in question. In August 1987 the Director of Leicester UDE wrote to the Secretary about an English and communications option in their secondary PGCE. When Group A had reviewed the PGCE some time before we had seen this subject as mainly concerned with FE and consequently excluded it from our proposal, but all students now did the substantial part of their teaching practice in schools and the UDE wished the course formally recognized on the grounds that it was meeting a growing need, especially among those in the 14–16 age-range with special needs. We continued to have some anxieties about this course, for enquiries revealed that about two-fifths of the teaching practice took place in FE, and there could be no guarantee that the lecturers with whom students were placed would themselves be qualified teachers. However, about three-quarters of the time in FE was with 16–18 year-olds and final teaching practice took place in an 11–16 school; we thought this just acceptable. Our proposal did not prove a difficult one to get through Council, and the DES Assessor indicated a welcome for the course.

A similar case to come before Group A was at the University of London Institute of Education, where there was a PGCE route with an FE interest, and while students following this secondary/tertiary route undertook two weeks' preliminary school experience in a primary school and at least eight weeks in schools, the balance was spent in tertiary/FE/ sixth form colleges. When we met representatives in December 1988 they told us that teaching practice in FE varied both in length and in the stage in the course at which a student took it but they confirmed that assessment was made on teaching practice in school. They sought to ensure that practice in FE was related to school work, although, like Leicester, they could not guarantee that all the staff involved in supervising students while they were in FE institutions would be trained teachers. Further written information for which we asked made it clear that the number of students involved was relatively small. The emphasis in terms both of curriculum and of teaching practice was on the secondary aspect of the course, with the focus on the whole 14–19 age-group. The tertiary institutions selected for placements had long associations with the Institute. Having particular regard to the assurance that the final practice for all students taking the course would be in a school, we made a positive proposal which was endorsed by the Council in June 1989.

CATE policy in this area may thus be seen to have developed pragmatically, with each submission being examined flexibly on its merits. Wolverhampton Polytechnic ran a PGCE which it described as for FE and secondary, since the institution was strongly committed to the principle of joint training of intending teachers in secondary schools and FE. However, Group A ascertained in September 1989 that the FE students spent only two weeks of teaching practice in schools, and this side of the course was therefore clearly outside CATE's accrediting remit. The converse arrangement for the secondary students to spend two weeks in FE was seen as entirely acceptable.

In Group conversation in October 1987 Bill Wright raised another side to the question. There was a growing trend towards provision for 16–19 year-olds to be in tertiary colleges: it was being planned in Sheffield and Leeds and to some extent in his own borough of Wakefield. At such institutions they might be taught by people trained at FE colleges or on FE courses which were not subject to the Criteria. It was pointed out that these young people were by definition over school leaving age, but Bill still considered it to be an anomaly. It was not one which CATE ever formally addressed.

Chapter 24

Staff Development
('Recent and Relevant')

The staff of training institutions who are concerned with pedagogy should have school teaching experience. They should have
enjoyed recent success as teachers of the age range to which their
training courses are directed, and should maintain regular and
frequent experience of classroom teaching. If some members of
staff cannot satisfy this requirement, the employing institution
should provide them with opportunities to demonstrate their
teaching effectiveness in schools, for example by means of
secondments to schools or schemes for tutor/schoolteacher
exchange. (DES, 1984a)

Second only to the requirement for subject studies, this became the most
famous or notorious of the Criteria. It was the White Paper, *Teaching
Quality*, which described the school experience required of a sufficient
proportion of training staff if ITT were to be successful as 'recent,
substantial and relevant', thus giving rise to the phrase by which this
criterion was commonly known. I recall the Chairman reporting to quite
an early meeting of CATE that he had heard teacher trainers referring
in a matter-of-fact way to their recent and relevant, using the term as a
substantive.

It was evident that rapid implementation of this criterion could not
be expected, as was confirmed when proposals began to come forward in
the spring of 1985 in respect of the first round of submissions. It was
agreed that in cases where institutions were having difficulty in meeting
the criterion fully the Council needed to be satisfied that it had a coherent
policy. Reporting Groups should look for a detailed staff development
plan giving numbers of staff involved and evidence of an acceptable
rolling programme. Progress towards achieving this became a very common condition attached to recommendations for the approval of courses
in the early stages of CATE's work. The situation had been made more
difficult for many institutions by the paucity of new appointments during

the early 1980s, and it was correspondingly eased when older and possibly more recalcitrant tutors came up for retirement and could be replaced by people coming fresh from schools.

Catenote 4 on links between institutions and schools, as explained in chapter 20, was published in January 1986. In a section on 'teaching opportunities for tutors' it noted the risk that not having held a recent full-time teaching appointment in a school could lead to some reduction in confidence on the part of college staff concerned with pedagogy, or to some reduction in their credibility in the eyes of both students and practising teachers. The original draft version adhered closely to the wording of the Annex by going on to refer to 'opportunities to demonstrate their teaching effectiveness'. Being still a fairly new member at that time, I was less conscious of CATE's constant concern not to appear to add to the requirements for which we had a warrant in the Criteria and I felt that this form of words placed too much emphasis on the presentational side of the exercise. I suggested that we say 'demonstrate and reinforce'. The final version of the paragraph adopted a slightly expanded statement, but I may count the inclusion of the verb 'reinforce' among my personal contributions to the development of ITT.

The Catenote went on to instance a number of ways in which such opportunities might be provided — secondment to classroom teaching in various forms, participation in IT/INSET, consultancy work, action research. In all cases the experience should as far as possible be related to the particular phase, subject or other specialisms of particular tutors, should be monitored and evaluated and should inform the tutors' subsequent work, including their approach to theoretical aspects of the course. Since it would not normally be practicable for all the staff of an institution to be involved in such schemes at the same time, staff development plans would often have to be devised which could be fully developed only over a cycle of some years. The Council therefore attached great importance to the existence of realistic plans which met both the collective staff development needs of the institution and those of individual members of staff. A final paragraph advocated the development of close and effective relations between training institutions and schools as a means of furthering this form of contribution to the effectiveness of ITT.

There was some opposition to the criterion in principle. In 1986 Professor Jean Ruddock of the University of Sheffield was quoted as saying at an SRHE conference, 'Some of my colleagues have not taught in school for five, seven or even ten years, but thirty days teaching will not make them credible class teachers. To think they can become practising class teachers so readily is an insult to teachers.' (*Education*, 1986) West London IHE pointed out to Group A in April 1987 that 'renewal of teaching experience is only one aspect of a tutor's staff development needs (for example, empirical research, the pursuit of higher degrees, the participation in conferences, the liaison with local teachers' centres, the continuing dialogues with schools over teaching practice placements)'. In October 1987 we heard of a complaint from Southampton UDE that the requirement for renewal of classroom experience was divisive between ITT course staff and other academic staff in the University. The conference of local committees in May 1988 (see Chapter 25) drew attention to the lack of a research base and to the difficulties for institutions of facing in different directions. In a document given to Group A in January 1989 the University of London Institute of Education incorporated the following manifesto:

> ...the Institute does not assume that the tasks of a teacher are the same as those of a teacher trainer. Although there are similarities, the tasks of a teacher trainer involve not only, for example, the demonstration of teaching strategies and of classroom management techniques, but also the coaching of student teachers into good styles of teaching, their support on teaching practice and the development of those personal qualities necessary to the good practice of teaching. Thus it is not accepted that the simple exchange of school staff and Institute staff would be a satisfactory form of staff development, since the aim is to develop the teacher training qualities of staff and not just their capacities as school teachers.

When I referred to this argument during the Council's review of the Criteria the Chairman conceded that someone good at teaching 7-year-olds was not necessarily good at training others to teach 7-year-olds, but in general he took a robust line in defence of the 'recent and relevant' criterion. He held forth to one visiting group about the irreplaceable nature of the experience of facing a class from nine till four, for five days a week, week after week; he believed that there was no substitute for being 'locked up' with a class in this way and for the responsibility which went with that. It was clearly possible to accept this argument without believing that the experience necessarily made better tutors.

However, these issues of principle rarely surfaced in our meetings with institutions or in Council's consideration of particular submissions. Then, as with the other criteria, it was on particular aspects of interpretation and implementation that attention focused. Reporting Groups knew from information supplied in Cateform 1 how many of the staff of each institution were concerned with pedagogy and how many of these had been away from the classroom for more than three, six and ten years. Often the institutions went to much trouble to prepare detailed schedules itemizing what these members of staff had done in schools over a period of time but our commonest difficulty was that the information did not take the form of a strategic plan. What we felt we needed was an institutional view of priorities projected into a rolling programme, an explicit statement that every member of staff engaged in pedagogy would be involved and some account of a process of structured evaluation of each person's experience. Consequently we had not infrequently to make repeated requests for supplementary written statements which we hoped would provide the necessary assurances. At times the ever courteous and helpful letters written by CATE's secretariat gave such broad hints of what we were looking for that it was difficult not to impute to the institutions a degree of obtuseness in not coming back with an acceptable form of words. In the end this was usually coaxed out, but at times with a lack of complete conviction which prompted us to propose to the Council taking another look a year later.

When Alan Marshall became CI for teacher training at the beginning of 1987 he queried this insistence on the provision of a plan, since our warrant for it was in Catenote 4 rather than in the Criteria themselves. But the justification in the Catenote was that plans were needed because everybody could not be released from an institution for renewal of experience at the same time. We sometimes gained the impression — and indeed were told — that our hard line on this issue was welcomed by a head of department or institution because of either the leverage which it provided for obtaining resource or the support which it gave in enticing some members of staff to get back into the classrooom.

Another issue which arose from time to time was what actually constituted an acceptable form of classroom experience and the allied question of consistency among the Reporting Groups. In May 1987 Group B, in introducing a proposal about the PGCE at York UDE, reported that the institution had been reluctant to be pinned down on the provision of school experience but now accepted a ten-week minimum period with three days per week teaching in schools. Group A had not evolved any standard which we would regard as minimal compliance, though we did look closely at whether being in school actually meant teaching as opposed to observing, assisting, researching or otherwise falling short of full class management. In January 1988 the Chairman mentioned in reporting on a conference which he had addressed that at least one person present had evidently had the impression that the only form of renewal of experience which CATE would accept was a second-ment of not less than three months to an appropriate school. He sought confirmation from those present that this was not the position — that while 'total immersion' was valuable, other arrangements were accept-able. This was agreed, but some light was subsequently thrown on how a different impression might have been given when Peter Scott indicated that Group B had in fact adopted three months as a rule of thumb for an acceptable minimum. In practice judgments had to be made about the adequacy of particular arrangements, especially when they took a serial form. In March 1988 I was with Group C when an instance came before them of a former secondary head who had been in a college since 1974 spending half-a-day a week in a primary school for one term; this was described by one member of the Group, without dissent from the others, as 'totally inadequate'. In October 1989 we heard from Group B that Reading UDE had been relying too little on block teaching and too much on teaching in small units.

Courses with a strong school focus paradoxically presented a specific difficulty. Introducing positive proposals in March 1988 on behalf of Group B about the PGCEs at the University of Sussex, Derek Mortimer explained that because of the UDE's unique approach in integrating its staff with serving teachers the Group had had a suspicion that they might be ducking their own responsibility to renew their experience in the classroom but they were now satisfied that this was not so. Group A had a similar problem when it reviewed the PGCE at Oxford UDE with its internship scheme, described in chapter 20. It appeared from their original paperwork that they relied almost entirely for providing their staff with relevant classroom experience on the internship arrangements, 'working alongside Interns and their Mentors or other teachers in classrooms'. When we met the UDE's representatives in March 1989 and pressed the point they conceded that though most tutors did undertake classroom teaching as part of their work with interns this could not be guaranteed in all cases. I asked them to reflect and see if they could incorporate in their procedures a process of annual review which would enable them to identify which tutors were 'actually teaching' and to arrange where neces-sary for this to happen. They agreed somewhat reluctantly to do so and in due course supplied us with a supplementary statement in which they accepted that what they were doing needed to be evaluated and to this end they proposed a three-stage process of internal review which we considered to be satisfactory. As reported in chapter 20, our positive proposal for the Oxford PGCE had a somewhat sceptical ride at Council. Members of other groups questioned whether we were being consistent in allowing this version of 'recent and relevant' to pass. I pointed out that Catenote 4 had allowed for more flexible forms of classroom experience than straight class teaching; what was unusual here was that the institu-tion relied exclusively on these. The proposal was in the end endorsed, though without total conviction.

Reference was made in chapter 8 to the flurry of alarm caused by the second HMI report on Birmingham Polytechnic which cast doubt on whether a staff development policy, as indicated to Group A at the time of the original CATE review, was actually in place. Their reply to the Chairman's letter of enquiry had in it something of the double defence that HMI were mistaken but that they were putting it right anyway.

After some further exchanges we met representatives again. It emerged that though they were upset by what had occurred their philosophy was against long-term planning in this area: they thought that renewal of individuals' classroom experience arose more profitably from their immediate needs, which were discussed in annual interviews with heads of department. However, we discovered that they had a Staff Development Committee with an annual plan, that they did prioritize where staff lacked recent experience and that they recognized the need for change if the new criteria, by then in draft, came into force. On balance we thought this gave us enough for a positive proposal, and this was endorsed by Council in October 1989.

What was prescribed by the draft new criteria represented a tightening and clarification of the rules. Classroom teaching, while not the only form of school experience, should form the major element in each tutor's development programme, and this should encompass the equivalent of one term's school experience in five years. These requirements, which remained intact in Circular 24/89, clearly had an impact on the thinking of those institutions with whom we were dealing at the end of our term.

The last item in this area to appear on our agenda was the HMI report on the *Renewed Teaching Experience Scheme at Trent Polytechnic*, which was circulated to members after the October 1989 meeting of the Council. It was noted virtually without discussion in November along with the fact that Trent Polytechnic had now become Nottingham Polytechnic. The scheme had been a joint initiative between the Polytechnic and Nottinghamshire LEA to provide opportunities for tutors involved in ITT to renew their teaching experience through one-term secondments to schools in an arrangement which also provided staff development opportunities for the teachers thus released. At its best the partnership was seen to have been mutually beneficial, but however good a model it had been we were told that it was now under pressure through lack of resources.

Chapter 25

Local Committees

A DES Circular of 1975 had called for the establishment of professional committees which would bring the interests of ITT institutions together with those of teachers' organizations, LEAs and the community at large. *Teaching Quality* announced the Government's intention to re-establish the professional committees with fresh guidelines and with constitutions to be approved by the Secretary of State, and Circular 3/84 duly declared:

> A course will be considered for approval only if it has the support of a local committee on which the training institution, the local education authorities in the area, local practising school teachers and individuals from outside the education service are all represented. Details of the constitution and membership of such committees will be for local determination but each institution will need to satisfy the Council that suitable arrangements have been made for a body of this kind to meet regularly. The committees should be encouraged to discuss all aspects of initial teacher training and should play a particularly important role in promoting links between training institutions, schools and the community. It is not intended that they should act in any way as sub-committees of the Council, which will deal direct with the institutions on course approval matters. (DES, 1984a)

At the first meeting of CATE David Shadbolt suggested that the structure and functions of local committees were one aspect of the Criteria on which early guidance would be particularly valuable to institutions. A paper on the subject was called for, though there was general agreement that the Council's approach would need to be flexible. At the Council meeting in December 1984 some textual amendments to a draft were made and the paper was published as Catenote 2 in January 1985. It was fairly brief, extending to only eleven paragraphs, and stressing the independence of local committees from CATE. Several patterns would be acceptable in principle, including the possibility of a committee serving more than one institution. Every LEA in the area need not be in membership but all should be consulted, and there should be an appropriate balance of member, officer and professional adviser representation. Teacher representation might also be secured in various ways, but the institution and its maintaining LEA, where appropriate, should be in agreement about its basis. The range of external membership should be as wide as practicable. Terms of reference ought to include regular review of the courses provided by each member institution and links with schools; the latter should include the participation of teachers in the selection, training, supervision and assessment of students, the provision of opportunities for renewal of classroom experience on the part of tutors, and school experience for students.

The final paragraph of the Catenote said that before CATE considered a course for accreditation it would ask the institution to provide a statement from the chairman of the local committee concerning the committee's support, its views on the course and the processes by which these views were formulated. I was not myself a member of CATE at this time, but much later I heard Renford Bambrough recall that the Council had earnestly debated the meaning of the word 'support' in this context, and had concluded that it was to be taken as analogous not with that given to a football team but with that given to an edifice. The Catenote also stated that while CATE would normally expect the requirements of the paragraph quoted above from the Criteria to be fully satisfied before recommending the approval of a course it recognized that in the initial stages of its work it might be sufficient for it to be assured that suitable arrangements for the early establishment of a local committee were well in hand. Nevertheless, in dealing with one of the first group of institutions to be reviewed, Kingston Polytechnic, the Council laid down as one of the conditions for a positive recommendation that substantial further progress should be made towards including in the membership of the local committee more teachers and members from outside the education service. Reservations of this kind were for some time not uncommon and the Council attempted to keep a close watch on local committee arrangements.

Early in December 1986 the Council secretariat organized a conference in Regent's College, London for local committee chairmen. After background introductions from the Chairman and Derek Mortimer the chairmen of the local committees associated with the University of Newcastle and Sheffield Polytechnic respectively recounted their experiences of the committees at work, and CI Pauline Perry gave an HMI perspective. We were addressed in the afternoon by Bob Dunn, MP, Parliamentary Under-Secretary of State at the DES, and institutional views were given by Leonard Marsh of Bishop Grosseteste College and Professor Maurice Galton of Leicester UDE. The invitation to the former was quite a brave one in view of his known reservations about the Criteria, and both speakers did in fact express some criticisms of the impact of CATE, but in general they were fairly constructive, though neither had much to say about local committees as such. In the final discussion session I was the only member of CATE to raise a question from the floor, asking what the local committees saw as their role after their institutions had been Cated. The Newcastle Chairman replied in effect that it was too early to tell, but probably not much; Leonard Marsh said his College had had a committee for several years and there was an ongoing role, for example in vetting school experience.

Meeting a few days later, Council members agreed that the conference had been a success; only five institutions had not been represented. The communication process had been two-way. The minutes recorded that 'there was some evidence of "conversion" among the audience'; on the other side Council members had learnt something about the operation of local committees. I drew attention to one point which had emerged, that many committees were chaired by the head of the institution concerned. It was agreed that whilst this was not contrary to the letter of the Criteria it was inconsistent with their spirit, since the likelihood of critical views being expressed in such circumstances was clearly reduced.

At the meeting of Group A on the morning of this Council day we had finalized proposals in respect of Edge Hill and St Martin's Colleges, but in both cases satisfactory evidence of local committee support had yet to be received. I queried whether it was still reasonable that such delay should be experienced; after two years of CATE in operation might we not expect that institutions should have completed this formality by the time we came to review their courses? The Group agreed, and in presenting our proposals to the Council Bill Wright mentioned the matter as one of principle, adding that if a course was known to have been approved by CATE before it came to the local committee this would put considerable pressure on the committee to fall into line. Again the point received general agreement, but the minute was worded in such a way as to commit the Council to not finalizing recommendations to the Secretary of State rather than not completing its own review procedures before receiving assurance of local committee support. This was already our practice and it did not alter.

At the Council meeting in October 1987 Ernie Grogan reported that he and Michael Pipes had paid a visit to the West Sussex IHE Local Committee, which also served the University of Southampton and La Sainte Union CHE. Among the matters raised had been a complaint that local committees heard nothing direct from CATE and that more detailed reasons should be given when a course was not approved. Although, as stated in Catenote 2, communications from the Council were normally direct with providing institutions, there was on this occasion agreement that letters to heads of institutions conveying the substance of Council recommendations should be copied to local committee chairmen. Another aspect of the relationship arose in November 1987 from the difficult situation in which Group A found itself, as described in chapter 16, in relation to the design and technology course at the University of Bath. One of the HMI concerns reported to us was that the local committee had been given inadequate documentation. This led Bill Wright to ask how far our responsibility extended: if a local committee supported a course were we to vet the local committee? There was in fact some warrant for this in Catenote 2, but the Chairman pointed out that HMI had representation on local committees: was it not for the local HMI to make it clear either that more information was needed or that the course ought not to be approved?

In January 1988 the Chairman suggested holding another conference for local committees, though on this occasion not necessarily chairmen. This was agreed, with the SI advocating what he called 'an earthy conference': he was hearing from colleagues of signs that were not good, such as poor attendance at meetings. In March, when we were considering more detailed arrangements, Peter Griffin said he thought there was a danger that local committees could be too much a matter of old pals together. Renford Bambrough thought they might have a sharper edge in those cases where a committee dealt with more than a single institution. The Chairman reverted to the undesirable practice of the local committee chairman being the head of the institution: Council would receive the letter of support which was required but it might emanate from a half-hour meeting. He also alluded to the question of the role of committees after their institutions' courses had been accredited. All these were good reasons for holding another conference, and it duly took place in May 1988, again in Regent's College.

The programme was wider-ranging than the role of local committees themselves, but in his opening remarks the Chairman suggested eight functions which they might serve.

1   To give support to the institution.

2   To monitor and comment on changes and developments in its courses. This would involve receiving regular reports from the institution.

3   To emphasize the concept of partnership in teacher training.

4   To help integrate the stages of teacher education (selection, ITT, induction, INSET).

5   To make a local input into whatever machinery succeeded CATE.

6 To provide a focus for special interests and the needs of particular groups.

7 To initiate and encourage debate on new developments in teacher education.

8 To take up issues with CATE and the DES.

Speaking after him, CI Alan Marshall told the meeting of some of the results of a recent HMI survey of local committees. First, as he put it, the good news. The vast majority of local committees were highly supportive of their institutions, and some had gone out of their way to inform themselves about their work. Some had taken specific initiatives such as help with interviewing techniques, seminars on educational issues to help members, the appointment of smaller groups to address particular issues like staff development or links with schools, in the case of a voluntary institution the contribution of the church and in another case help with recruitment strategy. On the other hand there were items of not such good news. Some committees found difficulty in sustaining regular attendance, not least on the part of teachers and LEA representatives. There was the difficulty experienced by non-educational members in contributing to discussion: sometimes they were not effectively drawn in. Not all local committees were sure of their role in relation to CATE — some even called themselves 'CATE committees', as if they were sub-committees of the Council. Some did not invite the local HMI — or invited him but did not send the papers! Alan also thought, while conceding that this was really a matter for CATE, that local committees might usefully provide the Council with more information about issues which they had examined. Looking to the future, he suggested that communications with local committees could be improved. He thought it useful when a committee served several institutions, as this facilitated comparisons among them. But the role of local committees needed clarification and he welcomed the Chairman's attempt to achieve this. He would have liked to see them make better use of their non-educational members, taking up special issues on which they could offer help, providing institutions with feedback on courses, performing an integrating function and helping to overcome teacher shortage through assistance with recruitment.

A further contribution came from Mr J.H. Aldam, the Chairman of the local committee which Ernie Grogan and Michael Pipes had visited, and a former Chief Education Officer. His was a witty speech in which he managed without rancour to convey a sense of both isolation and frustration in his present role. He thought it significant of the regard in which local committees were held that they were not addressees of CATE documents. The suggestion made that day that their comments would be welcome was news to him. He pointed out that local committees had no resources whatsoever at their disposal except through the good offices of the institutions which they served. The Circular was unrealistic in ascribing to local committees a particularly important role in promoting links between the institutions and the schools; the lead must surely come from the institutions themselves. A sense of partnership with CATE was lacking but the future of local committees was bound up with that of the Council itself. The current political climate was one of centralization and in his view the Government should either abolish local committees and centralize the accreditation process or build them into a devolved national system.

Since this broadside, however elegantly expressed, constituted a strong criticism of CATE's administrative arrangements, Ernie Grogan intervened as soon as Mr Aldam sat down to explain that a deliberate decision had been made at the outset to communicate with local committees through the institutions; in any case, until each submission was received — a process which even then was not complete — he had no means of knowing who the chairs or members of local committees were. Perhaps in some cases heads of institutions had slipped in not passing papers on; perhaps in some cases, he added naughtily, they did not want their committee chairmen to know what was going on. David Winkley also made a useful contribution in which he suggested that local committees had a positive and reconciling role, and explained the part which they could play in promoting school links. Other speakers reinforced themes already introduced. Dr Mike Preston, the Principal of Rolle College, felt that CATE should give more recognition to the competence and potential role of local committees. Professor Paul Hirst of Cambridge put the emphasis rather on the lack of definition of this role: the committees were not 'local CATEs' yet they were being told that in a sense they should be. There was a need for clarification.

Since the main message of the day seemed to be that CATE should establish direct links with the local committees the Chairman reported at the following Council meeting that the Secretary was writing to institutions asking for the names and addresses of their committee chairs. He also suggested that in future Reporting Groups should be more ready to ask for local committee views and even copies of their minutes. I am not sure whether Groups did change their practice much in this respect but it was noticeable towards the end of our term that chairmen or other representatives of local committees more frequently appeared as members of delegations from institutions who came to Elizabeth House to meet us, and when this happened one naturally gave them an opportunity to contribute to the discussion. In July 1988 the Chairman reported that there had been a good response to Ernie's letter and a list was being compiled. Later in that meeting he proposed the further role for local committees in relation to exceptional entry which is described in chapter 19.

In January 1989 it was reported that the secretariat had completed their own survey of local committees. This revealed that seven were without a chairman, only nine served more than one institution, and twenty-five had a member of the institution's staff as chairman. Membership ranged from twenty-four to forty-eight. Alan Marshall indicated continuing concern on the part of the Inspectorate that all was not well in this area and the Chairman said the committees did not all seem to know what to do after courses had been approved. From this time onwards consideration of the role of local committees and of their relationship with CATE became subsumed in the wider debate about structures for accreditation after 1989. This is described in chapter 30.

Chapter 26

Resource Implications of the Criteria

To the extent that the policies set out in this Circular may require local authorities to incur some relatively small additional expenditure in future years, in particular on the release of school teachers and teacher trainers, the Secretaries of State will expect this to be contained within the provision for those years, including the cost of employing teachers. It will be for local authorities to decide where any necessary savings should be made...(DES, 1984a)

This somewhat grudging statement constituted the final paragraph of Circular 3/84. Clearly these possible minor financial implications of the Criteria were not intended to be the concern of CATE, but it soon became obvious to the Council that they loomed large in the consciousness of the institutions to which the Criteria applied, and they were the subject of various queries and observations made to and concerning the Council as it set about its work. In March 1985 the Chairman reported on a recent discussion with the Secretary of State at which he had mentioned these concerns. Sir Keith Joseph had indicated that if the Council concluded that lack of resources was indeed a serious impediment to implementation it would be open to us to report the matter to him formally.

It was evident that it would have been premature to consider any such report at that time, when no institution had yet been reviewed, but representations continued to be made to us, for example by some of the professional bodies whom we met and from one or two local committees. These concerns were exacerbated in 1986 by the introduction of grant-related in-service training (GRIST), among the effects of which was to reduce the resources made available to some public sector institutions by their LEAs. At the first local committee conference, in December 1986, CI Pauline Perry acknowledged that there were clear resource implications in the concept of partnership in ITT, while diplomatically adding that whether responsibility lay with the DES, LEAs or the institutions themselves was a political question. Though GRIST did not apply to the universities they too had their problems, as Tony Becher and the Chairman mentioned in the Council in February 1987; the former explained that although the UGC was allowing in its funding for increased expenditure on ITT the universities were not necessarily passing this on to their UDEs. It was also recognized that in this context resources did not mean only money: various forms of pressure on schools made the release of teachers increasingly problematic, and in May 1987 Tony pointed out that the kind of partnership schemes which Sussex UDE had fostered, being entirely dependent on goodwill, were becoming more difficult to operate.

These problems were brought to the attention of the Minister of State when she visited CATE in October 1987, and at the following Council meeting Andrew Collier, who had not been present when Mrs Rumbold was with us, drew attention to a reference in the minutes to resource constraints and to what was described as 'the lack of any formal machinery for bringing them to the attention of the DES'. The minute added, 'It was agreed in discussion that the Council should not seek to act as a focal point for such concerns'. Andrew said he considered resource constraints to be a serious and growing problem and he offered to write a note on the subject for the next meeting. The Chairman had clearly been forewarned and responded sympathetically. Peter Scott, from another LEA, confirmed that shortage of money was indeed a severe problem, and CI Alan Marshall conceded that the effect of GRIST on LEA secondments was a cause for concern.

Andrew's paper duly accompanied the agenda for the next meeting, in January 1988. He had entitled it 'Links between training institutions and schools', and it began by referring to the relevant aspects of the Criteria. Having then quoted the words from the Circular with which this chapter begins, he remarked that even in 1984 the expressed expectation had been unrealistic, not least because the financing of the release of teacher trainers from universities and voluntary colleges was not the responsibility of LEAs. He went on to refer to the difficulties experienced in present circumstances by schools and training institutions alike. Finally he drew attention to relevant aspects of the Education Reform Bill then before Parliament — the proposed removal of nearly all ITT courses from the LEA sector, the effects of financial delegation to secondary schools, which would reduce the ability of LEAs to direct resources towards the release of school teachers, and the creation of the new category of grant maintained schools which would be independent of LEAs. In these circumstances, he concluded, it would be appropriate to ask the Secretary of State to review the relevant terms of the Circular, one possibility being that the costs of teacher release should become the responsibility of the training institutions, which would then have to seek recognition of this in their funding.

Unfortunately Andrew had given notice that he would have to miss both this and the following meeting of the Council, and so it was agreed to postpone full discussion until the spring, though several members confirmed from their own experience the reality of the problem he described. When we returned to the subject in Andrew's presence in April 1988 he placed the emphasis in introducing his paper on the point that after the Gerbil was enacted LEAs would, as he put it, virtually cease to be involved in ITT, and that consequently links with schools would have to be funded by the institutions. The Chairman observed that this was not a matter for CATE *qua* CATE, but Andrew argued that the Council had a locus in the matter on two counts — that the reference in the Circular to resources would have no validity after vesting day and that we had accumulated experience of institutions' problems in this regard. The Chairman then suggested that he should write to the DES drawing attention to the altered situation; to avoid the danger of appearing 'political' he would refer to the paragraph in the Circular about resources as one instance of change resulting from the proposed legislation. The DES Assessor said he assumed that the Chairman would not be expecting a substantive reply to his letter!

It was a couple of weeks after this that members of CATE met representatives of the UGC, CNAA and other bodies and some rather technical discussion took place about the extent to which the funding of either universities or public sector institutions took adequate account of the staff development requirements of the Criteria. At the Council meeting at the beginning of June 1988 it was reported that the Chairman had written to the Department reflecting the concerns expressed in Andrew Collier's paper and the discussion arising from it; the Department's reply had assured him that they had been noted. Problems encountered by individual institutions continued to come to our notice — for example, in connection with their ability to secure the services of enough teachers to participate in selection interviews. The CNAA man had hinted that some institutions were already paying for such services in cash or in kind, and in November 1989 Group B reported a specific instance: Nottingham Polytechnic was being required to pay for the use of teachers in student interviews. This was recognized as a growing problem, and one that was likely to become worse as the impact of the local management of schools (LMS) made itself felt. It would be a matter for the reconstituted Council to keep under review.

By this time the Council had held the discussions about the new criteria which are described in chapter 30, and in that context our concerns about resources had been firmly expressed in our response to the consultation document.

Chapter 27

New Types of Course, New Routes of Entry

It was the practice near the beginning of each Council meeting for members to report on any relevant conferences which they had attended. In February 1987 we heard from Derek Mortimer and David Shadbolt about one in Bournemouth on shortage subject training initiatives. They had found it helpful to be involved in formative discussion of new patterns of course. These were to be mainly BEds shortened to two years for those already possessing an HND or something similar in the areas of science, mathematics or CDT and PGCEs extended to two years for students with an element of these subjects in their first degrees. The Council would have to see how these new courses matched the Criteria, for they had not been envisaged when Circular 3/84 was drafted; it was foreseeable that they would raise some interesting issues but our two representatives seemed hopeful that the courses could be acceptable in our terms. At almost exactly the midway point in the Council's life this was the first specific evidence we received of a new climate of supply and demand for the teaching profession which became increasingly prevalent during the second half of our term.

Within the next few months Groups began to receive submissions in respect of the new-style courses. It was found that in the case of the new variety of two-year BEds it was relatively straightforward to infer how the Criteria should be applied, but the new PGCEs were not so closely analogous. A particular problem arose over qualifications for entry, for if an institution expected only 'A' level or equivalent in the relevant subject and included a year of subject study in the two-year course the students would experience no more than about half the study of the subject they were going to teach that students on a normal secondary BEd would undertake. CATE's first reaction was to conclude that we should need to take a flexible approach in applying the spirit of the Criteria to these exceptional circumstances. However, in the autumn of 1987 we received copies of a letter from the DES providing more specific advice. It stated that in giving temporary approval to some eighty courses in shortage subjects the Department had taken the Criteria into account as far as was possible. In the case of the two-year BEd, institutions had been told to ensure that students who were admitted had not only the normal entry requirements for a BEd but also a recognized qualification equivalent to one year in higher education in the relevant subject area and significant relevant industrial experience. In the case of the extended PGCE, institutions should be looking for students whose original degrees contained one year of relevant subject study — for example, a degree in economics, statistics or psychology might meet the test for a maths PGCE, or a degree in geography or biology for a physics one. This fairly explicit guidance was obviously of assistance to the Council from that time onwards though difficulties did not disappear.

In November 1987 the Chairman reported to us on a UCET conference which he had recently attended. One of the dominant issues had been teacher supply in the 1990s; it was clear that there would be an urgent need to increase the flow of both school-leavers and graduates into the teaching profession. He indicated that this was an area which was being given greater policy priority, and members may have recalled this if they saw *The Times* of 29 December 1987, for the main headline on the front page read 'Storm looms over plan for new teachers — Baker aims to recruit retired executives'. The story, by one of the paper's political correspondents, was that the Government was planning radical changes in teacher training. Redundant executives, retired police officers and former miners were among those who would be encouraged to train under proposals designed to bring more mature people into the profession and equip it with a more dynamic, managerial image. The plan, it was claimed, was to bring these people into primary schools, where they would work under supervision while achieving teaching qualifications through correspondence courses, night classes and the Open University. Because ministers wanted greater emphasis in the classrooms on the work ethic rather than purely academic subjects they were anxious to encourage student teachers to spend a greater period in schools rather than in colleges learning theory (Ford, 1987). On the following day *The Independent*, quoting some critical comments on this report by the General Secretary of the NAHT, also quoted a DES spokesman as saying 'it was no secret that the Government was trying to encourage people to come into teaching from industry' (Midgley, 1987). When the Council held its first meeting in 1988 some ten days later the Chairman referred to the report in *The Times* and said his enquiries suggested it was not true, although the Government was no doubt considering a range of possible approaches to recruitment. The DES Assessor confirmed that there was already provision under the appropriate Regulations for teachers to be recruited direct from industry, although this route then accounted for only about 200 new entrants to teaching each year.

At the March 1988 meeting of the Council reference was made for the first time to another form of innovation when the Chairman asked whether any group had encountered distance learning methods in submissions so far dealt with. Though no examples came to members' minds it was felt that resubmission of a course already approved might be required if the nature of its delivery as distinct from the material used were to change in any material respect. Knowing that the Open University was becoming involved in this form of project I undertook to provide a paper for the April meeting. In this I explained that the OU had just launched a new generic introductory education course entitled *Frameworks for Teaching* which was to be presented in January and September of each year as a joint initiative with a number of ITT institutions. This was part of the OU's response to the shortage of teachers in mathematics and physics and was based on the belief that many OU and other graduates would be interested in entering teaching if they had the opportunity to take a part-time PGCE. The idea was that students should register in the ordinary way with the PGCE provider but in effect the institution would contract out to the OU the provision of material for one or two components of the course. Brunel University and Thames Polytechnic had started to use the Open University course in this way at the beginning of that year for part-time PGCEs in physics with technology and in mathematics respectively, and others, including the University of London Institute of Education, were to start in September. In my paper I listed those Criteria which in the opinion of the OU course team chairman an institution might seek to meet in whole or in part through the use of the OU course, but I assumed that, as with any part-time PGCE, the onus would still be on the providing institution to satisfy the Council that all the Criteria were being met, including an equivalence to a full-time course of thirty-six weeks' duration. In practice no PGCE courses run in conjunction with the OU appeared to present any intrinsic difficulties for CATE.

Early in May 1988 a very senior official of the DENI remarked to me in conversation that he thought the whole CATE exercise might be overtaken by events; his reading of the political scene was that more attention was to be paid to linking teachers with industry and getting away from the school-college-school syndrome. This was exactly the question which had been put to us by Lord Beloff during our parliamentary briefing a couple of weeks earlier (see chapter 28); and at the second conference for local committees a few days after my conversation in Belfast the Minister of State at the DES, while claiming that the Criteria had had a major impact, stressed the importance of links between ITT and industry and commerce. CATE, Mrs Rumbold believed, had helped to make the former more outward looking, and the local committees could do much to strengthen its practical orientation. *The Daily Telegraph* reported this on the following day under the headline 'Train teachers "to be geared to industry"'; and *The Times* gave its report an obvious link with its earlier story by the headline 'Bosses tired of stress may find new job in classroom'. Ministers were said to believe that teaching would soon require an infusion of new blood if schools were to meet the challenge of the National Curriculum; they were examining ways to relax the rules governing a little-used route into teaching for mature entrants so that they could bypass the usual training requirements.

Further light was shed on Government thinking by the publication on 24 May 1988 of a green consultation document innocently entitled *Qualified Teacher Status*. It set out the Secretary of State's proposals for significant revisions to the regulations on the granting of this status 'to produce a simpler, more effective system'. The vast majority of entrants to teaching would still qualify by successful completion of a course of initial training; the intention was to rationalize the 'non-standard' routes, which included possession of a qualification gained outside England and Wales. The document noted that there would be a continuing need in the schools not only for re-entrants to the profession but for mature entrants making a career change 'for whom a period of full-time study would be a disincentive to recruitment'. The essential proposal was to confer upon LEAs and governing bodies the right to recommend that first a person be granted a licence to teach, subject in some cases to undertaking 'a pro-gramme of training tailored to their needs', and then that after two years he/she should be granted QTS. Subject to the outcome of consultation, these new arrangements were to come into force by the spring of 1989.

Most of the educational press seemed in no doubt about the signi-ficance of the Green Paper. 'Unqualified cavalry to ride to the rescue' was the *TES* headline for Bert Lodge's report. In the following week's edition Professor Bob Moon of the Open University asserted that 'the policy problem behind the paper is not status but supply'. When CATE met at the beginning of June 1988 most members had not yet seen the Consulta-tion Document and it was agreed to defer substantive discussion until our next meeting. The Chairman, however, seemed anxious to defuse the issue. He thought reactions reported in the press (from some teachers' associations among others) had been premature and ill-considered. He quoted a college principal as saying to him conversationally, 'I see you're out of business'! But the proposals, he declared, were not concerned with the categories of entrant to teaching for which we were responsible but with tidying up a number of other miscellaneous routes into the profes-sion; it was intended to be a clarifying statement, not, as some had seen it, a move towards 'deregulation'. The DES Assessor confirmed this interpretation, and Peter Griffin was the only member to speak and sound unconvinced. On my way home that evening I met in the Belfast depar-ture lounge at Heathrow the Northern Ireland civil servant who had expressed some forebodings a month earlier. When I mentioned the tenor of the Chairman's remarks on this subject he observed, though not a man given to indiscretion, 'I'm surprised that Bill Taylor should have fallen for that line of propaganda'.

When the Council returned to the subject in the middle of July 1988 the Chairman again seemed anxious to anticipate controversy. He began by pointing out that CATE's views on the Consultation Document had not been formally requested and he suggested that anything we had to say might be incorporated in our final comments and recommendations. The DES Assessor said the Document was about the non-standard routes into teaching whereas CATE was concerned with the standard ones. In spite of this discouragement to debate Andrew Collier ventured to observe that though he did not dissent strongly from the proposals in the document he felt that the non-standard routes ought to be related to the standard ones, but Michael Pipes said that after looking at the paper very carefully in order to judge how the NAHT should respond he too had concluded that it was essentially an exercise in rationalization. The DES Assessor said the main problem from the Department's point of view had lain in trying to determine the comparability of courses of ITT outside England and Wales. Andrew suggested that more emphasis was needed throughout the document on candidates' suitability for teaching. The Chairman commented that ITT was not all that was required to make a teacher. Michael added that a shortage of teachers was certainly coming and someone had to find them, but it was important that in dealing with the problem the good things brought about by CATE should not be lost. That seemed to be as much as anyone was prepared to say. Some months later the Chairman returned to the theme of misleading reporting of the licensed teacher scheme in the press and read to us part of a speech made by the Secretary of State to the Society of Education Officers in which he had sought to clarify his proposals.

The impending supply crisis figured prominently in educational comment after the 1988 summer break. In September the Labour Party published figures indicating that in 1986/87 four out of ten newly-qualified teachers did not take up a teaching job, and Jack Straw, MP, the Shadow Education spokesman, warned of teacher shortages engulfing the education service. The Secretary of State subsequently disputed these figures, claiming that a large proportion of newly qualified teachers went into teaching eventually and that real wastage was only 20 per cent. At CATE's September meeting, however, Michael Pipes enquired about the figures, suggesting that if a substantial proportion of trainees were not taking up teaching posts it must say something about the training courses and must therefore have implications for us. The Chairman remarked that Jack Straw went to a lot of trouble to collect figures but did not necessarily draw the right conclusions from them. He also remarked that one of the things we looked at now was 'funny' degrees possessed by entrants to teaching, though usually the institutions had a sound explanation; he wondered whether the supply situation might lead to an increase in the number admitted with funny degrees.

At the January 1989 Council CI Alan Marshall told us that HMI was about to publish a paper on a teacher apprenticeship scheme in the American state of New Jersey. This was duly circulated to us. Known as the Provisional Teacher Program, the scheme aimed to attract highly qualified graduates into teaching by offering a reasonably competitive salary and to provide them with on-the-job training. Not surprisingly, this 'alternative route' was found to make heavy demands on the practising teachers involved in the training, but HMI concluded that such a method of entry could command the respect of the teaching profession 'provided that it has a coherent framework, is capable of implementation and adjustment to meet local needs, and is comparable in demand and content with traditional routes of good quality'. At this meeting the Chairman observed that while CATE was not a policy body he was taking the line, if called upon to comment, that secondary routes into teaching were not a substitute for mainstream PGCEs and BEds. This was greeted with murmurs of agreement.

On the last day of February 1989 the DES published the first HMI Annual Report, which related to 1987/88. It stated that the education service would collapse unless there were enough qualified and competent teachers. It also included an assertion which could be construed as a pre-emptive warning from the professional arm: 'Standards of learning are never improved by poor teachers and there are no cheap high quality routes into teaching.' However, a DES letter near the end of June 1989 intimated another initiative on lines which had been advocated in some right-wing circles. This was to encourage more school-based courses of ITT, and bids were invited for pilot schemes in which 'articled teachers' would enrol for PGCE courses, usually of two years, when they would spend as much as four-fifths of their time in school, with training being delivered both by staff from the training institution and by selected teachers. This letter was on the agenda for the July Council meeting but in introducing it the Chairman drew attention to the statement that standard arrangements for accreditation would apply to these courses. No one asked how all the Criteria were to be applied in the circumstances envisaged. The DES Assessor said that as the bids invited were for 1990 starts institutions might for a time make fairly minor changes to existing courses and use the temporary approval mechanism. He indicated that there was no lack of interest in the project and that the Department might have to ration the courses, with priority given to shortage subjects. This was an experiment, and issues, including costs, would be noted. We were told in September that thirty-one bids had been received; these would not come to us, but those selected would come to the new CATE. (By November 1990 a Minister at the DES was saying that the Department was looking to develop the Articled Teacher Scheme into *a* main, perhaps *the* main, way of teacher training — DES, 1990b.)

In the meantime that Council had dealt with a substantial number of the new-style BEds and PGCEs. Many of these proved to be relatively unproblematic but the detailed consideration of others threw up two areas of difficulty which exercised Groups not a little during the last few months of the Council's life. One was the question of satisfying the conditions for entry laid down by the DES. Group A discovered, for example, that the requirements for the two-year PGCE at Birmingham UDE were 'A' level in the appropriate subject plus 'evidence of post "A" level experience', which would normally be in the form of undergraduate study, though in the interests of access other evidence of relevant study or experience would be considered. Bernice Martin reported to Council that Group B had encountered the same approach: some institutions wanted to allow 'experience' instead of subject study. The DES Assessor confirmed that this would not do.

An associated difficulty related to subject study within the extended PGCEs. To quote again from Group A's experience with Birmingham UDE, we were told that subject studies were designed to ensure that students reached a level of knowledge and capability at least equal to that of BEd Honours students; external examiners were said to believe that students compared favourably with those on the one-year PGCE course. We were also told that in the two-year version a range of courses from the respective undergraduate departments was used. This caused us to seek assurances that the students were progressing beyond their pre-existing knowledge base. Group B had similar concerns in relation to the extended PGCE in mathematics at Sheffield City Polytechnic, where again a range of courses was offered and individual students could take those best suited to their needs.

When I introduced a positive proposal in respect of the Birmingham courses at the Council's final meeting I drew attention on behalf of Group A to the difficulty we had now experienced with two or three institutions in satisfying ourselves about the entry qualifications of students on these shortage courses. This seemed to reflect the difficulty of the institutions themselves in recruiting candidates who complied with the letter of the law in having a year of higher education in the relevant subject. As a result their emphasis was on output — on the standard to be achieved at the end of the course — and on the structures necessary to facilitate this. There were nods around the table to suggest that members of other Groups recognized this account. I added that the point was perhaps one not so much for the new Council as for the DES itself if they really wanted these courses to make a significant contribution to teacher supply. Our assessor took note.

It was as late as September 1989 that the Council first received proposals in respect of one of the oldest of all the innovative degrees — that offered by Keele UDE. Group B had concluded that their BA/BSc with Certificate of Education was a concurrent course resembling the model of an extended PGCE rather than a BEd. Consequently the requirement for two years of relevant subject study was not breached by the fact that only one of the two principal subjects in the degree need be a 'school' subject. This was a unique formula.

In October 1989 Group A was happy to encounter another new variety of course about which there did not seem to be any cause for concern. This was submitted by Warwick UDE, which wished to present an MSc in mathematics, education and industry with QTS for intending secondary teachers. Introducing this to the October Council I said we thought it an exciting concept, and the Chairman agreed that it was also unique — the first MSc leading to QTS in the country. He observed that it illustrated once again the falsity of the suggestion sometimes made when CATE was first established that there could be only one acceptable pattern of course to satisfy the Criteria. This one was recommended with enthusiasm.

At the same meeting Group C outlined the background to yet another variety of non-standard submission, this time from the University of Exeter. The unusual feature in this case was that one course of study could lead to any of three qualifications. It was agreed to recommend the course as a two-year BSc plus Certificate in Education with three strands in maths, physics and technology respectively, but an alternative BEd route within the course was referred for further investigation. In subsequent correspondence the UDE justified the several routes through the course because of the need to cater for two types of student on entry — those who had had at least two years of main subject study and those who had had a least one. The former were eligible for entry to the BSc(Ed), and it had been decided that the latter should receive a BEd (Ordinary). However, if this latter group successfully completed a school-based dissertation during a part-time year following on immediately after graduation they were awarded a BEd (Hons). After some initial misgivings the Group concluded that the University had demonstrated the existence of three distinctive pathways within the one course, and the two BEd routes were accepted by Council at its final meeting in December.

In November 1989 Group A met representatives of the College of St Mark and St John. Among their courses was a two-year secondary BEd in design technology. We discussed the entry qualifications for this course and asked for written assurances, which we later found satisfactory. However, a curious point of interpretation arose from this in relation to the revised criteria which had by then been published. The College statement said that exceptionally, 'and in accordance with Circular 24/89, 7.9 and 7.10', they might consider applicants without the normal year of prior study in higher education if they were able to demonstrate that they had the academic capacity to complete the course successfully. These were the paragraphs which permitted exceptional entry by mature students to undergraduate courses and they followed without any sub-heading after paragraph 7.8 which dealt with admission to shortened BEds; 'Marjon' had therefore read the three paragraphs together. Prima facie this was not an unreasonable interpretation, but we were fairly sure that it was not the intention of the Circular — otherwise students would not have two years of subject study — and so we brought the point to the attention of Council at its final meeting; the DES Assessor confirmed that we were right to suppose that this was not the way the Circular was meant to be read.

It seemed fairly clear that the new types of course and new routes of entry to the teaching profession would figure prominently among the preoccupations of the new Council.

Part Four

'What CATE Did'

Chapter 28

Public Relations and Repute

I have already remarked that when I attended my first CATE meeting, in July 1985, it was evident that it had developed a strong sense of cohesion. Nine months of working on a demanding task under an incisive yet informal chairman might have been expected to achieve this. But I soon realized that there was another aspect to the group dynamics — a feeling of being misunderstood and under attack by the world outside, and therefore of members clinging together for mutual reassurance. The importance of publicity had been obvious from the outset and the Chairman had immediately begun taking advantage of opportunities to speak about the Council at conferences and the like; members were asked to do the same. In December 1984 a general desire had been expressed that the Council should interpret and disseminate its role in positive terms. A key factor in securing improvement in ITT would be the willingness of institutions to effect change; CATE would need to encourage the professional commitment to such change of those working in the field. But now, some six months later, the Council had just completed its first round of course reviews, and this had resulted in misleading headlines such as 'Exeter alone gets CATE seal of approval on training' in the *THES*, and some reporting had been inaccurate. There was discussion about how bad publicity might be prevented, though a resigned acceptance that it probably could not.

At the beginning of November 1985 there were reports of a highly critical debate at a conference on the impact of CATE run by the Society for Research into Higher Education at which CI Mrs Perry had been thrown to the teacher training wolves. Shortly after this the Chairman met hostile questioning when he spoke at a SCETT conference, and several members were present at a UCET conference when the Permanent Secretary of the DES received similar treatment. The criteria which came in for most adverse comment, as earlier chapters in this book will have indicated, were those concerning subject studies in the BEd and renewal of classroom experience for tutorial staff. These two aspects had also been the main subject of an editorial in the *TES* on 'Recent experience of CATE' in November 1985. While acknowledging the need to improve the quality of teacher education in some institutions, the writer declared: 'The question is whether Sir Keith, and his CATE, are setting about it in a productive way'. The demand for recent and relevant experience might be a necessary incentive, though the CATE approach was very rigid, but the subject studies criterion was 'more problematic'. Greater flexibility might be the Council's long-term intention; 'but it is a pity that, because of the way it was set up, it is seen as the mouthpiece of the Secretary of State rather than the watchdog for professional standards, and that its operating style, like his, has had to be all stick and no carrot' (*TES*, 1985).

The situation was discussed at the following Council meeting. The general view was that much of the criticism derived from anxieties and misunderstanding about the Council's work which would gradually be allayed as more courses were reviewed and our policies and procedures became more widely known. It was felt that members should continue to accept invitations to speak at meetings, and members' reports from conferences became a regular part of the miscellaneous items at the start of each Council agenda. On this occasion it was also noted that the subject studies criterion had recently arisen in a parliamentary question and in ministerial correspondence; it was agreed that every effort should be made to prevent the Council's work from becoming a subject of political controversy. In one sense, however, this horse had already bolted, for reports began to appear in the educational press of evidence being given by various bodies to the House of Commons Select Committee on Education, Science and the Arts, which was preparing a report on primary education. Some of the evidence related to teacher training and was critical of CATE or of the Criteria. Even HMI were reported as admitting that some courses which they had judged good did not precisely meet the CATE Criteria, and conversely CI Pauline Perry had said that courses approved by CATE might not be judged by the Inspectorate to be of sufficiently high quality. She and the Senior Chief Inspector emphasized that the Criteria were only one element from which they formed their judgments and they agreed that the Criteria had caused anxiety among teacher trainers. Mrs Perry had, however, defended the subject studies criteria as a response to the needs of primary children and of schools.

CATE itself was invited to give evidence to the Select Committee at the beginning of February 1986. A written submission of an explanatory nature was approved by the Council in advance, and subsequently we received a transcript of the lengthy discussion held with the Chairman and the three Group Convenors. The Chairman told us that rather surprisingly the MPs had shown no interest in the subject studies issue, though our witnesses had been primed to deal with it. We also received the evidence submitted by a number of training institutions, which included further criticism of CATE — the under-representation of teachers in its membership, a mechanistic and inflexible approach to the Criteria and a lack of clarity and consistency about their application, delays caused in course approval, the lack of advice prior to formal reviews and of dialogue generally, the resource implications of some of the Criteria, potential conflict between accreditation and validation; above all there was almost unanimous hostility to the two years of subject study and the pressure which this requirement put on other aspects of ITT. It may have been the public battering which CATE was receiving at this time which prompted the Secretary of State to speak publicly in its defence. He referred to the Council in his speech to the NASUWT conference at Scarborough at the beginning of April 1986 and reminded his audience that the Criteria and the whole accreditation exercise were based on the work of ACSET, on which the Association was represented. 'I believe [the Council's] work is already having a powerful and beneficial effect', he said (DES, 1986).

Discussions with representatives of organizations wishing to talk to us frequently occurred at this time after Council meetings. CATE was normally represented by the Chairman and the Convenors of the Reporting Groups together with any other members who could spare the time to stay on for an hour or so. A meeting of this kind took place with UCET in March 1986, with the SRHE in April, with the CNAA in May, with NUS in September, and with the World Education Fellowship in October. Aspects of these discussions which bore particularly on the subjects of other chapters are mentioned in the appropriate places. In general they were polite and somewhat stilted; it often seemed that the points or at least the emotions which our visitors had come to register were blunted or evaded by the formalities of the situation. If they left at all reassured it must have been more by the professional courtesy with which they were received than by the substance of the exchanges.

Adverse comment continued to appear regularly in the press. On the day of the Council meeting at the end of May 1986 there was a report in *Education* of a meeting of the SRHE teacher education group; recent talks with CATE 'had evidently failed to clear the air'. Professor Jean Ruddock of the University of Sheffield was said to have described the logic of the Criteria as 'crude and unformed' and the Council's way of implementing its decisions as 'highhanded'. She had stated that it was 'important to maintain a spirit of constant challenge in dealings with CATE' and she had offered a critique of several of the Criteria, which she expanded in the *TES* in July. Another speaker had described the Criteria as short on rationality and offering no ideal model; he called for both rejection and action, claiming that 'if we just accept these criteria we will be selling ourselves a long way short' (*Education*, 1986). Andrew Collier observed at Council that it was not the experience of his Group that the Criteria were challenged when they actually met with institutional representatives, and Group A might have said the same; but perhaps it would hardly have been realistic to expect delegations to be openly aggressive when the future of their courses was at stake. A more telling point may have been made by Group A's HMI Assessor, that people who agreed with the Criteria did not on the whole write about them; she quoted a colleague who had found a Polytechnic tutor much excited by a course revised in the light of the Criteria — he thought it was now significantly better.

A few days before this meeting, in a minor ministerial reshuffle, Sir Keith Joseph had been replaced as Secretary of State for Education and Science by Kenneth Baker, MP. HMI told us that Mr Baker was to be briefed about CATE in a few days' time and the Chairman said he had prepared a letter for him reporting on our progress. The Chairman thought the new man would be seen as more open to accept criticism of CATE than his predecessor, who had established it. (He and two of the Convenors met with Kenneth Baker shortly before Christmas.) The Chairman also told us that he had personally made contact with each political party in an effort to ensure that none of them went into a general election campaign saying 'We shall abolish CATE' — in other words to persuade them that there was not enough resentment in the field for them to feel that there might be something for them in such a pledge in terms of votes. (This was not minuted.) Early in June Maureen O'Connor had a piece in *The Guardian* reviewing Sir Keith's attempts in office to improve the quality of the teaching profession. Doubts about CATE were quoted from Professor Ted Wragg of the University of Exeter in respect of the ability which the mechanism gave to a Secretary of State to impose his personal whims on the system, from Len Marsh of Bishop Grosseteste College in respect of its centralizing tendency and from Professor John Tomlinson of the University of Warwick in respect of the effect of the subject studies criteria on courses which attempted to blend subject teaching and professional training. Bill Taylor was allowed to express the view that a greater variety of arrangements were possible within the Criteria than their critics assumed. The article concluded that there were other and grave problems affecting the teaching profession and the verdict on CATE must still be not proven (O'Connor, 1986).

Towards the end of September 1986 the report of the Select Committee was published. 'Select Committee suggests phasing out of CATE' was the headline in the *THES*. The Committee's conclusion had in fact been:

> that CATE had been given a difficult but important task to do in a way that makes it nearly impossible to do it well. There is a serious and potentially damaging breakdown in understanding between the Secretary of State, HMI and CATE on the one hand and the training institutions on the other

— and it recommended that the Council should not be continued after its initial term of appointment expired. Its task should be taken over by the CNAA and the other validating bodies. The report stated:

> While some of the criteria merely codified existing requirements and good practice, their cumulative effect and the manner of their application place unprecedented restrictions on the ability of individual institutions to plan and to change courses on the basis of their own perceptions of what is needed. A new and untried body with limited resources for advice and explanation had been given the responsibility of applying this code of rules to individual courses and then imposing decisions which critically affect the future of individual institutions. It has not been surprising that many institutions have objected strongly both to the degree of central direction and to the methods chosen to implement it.

It went on to quote many of the objections and criticisms which the Committee had received, especially with regard to 'the compulsory two years of subject study', and to CATE's methods and composition (House of Commons, 1986b).

At the beginning of October 1986 the *THES* carried a leading article entitled 'CATE on trial' which began with the observation. 'The Council for the Accreditation of Teacher Education was intended as an irritant institution, and it has duly irritated.' The Select Committee had recommended its abolition, 'no doubt overwhelmed by the sheer weight of the hostility to the CATE among teacher educators'. But the new Secretary was unlikely to take this advice because he would be told by his officials that CATE was the way to maintain —

> two essential strands in the Government's policy on teacher education, that the academic standing of the BEd be strengthened by stiffening it with 'subject studies', and that a much more intensive relationship be encouraged between teacher training institutions and the schools.

According to the article there was broad agreement on these two aims — no 'grand ideological struggle for the soul of teacher education' — but far from helping, 'CATE's inquisitorial and bureaucratic style and the abrasive obscurity of some Catenotes' had produced 'confusion rather than coherence'. In setting up CATE the DES had undermined the work of the CNAA, compromised the Inspectorate and disrupted the NAB. 'Like most short, sharp shocks the CATE experiment is at best irrelevant and at worst counter-productive' (*THES*, 1986).

The Chairman lost no time in responding to this outburst and his reply was published in the following issue. He reminded readers that

CATE was set up not to irritate or offer shocks but on the recommendation of ACSET. There had been no consensus for CATE to undermine and we did not look for uniformity. He made a vigorous defence of the subject studies criterion and of our working methods (Taylor, 1986). When the Council met later in the month we were told that in accordance with normal procedures the DES would be making a formal response to the Select Committee report within six months of its publication but that in a few days' time the Secretary of State planned to make a statement in the House defending the Council; other suitable opportunities would be taken by ministers to reinforce the message. As the Chairman said, there was therefore no immediate problem of Government support, and he also indicated that he had obtained at least tacit understanding from the spokesmen of other parties, but we could not afford to be complacent: we must ask whether we had got our procedures right and do all we could to avoid our public image deteriorating to the point at which we became politically embarrassing.

Time was allowed at this meeting for some discussion of the situation. Michael Pipes observed philosophically that the application of the Criteria was part of the general movement in education from norm-referencing to criterion-referencing and it was bound to cause resentment in those who failed. Derek Mortimer wondered if there were ways in which we might become more open, and I suggested that to meet the criticism that we operated on a checklist and did not look at courses as whole we might include in our submission-requests an invitation to make a general statement about the underlying aims or rationale of a course. (This was not taken up.) The possibility of adopting a more developmental role was also raised, but Derek suggested that the hidden agenda behind much of the criticism was the question of centralism — who had control? Summing up, the Chairman said he detected no sense of our having erred. We should exploit all possible opportunities for maintaining and improving our communications — members should be ready to write about CATE and speak about CATE. Perhaps we could improve our image — glossy Catenotes! He ended by reaffirming his faith: he thought the Criteria were justified and the impact of CATE was positive. There were murmurs of 'Hear, hear' from around the table.

On 30 October 1986 the Secretary of State gave a written answer to a parliamentary question on the future of CATE by saying that while not anticipating a detailed response to the Select Committee report he wished to make plain his confidence in the Council, which had been established after full consultation with interested parties.

> I believe that the Council is contributing substantially to the improvement of initial teacher training. It is carrying out that important task effectively and with tact and consideration. It has my full confidence. In due course the Council will complete its

remit. I will then review the situation, but meantime I propose no change in its terms of reference or the criteria to which it is working. (Hansard, 1986)

At the first of our conferences for local committees, at the beginning of December 1986, the Parliamentary Under-Secretary of State at the DES, Robert Dunn, MP, reiterated that CATE had the Government's full and confident support. Our critics can therefore have been left in no doubt that the Council would continue in being.

This, of course, did not mean that they were silenced, though after the December 1986 Council we had another of our meetings with professional bodies at which I thought there was more of a meeting of minds than at most of our previous encounters. This was with the Standing Conference of Principals and Directors of Colleges and Institutes in Higher Education, which, as SCPDCIHE, had been affectionately known to Branch and the Inspectorate as Scoobidoo, but had recently assumed the more dignified acronym of SCOP. Even at the start of the discussion they were not hostile and at the end of the session they seemed considerably reassured by evidence of our flexibility. However, in the spring edition of *Forum* there was an article by the Chairman of UPTEC, entitled 'What CATE is doing to schools', and his answer was in effect that it was damaging primary education because of the over-emphasis on subject studies (Hallett, 1987). A less hostile assessment appeared in the spring number of the *Journal of Further and Higher Education* (McGuckin, 1987). Members of CATE for their part wrote letters to journals and spoke at conferences. The Chairman in particular was tireless in this respect. In April 1987, discussing our progress towards completing our task, he remarked that it was process which was important rather than outcome. In other words, as he saw it — and that was not the only occasion on which the point was made — the very existence of the Council was having a salutary effect on course development.

At the beginning of September 1987 the extension of the Council's term till the end of 1989 was announced; as the *THES* put it, 'Stay of execution for CATE'. This headline provoked another letter from the Chairman explaining why our work was taking longer than originally expected. He referred to various benefits already accruing from the Criteria and claimed that whatever arrangements were decided upon for the future would have to build upon 'the vigorous course scrutiny and development' which had resulted from them (Taylor, 1987a). The Council met on the day on which this letter was published and the Chairman informed us that that morning he had given an interview to Bert Lodge of the *TES*, who had wanted to write a profile of CATE to mark its birthday. The Chairman had told him that accreditation bodies could not expect to be loved, and this remark may have inspired the headline which appeared the following week: 'An unloved baby grows into a bearable child'. The meddlesome infant godfathered by Sir Keith Joseph was now three, Lodge reported. Sent to discomfit, it had not, of course, been a wanted child; but the article traced, not unsympathetically, the background and progress of our work and its public reception. It ended with Bill Taylor's own summing up: 'I think we have raised quality and raised expectations' (Lodge, 1987). This piece gave a balanced impression, and at the September meeting the DES Assessor had disclosed that the Secretary of State had written to the Chairman of the Commons Select Committee defending CATE's role. Mary Hallaway also drew attention to an article in a professional journal which she considered more sympathetic than most which had appeared from such quarters, and I was able to report from the Education Section of the British Association, which had been meeting in Belfast during August; Professor Fulton of Queen's University had spoken of CATE in fairly positive terms and no one had voiced any criticism of it.

Any incipient euphoria which these more hopeful portents might have induced was slightly dented a week or two later by a curious piece contributed to *New Society* for its twenty-fifth anniversary edition by Lady Warnock, the distinguished philosopher and chair of the committee of enquiry into the education of handicapped children and young people which had reported in 1978. In this article she produced a critique of teacher training and her own remedy for its shortcomings ('teaching schools', analogous to teaching hospitals) without showing any awareness that CATE existed (Warnock, 1987). The Chairman wrote to the *Daily Telegraph*, which carried extracts from Lady Warnock's piece, explaining politely what was going on (Taylor, 1987b).

Just at this time the Prime Minister addressed the Conservative Party conference in Blackpool and announced that the Government's most important task in the ensuing Parliament was to raise the quality of education. Mrs Thatcher went on to outline the main provisions of what was to become the Education Reform Bill, including the establishment of a National Curriculum. It was clear that education was to be prominent on the political agenda for some time to come. It may not have been accidental that a few days after the Prime Minister's speech part of the Council's October 1987 meeting was attended by the Minister of State at the DES, Mrs Angela Rumbold, MP. She alluded to the need to defend CATE — against the Select Committee, against Baroness Warnock; she reiterated the importance attached to our work by the Government and was pleased that members had agreed to continue to serve. In particular, ministers continued to believe that intending primary teachers should have subject expertise and that pressure to abandon this policy should be resisted. When she spoke to the local committees conference six months later Mrs Rumbold said she had been impressed by the care and thoroughness with which we discharged our responsibilities. The Secretary of State and she were encouraged by the progress we had made. From the autumn of 1987 the enormous implications of the legislative proposals before Parliament and the anxieties which they aroused began to dominate educational discussion. This may have had the effect of taking some of the heat off CATE. Peter Scott remarked in November 1987 that 1984 was now an aeon away in education. Michael Dixon quoted Sir Keith Joseph, whom he had recently interviewed in retirement and for whom, unfashionably, he had rather a soft spot, as saying that they had not got teacher education right. The Chairman said it was no secret that there was a political push to have another look at the whole area, and I have referred in chapter 27 to some of the reports which began to surface shortly after this.

When we assembled for our first meeting of 1988 the Chairman reported what he considered to be a revealing incident at a recent conference which he had addressed. A delegate had raised a point from the floor, and in responding Bill had asked him which institution he came from. There had been a gasp from the audience. The Chairman had sought to explore the reasons for the gasp; he concluded that it revealed a still confrontational view of CATE's activity. He had written a short paper for the January Council to elicit our views on whether to make arrangements for a variety of seminars and conferences. One proposal was for the second meeting for local committees which I described in chapter 25; another was for a parliamentary briefing, which, as he said, was a new idea, prompted by the fact that he had received a number of informal enquiries and comments from members of both Houses. It was agreed to pursue the idea, and the briefing was duly arranged in a committee room in the Palace of Westminster on 21 April 1988 between 4.30 and 5.30 pm, after which all present were invited to a dining-room for drinks. Only two parliamentarians stayed for the whole hour. We had been warned that it was quite normal for members to wander in and out of such events and we were subsequently told that on this occasion a total of seventeen did so, but most stayed for only a few minutes so it seemed doubtful how much light had been shed. However, questions began to flow as soon as the Chairman and Derek Mortimer had made opening statements, and the rest of us (ten in all) were drawn in piecemeal. Our guests were interested in why courses were being turned back and what happened to these courses and to the students on them. Lord Beloff wanted to know our views on the desirability of teachers having experience of industry and commerce as opposed to having followed the school–college–school cycle, while a few questions were of the variety, 'One of my constituents...', 'My daughter is at college...' Renford Bambrough stressed that we now had more support from parents and trainers than we had had initially, when teachers were lukewarm. Not lukewarm, said the Chairman: red-hot against! Reporting to the Council on the following day, he mentioned that in the bar after the formal presentation the question had arisen what happened if an institution failed the second time round — an eventuality which had not yet occurred, though, as the Chairman observed, it could well happen before the end of our term. He also remarked that he had told politicians on the Government side that as they had been critical of the Opposition for conducting its campaign on the health service in terms of anecdotes they should avoid doing the same themselves about teacher training.

In May 1988 the second conference for local committees exposed the Council to another opportunity for critical scrutiny. One perspective derived from a questionnaire which SCOP had sent to its members. Not all the feedback thus obtained had been hostile, though institutions were said to be unanimous in identifying the dominating and distorting effect of the subject studies criteria on undergraduate courses for primary teachers, especially for the early years phase. But the most incisive critique came from Professor Paul Hirst of the University of Cambridge. In part he was concerned about the arrangements which would succeed CATE, and he conceded that behind the criteria which we were appointed to apply had been ACSET, a representative advisory body; he reported the UDEs as being of one mind about the importance of having an accreditation body, he thought the right sort of people were on CATE, the Criteria were necessary, and HMI visits, though originally regarded by the universities as something of an attack on their autonomy, had proved to be useful. In many ways, therefore, the CATE exercise had been successful. But its membership ought to be representative of professional interests and not nominated by the Secretary of State; it was because CATE was not representative that it had seemed remote. There was also concern about its bureaucratic procedure, the endless demand for bumf; this needed to be streamlined and coordinated. He thought that accreditation visits should not be made only by HMI but should include teachers and teacher trainers. Most fundamentally he questioned the purpose for which CATE had been established: was it to improve quality or to ensure basic standards? The Criteria were a very mixed bag, ranging from saying that people should not pass initial training if they could not teach, to others which were not laying down minimum requirements but were principles or guidelines that could be satisfied in a great variety of ways. There were also problems about what ideas like partnership meant. If teacher training was to be a collaboration the respective roles of tutors and teachers needed to be worked out; each had a proper role and it was not obvious that standing in front of a class, which of course tutors could do, was their role. There was a need for review of the Criteria, a need for distinctions, a need for clarification of what it was all about. The Chairman later described Paul Hirst's contribution as iconoclastic and 'very Cambridge'.

At the same meeting, at the beginning of June 1988, he said he was now hearing the argument, why have obligatory teacher training at all? If it was as valuable as was claimed, schools would want trained teachers, but if they did not, let them appoint untrained ones: let market forces prevail. He added that he thought CATE more of a Van Gogh than a Picasso — the rewards would accumulate after we had expired. After this meeting, some members remained to see half-a-dozen representatives of SCETT. Among a variety of issues raised was that of communication between CATE and the system; there was a lack of feedback, and it was a long time since a Catenote had been produced. The Chairman was able to tell the visitors that another was in fact on the way, but he added that CATE had been set up in quango-hunting days with a low budget and a small secretariat — we had never been in a position to produce glossy journals, or glossy anythings. They assured him that our printed A4 Catenotes were fine, and suggested a subject for another (non-standard courses). They also thought attendance by CATE members at professional conferences was valuable — it had removed a lot of the tension in the early days. They now saw a need for the application of the Criteria to take account of recent developments like the publication of the Kingman Report and the still embryonic National Curriculum and associated proposals for assessment; the last of these they thought implied a need for understanding of child development. Renford Bambrough pointed out that the Criteria had a built-in adaptability through their reference to the (secondary) curriculum 'as it may be expected to develop'. The Chairman said they were general purpose and not too prescriptive, and Derek Mortimer added that they were a creation of their time and changes in one part of the system required change elsewhere.

In September 1988 we were told that the House of Commons Select Committee was preparing another report, this time on the supply of teachers for the 1990s, and it was agreed that the secretariat would prepare a short paper to enable the Chairman to respond to their request for written evidence. The paper was endorsed by Council in November. The Chairman said he had thought it desirable to spell out fairly carefully what CATE's role was so that the Committee did not think, as on the last occasion, that we had responsibilities far beyond our brief. In November we also received a report from Derek Mortimer, who had attended a CNAA conference in September on partnership in teacher education. He said a lot of cynicism had been expressed about the speed of change. There was a tendency to hear most from those who were moving, but the system as a whole had a long way to catch up.

Among the reports of this kind which we received at each meeting we still heard occasionally of hostility towards CATE, but in general it was at about this time that a change in the climate began to be discernible. Two HMI conferences on the Education Reform Act were held during November. CATE was represented at both and when members reported back in January 1989 it was to say that a more favourable attitude to our work was beginning to emerge. CI Alan Marshall even referred to people expressing the hope that CATE would continue — a turn-round, as he put it, in perception of CATE. This remark was greeted with pleased laughter: it seemed that we had arrived at last. We also heard at the same meeting about a conference organized just before Christmas by the University of Lancaster with the title, 'A future for teacher education?' Here again there had been a fairly sympathetic view of CATE, and a feeling that in the turmoil into which education had been thrown by the new Act and the proposals for licensed teachers the Council was to some extent a protector of educational standards. There had been a strong desire not to lose ground which had been gained, such as graduate entry into teaching.

After a special Council meeting at the beginning of February 1989 to consider future arrangements we held a press conference at Elizabeth House. This was very much the Chairman's idea, which he had broached in December 'so that the importance of initial teacher training and the experience of CATE could be kept in the public eye'. About ten journalists turned up. They were given a press release with background information about the Council and a summary account of its work in terms of the principal obstacles to the approval of courses which had been encountered and impressions of CATE's influence on training. When questions were invited the Chairman had some difficulty in steering them off the then topical issue of alternative routes into teaching, but presently Peter Wilby of *The Independent* fired off the observation that ministers were constantly going on in public and in private about there being too much theory in ITT and not enough practical preparation for the classroom: either ministers were wrong, he concluded provocatively, or we had failed. The Chairman responded by using slides prepared for the purpose to draw attention to the areas where he claimed we had made a positive impact on the system. Derek Mortimer supported him by referring to the lead-in time involved in a four-year course: few teachers who were the product of CATE-approved courses were yet in the schools. I did not observe the education correspondents taking many notes and the event did not appear to inspire much direct reporting, though the Chairman subsequently deplored some headlines which had evidently suggested an attack by him on the Secretary of State. Bert Lodge had a useful piece in the *TES* concluding that many teacher-trainers would now assent to the proposition that post-CATE arrangements for accreditation were needed to preserve the gains of the previous four years (Lodge, 1989). But it was clear from much that appeared in the press around this time that education correspondents saw the introduction of licensed teachers as a more significant development then did CATE under Bill Taylor's guidance. At our April 1989 meeting we received an extract from the HMI Annual Report for 1987/88, which boldly announced that since Circular 3/84 and the establishment of CATE 'there has been a considerable change for the better in initial teacher training courses'. This, as our minutes recorded, 'made encouraging reading'.

The publication in early May 1989 of a DES consultation paper on future arrangements for accreditation made it clear that a Council on something like the lines of the 1984 CATE was to be a continuing feature of the educational landscape and this obviously had the effect of changing the terms of the debate from whether to what and how. Nevertheless, even as we entered our terminal phase, the occasional brickbat continued to be tossed in our direction. A negative instance in early September was an article in the *TES* by Professor David Hargreaves in which he advocated the abolition of the BEd and the replacement of PGCE courses by teaching schools. He began by expressing surprise that Kenneth Baker's zeal for school reform while he was Secretary of State had not extended to ITT. This seemed a rather curious remark in view of the fact that Hargreaves had been a member of CATE during its first year of existence.

A letter published in the *THES* on the day of our September 1989 meeting expressed surprise that the consultation paper had not attracted more criticism. CATE, wrote the correspondent, had proved supine and unproductive (foolishly citing as evidence for this accusation that we had produced only five Catenotes in three-and-a-half years); and if CATE had been a bureaucratic impediment to effective teacher education the same was probably true of local committees. He attacked as wasteful and unnecessary the involvement of teachers in selection and of tutors in teaching, and concluded that the state of teacher training twenty years before had left little to be desired (Sharps, 1989). Some members of Council knew who the writer was and did not regard him as representative, but the *THES* had made it their leading letter with the heading, 'A bureaucratic brake on good training', so the Chairman said he would reply. His rejoinder, which appeared in the following issue, was in terms of our acknowledged impact and the scale of our work, but concluded that 'anyone who believes that teacher training twenty years ago "left little to be desired" is going to be pretty difficult to satisfy' (Taylor, 1989).

This proved to be our last foray into public controversy before our demise, but the two perspectives on our work continued right until the end. At our penultimate meeting in November 1989 Marian Giles Jones reported on the recent UCET conference at which the Parliamentary Under-Secretary of State for Education had announced the publication of the new criteria which were to apply from January 1990. There were still some anti-CATE voices, she told us. 'You took names', said the Chairman with a straight face. But at the same meeting we were joined for lunch by the new Permanent Secretary at the DES, John Caines, CB. He said that since taking up his appointment he had heard a lot about CATE from within the Department but less from outside and he thought it a pity that our work was not more widely known. He was very flattering about the time and effort we had all put into the Council.

Our apotheosis came on the evening before our final meeting in December 1989, when the Secretary of State, now John MacGregor, MP, held a reception in Elizabeth House for all members, assessors and officers of the Council, past and present. At the end of the event our attention was drawn to the fact that there was a souvenir present for each of us on a side-table; this proved to be a tasteful glass paperweight inscribed 'CATE 1984–1989'. In his short speech of thanks Mr Mac-Gregor said that we had proceeded with sensitivity and authority. At our Council meeting on the following day our Branch Assessor told us that the civil servants had supplied him for the occasion with a motto which he might have cared to apply to us, *Suaviter in modo, fortiter in re* (sweetly in manner, firmly in deed); but he had not used it. The Chairman had replied to the Secretary of State on the previous evening, and he also responded ably and comprehensively to a presentation made to him from us all at lunch-time that day. At the close of business on 13 December 1989 he told us he would not be otiose and repeat all that had been said, but this was the end of a chapter in the history of teacher training in Britain. One day someone would write a book about it...

Chapter 29

Good Practice

In one of the papers prepared for the Council's first meeting it was suggested that institutions could be helped 'through the dissemination of information on good practice'. The only way in which this was followed up initially was by the publication of the early Catenotes, the purpose of which was rather to offer an interpretive commentary on the Criteria. But in the autumn of 1985, when Catenote 4 on links with schools was under discussion (see chapter 20), a more specific point arose in the context of deciding whether to refer to IT/INSET as an acceptable form of school experience. Concern was expressed that by picking one model for favourable comment the Council might appear to be being prescriptive; some members felt that we should not give any examples until we were in a position to give several. In the end the reference was retained but carefully prefaced by the phrase, 'One among a number of examples of such collaboration. . .' The idea was mooted, however, that at some stage, perhaps in a later Catenote, the Council might publish descriptions of good practice which it had encountered in various aspects of teacher training. In October 1986, when the Council was discussing the critical references to CATE by the House of Commons Select Committee and considering how our public image might be protected, Mary Hallaway said that the publication of examples of good practice would be one way to promote the positive side of our work.

Two meetings later, in January 1987, the theme resurfaced in a more positive form from the chair. Before the day's business began I was having coffee with one or two other members in the little kitchen on the seventh floor of Elizabeth House when Bill Taylor arrived and immediately began to tell us of an idea which he was going to put to the meeting but had deliberately obscured on the agenda in order to avoid any risk of leaks. This was to establish a small group of members and external people to distil the experience CATE had now gained about good practice in ITT. I had the impression he wanted to ensure that at least a few members understood what he would be saying and were sympathetic. In fact we were all fairly non-committal; Bill Wright observed that much would depend on how it was done and what messages went out to the system. During the afternoon the Chairman introduced his initiative after reporting to us on the meeting which he and two of the Group Convenors had held just before Christmas with the new Secretary of State for Education and Science. In the context of Kenneth Baker's evident interest, of the forthcoming publication of an HMI survey of initial teacher training, of the substantial number of courses we had now 'seen', of the consideration which he hoped would soon be given to arrangements after CATE had terminated and of the fact that we ought to be evaluating what we had done, had the time come, he asked, to see what advice could be given to the field and to the Secretary of State about courses which satisfied the Criteria and were good courses? The message would be that there is a variety of ways of doing things but common features include such and such, and these would constitute good practice. He was not seeking to lay down a 'British' BEd or PGCE, but practice was in fact less diverse than had been supposed.

These remarks led to a lengthy discussion to which the Chairman himself made further contributions. Peter Scott was the first to respond from the floor, referring to the attempts of the working party of which he was at that time a member to illustrate good practice in the selection of students — the embryonic Catenote 5; he thought there was great demand for such material. Alistair Lawton, attending his first meeting, expressed the view that a system of reviewing and monitoring institutions' progress was needed. The Chairman suggested that this was HMIs' work, and CI Alan Marshall made a number of points. HMI were always on the look-out for good practice and anxious to draw attention to it. They also from time to time produced packages of good practice in the form of booklets on subject areas and the like; that this should happen in relation to ITT was a good idea. There was a possibility of revisiting some institutions after they had been Cated. Perhaps a recently retired HMI could be given the job but it must be done independently of CATE. Tony Becher said that two things worried him. One was CATE's resources: could we as a Council, given our heavily worked membership and small secretariat, undertake such a task (though we might commission others)? The other was the idea of disseminating a pattern — if not an ideal then at least one that was being commended as very good — since so much that happens is contextual. Andrew Collier said it would be a pity if we did not collect the experience we were gathering and he reminded the Council that this had been a strong recommendation of the Select Committee. Though the Chairman had drawn attention to the fact that we could not go beyond our terms of reference the Branch Assessor said he would like to hear about what was generalizable. He thought it would be within our remit to attempt this for two audiences — institutions which had not yet been Cated, and ultimately the Secretary of State.

This implied two timescales; to be helpful to the first group we should need to move quickly.

Renford Bambrough was against bringing in some outside person to do the job on a secondment: what was needed, he considered, was an articulation of our common mind, a systematization of the kind of remarks we all made in conversations about CATE and which people found helpful. Peter Scott expressed agreement, saying that if each Reporting Group went back over its cases it could unearth a wealth of experience. But Renford was not sure about 'good practice'; it was rather procedures which should be collected. Bill Wright thought it must be experience, and this could be collected only by Council members; but he returned to the question, had we the time to do it? Michael Pipes believed that agreement on a general teaching council was nearer than was generally realized; such a body might take over from CATE and a corpus of successful application of the Criteria would then be helpful. My own contribution was to suggest that there might be difficulties about describing good practice because our approach to the courses which came before us was a minimalist one, primarily satisfying ourselves that the Criteria were being met and probing where there were doubts rather than where there was excellence. To identify 'successful application of the Criteria' might therefore be a more realistic aim.

The Chairman summed up by saying he felt sufficiently encouraged by the discussion to write a paper on the subject for further consideration, and would do so in consultation with the Convenors and ex-Convenors. Renford Bambrough and Derek Mortimer both added that they did not think the exercise should be conceived as mainly for institutions which had not yet been Cated, partly for reasons of equity (they would then, as it were, have an unfair advantage over those which had been taken first). Peter Scott said he thought the secretariat should be involved. The Secretary said he thought HMI should be involved!

'Identification and dissemination of good practice' was on the agenda for the following meeting at the end of February 1987. The Chairman explained at the start of the meeting that at the end of the afternoon he was going to have a short meeting with the Convenors and ex-Convenors, as agreed at the previous Council, and he asked us to be thinking 'in the interstices of the agenda' about examples of good practice which he would invite us to offer before the formal business closed. When this point came he said that what he was looking for were examples from our experience in the Groups as markers for good practice, and preferably in areas not covered by previous Catenotes. A few suggestions were readily offered by members — selection at one university, schemes with industry at another, multicultural education at a college in a cathedral city as an example of good practice in a situation without strong representation of ethnic groups. At this point the SI who was with us that day intervened to say that as it happened she had been involved in the inspection of all three institutions to have been instanced, and she would have some hesitation in citing them as examples of good practice: the institutions were good at describing what they were doing but the reality was less impressive. The Chairman remarked reflectively that this had serious implications: in spite of the close involvement of HMI in our work were there still blatant examples of our having the wool pulled over our eyes? Michael Pipes and Derek Mortimer both suggested the moral was that we should not be talking about good practice but about good ideas. The Chairman said he thought it was important to get away from our image as people who turn things down. He believed that like children, and indeed like adults, institutions respond best to praise and support.

Ernie Grogan echoed the point I had made at the previous meeting: because our job was to ensure that each of the Criteria was being met the Council might not be the best body to identify things that were being done particularly well. The SI said we should think in terms of good practice in course design rather than on the ground; 'You have your spies', she added, meaning the Inspectorate. The Chairman said he would do a paper for the next meeting and Michael Pipes supported him in the view that we should not let the matter drop by stressing the need to demonstrate to the field that the Criteria could be met. Some more examples were then volunteered by members in relation to various aspects of the Criteria before the Chairman went into conclave with the Convenors. The entire debate was minuted in one paragraph, of which the last sentence read:

> ...it was recognized in discussion that the Council's terms of reference and methods of working were such that examples of good practice (as distinct from practice which simply met the requirements of the criteria) were not necessarily identifiable in individual submissions; and that the Council's capacity to distinguish between actual and described practice was limited.

When Group A next met, Bill Wright told us that as a result of the Chairman's meeting with the Convenors he would be approaching all members for examples of good practice. The questions had arisen whether there were areas where some refinement of the Criteria was needed and whether there was any evidence of the Criteria having a negative effect. Conversationally we commented on the startling incident at the Council when HMI had made her 'Wait a minute' intervention. I referred to the subsequent suggestion that we should refer not to good practice but to good ideas or descriptions. 'Yes', said Bill wryly; 'candidates who have done well in their written paper!'

At the April 1987 Council there was only a brief 'matter arising' to report that the Chairman had met with the Convenors, HMI and Branch officers. What had occurred was described as preliminary discussion of the possibilities for the identification and dissemination of good practice, and this had been linked with the question of a possible continuing role for the Council after the completion of its initial remit. The Council would need itself to address these issues in due course but the Chairman would shortly be inviting the present Convenors to begin the process of identifying examples of good practice. The May Council began with discussion of the HMI survey of ITT, which had just been published, and I commented on the implications for CATE of its statements about good practice. There was more in the HMI document about staff development than we had put in Catenote 4 and more about selection than we were likely to put in Catenote 5 (still, at that time, in draft). If we proceeded with the intention of putting out notes on good practice we should have to ask ourselves to what extent we were duplicating material in the HMI report and consider whether we were being consistent with it. The Chairman responded with 'Thank you, that's helpful', which I had come to recognize as an indication that he was going to pay no attention to what had been said. I had the impression that he was now very much committed to the idea of producing a CATE anthology, and perhaps saw it as our most valuable and lasting memorial. No one could doubt his conviction and determination that we were in the business of improving quality in teacher training.

Later that day the Chairman reported what he described as a helpful suggestion from HMI that we should ask certain institutions to write their own descriptions of practices which we thought particularly interesting and he asked for guidance as to who should be invited to write about what. The idea seemed to me to be somewhat at variance with the same HMI's earlier comment about the institutions which she knew personally but no one referred to this. The minute recorded that 'the Chairman undertook to write to members pursuing this suggestion', and such a letter did indeed follow. When Group A met early in July 1987 we agreed that it would save time and be more effective if we divided among ourselves the institutions with which we had dealt and Ernie Grogan agreed to draw up a schedule for our next meeting. When this day came Bill Wright simply took the alphabetical list which Ernie had prepared and allocated three institutions to each of us as we sat round the table. If we were to comply with the Chairman's request to convey our comments to Ernie by the end of July there would be no opportunity to discuss them collectively first, as we should have liked, but we agreed to compare notes at our first meeting in September.

In the meantime there was a meeting of full Council later that day when the Chairman's letter was mentioned and its message reinforced. Accompanying the agenda was a paper on which Ernie had listed the suggestions already made by members, but the hazards of the enterprise were again illustrated when Mary Hallaway drew attention to one institution on the schedule, saying she thought it was she who had mentioned it but that it had been as an example of what was *not* good practice! This seemed a suitable note on which to lay the issue to rest for the summer recess, but I for one attempted my homework before the end of the month. I was perhaps fortunate in that the luck of the draw had assigned to me two institutions — Bristol and Cambridge Universities — which we had considered to be very sound and in some respects outstanding, and brief reference to the files enabled me to put some comments together for the Secretary. When Group A met again in September these were tabled along with the others received. But only four of us had responded, and as David Shadbolt's was a 'nil return', Bill Wright's example of good practice was on the part of the DENI rather than of a particular college, and one of Peter Ward's nominations was considered by the rest of us to be not wholly appropriate, our total distillation of good practice was not very impressive. Ernie told us that only one other member of the Council had made a return at all. When the Council met a week later the Chairman reported that the result of his request for suggestions had been poor but he nevertheless renewed it.

The matter was the last item on our October 1987 agenda, and when we reached it we were already somewhat past the Chairman's estimate of the time at which he expected the meeting to conclude. Peter Scott reported that Group B, for whom he was speaking that day, had spent some time on the subject that morning and he was bound to say that they had some reservations about whether to proceed. Peter Griffin, from the same Group, said they had trimmed their long list down to one or two examples but anything published would require very careful editing and he wondered where the resource was to come from. They were also very conscious that it could only be impressions that they had to go by. The Chairman looked as if he were not unduly surprised by this rather negative response and by a glance round the table invited further comment. 'I don't want to say, "I told you so!"' said Tony Becher; 'but I've said it'. He went on to recall that in the original discussion of the topic he had advocated commissioning someone to do the work. We had accumulated a lot of material about ITT and he accepted that it would be to some extent wasted if it were not fed back into the system. He was in favour of an attempt at this being done but not by the Council. The Chairman said it looked as if we had to accept that no progress could be made. In order to test how far he had retreated from his initial thinking I reminded him of the HMI suggestion that we should invite institutions to write up their own accounts of what seemed to us good ideas. But the objection was that this would still carry the Council's imprimatur: it was a political point. The minute of this 'lengthy discussion' reported agreement 'that there were major practical obstacles to further progress'. It also recorded an undertaking by the Chairman to discuss the matter further with the Department and HMI and to give a further report at the next Council meeting. In November, however, he merely stated that he had no more points to come back with, and the matter was dropped.

Nevertheless, it transpired that it was not yet dead. In February 1988 Group A was given to understand that Tony Becher had suggested to the Chairman some form of 'jamboree', and this was referred to formally at the Council meeting in March. It was to be a get-together with representatives of bodies which had 'formal approval/accreditation/inspection functions' — namely, CNAA, DES, HMI, NAB, UGC, and WAB; an observer from the new PCFC was later added. The time chosen was the afternoon of a day on which Group A was meeting in the morning, so we were the only members present apart from the Chairman himself. In his opening remarks he ranged widely over the Council's experience and the issues which had arisen; of these he mentioned good practice last. Much was now in the public domain in the pages of HMI reports, but he felt that it was relatively little used; it was not being pounced on by researchers as he would have expected. At this point he invited Tony Becher to speak. Tony expressed the view that 'good practice' was a rather static notion, not least because of the impending imposition of the National Curriculum. He preferred to think of the relevance of good practice for future policy. To winnow this out from the material which CATE had accumulated was not a job for one person but could usefully be done through a task-force approach, perhaps over a couple of years. General discussion then reverted to the various other questions which the Chairman had raised, but as the meeting was about to break up Len Wharfe of the CNAA asked what was going to happen about Professor Becher's proposal in relation to good practice. Tony's answer seemed to be that funds would have to be sought from some external source.

In July 1988 Tony reported to the Council that with the Chairman's approval he had been pursuing the matter. What he had in mind was separate from any review of the Criteria: he was concerned with curriculum development in ITT as a possible first step to a future national policy on teacher education. The approach should be empirical rather than theoretical. He therefore advocated a proposal to a private foundation. It should be for an independent review, not constraining ministers to policy. There should be a working group representative of all the relevant interests — primary and secondary, university and public sector, BEd and PGCE — to produce a report on curricular good practice by the summer of 1990. The Chairman added that this idea was to be considered during the following week at a meeting representative of various interests including the DES. There was no further discussion by CATE on this occasion but everyone seemed content that this line of approach should be pursued. In September it was reported that an exploratory meeting with other interested parties had been held as planned and another was to take place in October with the aim of putting up a proposal to the Leverhulme Foundation. This would be for a grant to enable a study to be carried out by a small team led by Professor Paul Hirst of Cambridge, who was about to retire. A decision by the Foundation was expected in February, so that the project, if approved, might begin in the summer of 1989. It so happened that the October meeting occurred on a Group A day and before Tony left us to attend it he showed me a draft brief in manuscript. Although I did not have time to absorb this fully, it was clear that the project as now envisaged had moved some way from the original idea of collecting current good practice. The approach being proposed seemed more developmental — an attempt to establish objectives and an agreed curriculum for ITT. However, this was to come to naught. At the February 1989 Council the Chairman revealed that the application to the Leverhulme Foundation had been unsuccessful. The impression had been given that in the view of the Foundation a review of teacher training might reasonably be seen as a responsibility of government.

Members of CATE found this outcome disappointing but at the April 1989 meeting the Chairman announced that he was now exploring another path. The Jerwood Foundation had recently advertised an annual award and invited the nomination 'of individuals and institutions that have made an original and significant contribution to the theory and practice of education within the United Kingdom'. The Chairman had seen no reason why CATE should not nominate itself for this award, which was worth £150,000, and had made a strong case on its behalf. If this application were successful the idea was that CATE should bring together various relevant educational bodies with the aim of identifying, disseminating, and encouraging best practice in the preparation of the nation's teachers. Again, however, our hopes were frustrated. During May reports appeared in the educational press of the selected short list for the 1989 Jerwood award and it did not include CATE. By the time of the following Council meeting the agenda was dictated by the publication of the DES consultative document on arrangements for accreditation after our term expired. The issues involved for the Council in that paper are recounted in the next chapter. But it was proposed among many other things that part of the role of a reconstituted CATE should be 'to identify and disseminate good practice in initial training'. This aspect of DES thinking attracted no specific comment in our debate other than a general welcome for the wider remit that was envisaged; I was the only member to ask, rhetorically, how our successors might tackle this issue more successfully than we had done.

Chapter 30

Retrospect and Prospect

Circular 3/84 provided that after CATE had reviewed all existing ITT courses the future of the Council itself would be considered. At the first conference for local committees, in December 1986, the Chairman said he hoped that a decision about future arrangements would be made soon and not deferred until 1989 with consequent loss of momentum. He repeated this point at a Council meeting a few days later, saying that consideration of 'life after CATE' should be seen as part of the remoralization of the profession and expressing the expectation that the Council itself would be enabled to make some input into the debate. At its next meeting the Council was told that when the Chairman and Convenors had seen the new Secretary of State they thought Kenneth Baker had taken their point about the need for an early look at what was to happen after CATE.

However, 1987 passed without any more being heard on the matter. In March of the following year, when we were discussing our approach to the forthcoming parliamentary briefing, Peter Scott and I both raised the question what our response should be if we were asked about the situation after our term ended. The Chairman said we ought not to be drawn into that; the decision was for the Secretary of State. In the event the Parliamentarians did not broach this issue but at the Council meeting the following day the Chairman reported that he was going to see the Minister of State, Mrs Angela Rumbold, about arrangements after CATE and that he had been asked to write a report for officers and ministers within the ensuing five months. At this time the legislation for a National Curriculum was before Parliament and it had become evident that a review of the Criteria would be required. We were also becoming conscious of the fact that CATE had no mechanism for keeping an eye on courses after they had received approval from the Secretary of State. At the second conference for local committees, in May 1988, Mrs Rumbold herself stated that before the end of 1989 the Secretary of State would be reviewing the procedures in Circular 3/84 and she invited the committees to offer advice. CI Alan Marshall spoke of improving the mechanisms for course approval and other speakers during the day addressed themselves similarly to what was to happen next. At the final session stress was laid on the importance of contributing to the process of review and to doing so while Government thinking was still at a formative stage.

Although we received continuing indications that future arrangements were under active consideration within the DES more time passed without any further discussion. After the November 1988 Council meeting Gillian Murton arranged for the three Group Convenors to remain behind for a short session with the Chairman and herself. I took the opportunity to ask how the Chairman envisaged providing an opportunity for the Council as a whole to make an input into the debate about future arrangements — would a special meeting be appropriate? Some discussion ensued, and early in December members received a notice that in order to allow time for a full and considered discussion of the questions surrounding 'life after CATE' a special meeting of the full Council had been arranged; it was to take place during the afternoon of 2 February 1989. When Group A met a couple of days after receipt of this notice Gillian explained that a DES consultative document on future arrangements was expected shortly and the Chairman was anxious that we should be clear about our views so that we were ready to respond to the paper. The implication of this way of putting it was that CATE's views would not be expected to play any part in determining what went into the consultative paper in the first place, though our Branch Assessor assured us, when this point was raised, that those responsible for drafting the paper would be there to hear the Council' debate.

At the January Council meeting the DES Assessor gave us some further insight into how the Deparment's collective mind was moving. He believed that ministers wished to continue with an external agency concerned with accreditation. They were also concerned that the prospect of new mechanisms and new criteria should not cast a planning blight over the remaining work of CATE. A consultative paper would be published after Easter allowing quite a short time for responses and the aim would be to have the new mechanisms in place for a smooth take-over from CATE. He thought the new criteria would be clearer — more susceptible of an 'is it or isn't it?' approach, and requiring less probing; new courses would need to cater for them.

The Council's First Debate

As mentioned in chapter 28, the Chairman decided to call a press conference for the same afternoon as the special meeting and the total time for discussion of our main business must have been less than an hour and three quarters. In setting the scene he said it seemed unlikely that the new criteria would be very different from the existing ones except to reflect the requirements of the National Curriculum by giving more emphasis to science and assessment and to incorporate the changes which had been made since Circular 3/84. This extent of agreement would assist our debate, which he then opened up by asking what difference CATE had really caused. Had we made an impact on the system? There were murmurs of 'Yes'. Mary Hallaway spoke up to say that in her view, which other members clearly shared, the requirement for recent and relevant experience was the aspect which had affected every institution. It was reckoned to be a good thing but it created considerable financial difficulties. Releasing staff from an institution to allow them to gain school experience had a cost in terms of the employment of other and perhaps less proficient part-time staff in their place. Bernice Martin suggested that often a difficult political game had to be played within institutions to meet the 'recent and relevant' criterion — its resource implications had to be combined with those of research in a rather uneasy package. Was the resource issue a serious impediment, asked the Chairman. Mary Hallaway and Tony Becher both replied that it was, and Tony said of links with schools generally that they were a good influence but they did cause resource problems. This led Andrew Collier and other members to develop the point about resources in relation to the impending funding changes — the virtual exclusion of LEAs from responsibility for ITT and the introduction of local management of schools.

Peter Griffin and Bill Wright thought that perhaps our interpretation of the 'recent and relevant' criterion had been rather narrow. Should we then propose a more liberal view for the future, the Chairman wondered. Derek Mortimer felt we had to be conscious of how such a message would be picked up in the field; a signal of apparent retreat from the position which had been achieved would be unwise. We were dealing with a backlog in terms of lack of teaching experience which arose from the academic thrust engendered by the introduction of the BEd in the 1960s. It was generally thought that the bottom line would be a continuing requirement for a comprehensive staff development plan. Mary Hallaway summarized what she saw as the problems connected with partnership among schools, institutions and LEAs by saying first that it had costs, and secondly that while it also had benefits they were benefits to the system and not necessarily to the institutions.

Peter Scott then suggested local committees as another question to which we might turn. He thought that a very varied picture of them had emerged, with some being used politically or manipulated by the institution itself. The Chairman agreed that this was an important topic: how could the role of local committees be beefed up? One step would be to ensure that the head of the institution was not the chairman. Andrew Collier had another solution — to scrap the local committees altogether. It was his impression that they had not proved very effective and he thought the essential elements of their role could well be assigned to governing bodies. Tony Becher disagreed, however: he would have preferred to see regional arrangements for local committees to serve several institutions. Would the result of that, the Chairman mused, not be rather like an area training organization? But that was not what Tony had in mind, and Andrew agreed that not regional but multi-institutional committees would have more to recommend them.

By now more than half the available time for discussion had passed and it was becoming evident that the Chairman was not intending to invite comment on the overriding structural issues to which I had myself been giving some thought. I therefore caught his eye at this point in order to say that while agreeing with the view that local committees should either be abandoned or beefed up, I should like to air some ideas about them which would involved broadening the discussion into other areas. As the Chairman nodded consent, I said it seemed to me that whatever good effects CATE had brought about, the exercise had been a highly bureaucratic and time-consuming one for us and for the institutions, and we should consider any means by which the processes could be simplified. Compliance with some of the Criteria could be checked with a fair degree of objectivity — the thirty-six-week PGCE, the amount of school experience, even curricular coverage in primary courses and the involvement of teachers in student selection. These issues were not always straightforward but they had become easier to deal with over the life of CATE, partly because our expertise had grown but partly also because institutions had come more fully to understand what was required. I wondered, therefore, whether a national body was any longer needed to enforce them. Could it not become part of the process of course approval that institutions should certify that these conditions had been met? In these circumstances, if there were to be a national body, as did seem necessary, it could confine itself to the quality issues such as staff development and links with schools generally. But even then, I suggested more tentatively, need the national body get involved in the nitty-gritty of every institution to the extent that we had done? Could that responsibility not be given in the first instance to the local committees, suitably strengthened in membership and terms of reference? The national body would then be free to concern itself with issues of monitoring and interpretation and with modifying the criteria in the light of circumstances.

Renford Bambrough said he agreed with much of what I had said. Until I spoke he had been going to make the point that one could not sensibly think about the role of local committees apart from the overall structures which were to be put in place. Derek Mortimer thought my ideas interesting but wondered whether they were not against the spirit of the times. The Chairman asked Andrew Collier how he thought my model could be reconciled with his idea of giving the role of local committees to governing bodies. Andrew confessed himself rather thrown by my remarks and had no immediate answer to the question. Bernice Martin queried my identification of simpler issues within the Criteria: she thought that they too could slip unless they were carefully monitored. Peter Griffin brought the discussion back to local committees as they had been operating; he thought they had been of service. The Chairman referred to the use of the word 'support' in the Criteria to describe their role in relation to courses; should they be given a more critical function? Renford said it was important to maintain the principle that responsibility for validation and accreditation should not rest in the same place.

The Chairman then suggested moving on to another topic — subject studies. This was honesty time, he encouraged us; what did we really think? Renford thought that among the Criteria it was second only to 'recent and relevant'; it had made a real impact on the system. Bernice agreed, and believed that on this point no quarter should be given; there was still some resistance, though it was less overt than it had been. The only notes of reservation were struck by Bill Wright, who doubted whether all students admitted to ITT were capable of benefitting from two years of subject study at a level appropriate to higher education, and by Andrew Collier, who thought the requirement least defensible in relation to training for the early years. But these were not general views. The Chairman said he had heard reports that the Inspectorate were not wholly behind the subject studies criterion, and asked if this were true. Alan Marshall admitted that there was some anxiety but in general the Inspectorate was strongly behind it.

We had now reached the time when it was necessary to adjourn. The Chairman confessed that there were several points on his draft agenda on which we had not even touched, such as curriculum studies and selection. We should have to get this day's debate written up and have another meeting. The DES Assessor, who had been taking copious notes throughout the afternoon, said he had found that day's debate invaluable. As the meeting was breaking up, Tony Becher remarked to me that what I had said about structures was rather similar to the ideas produced by UCET. These I had not known about, so Tony kindly sent me a copy of the UCET submission. The paper suggested that the best long-term solution would be for consultation on matters relating to accreditation to be with a general teaching council on the lines of the Scottish model, but that in the meantime there was a firm case for continuing CATE, albeit in a modified form. UCET wished to see the new body, which it hoped could be more professionally oriented, maintaining the close relationship with HMI but more distanced from the DES, and it did propose a strengthening of the local committees. Many of them could 'readily and efficiently carry out routine accreditation and re-accreditation work which fell clearly within the approved guidelines', while CATE would deal with less clear-cut cases and 'would monitor the work of committees to which powers had been devolved and would undertake five-yearly formal reviews'. It was interesting that UCET had moved to accepting that there should be a successor body to CATE, almost unthinkable three or four years earlier, and these ideas certainly bore some resemblance to mine. UCET hoped that its plan would result in a 'shift of emphasis from transactions across a table in Elizabeth House to an exchange of views in the place where training takes place'; and in relation to the Criteria in general they wished to see:

> more freedom to experiment, subject, of course, to the final evaluation of the product. CATE, and HMI, should not find themselves agonising over whether a certain practice is or is not in keeping with what the then Secretary of State had in mind when drawing up the criteria. The focus should shift away from construing phrases in historical documents to assessing innovations in current practice.

The Council's Second Debate

The Council's debate was resumed on the afternoon of its ordinary meeting in February 1989. The Chairman hoped that on this occasion we might deal with selection, educational and professional issues and secretarial support. Michael Dixon opened up on selection with what he described as an outsider's view in terms of the education system, though he had been writing about it for many years, by recalling how shocked he and the other 'industrial' members of CATE had at first been by the higgledy-piggledy and ill-defined basis of selection for ITT when compared to the well-tried methods employed in industry. It should be possible to compare the qualities of good and poor teachers so that measures could be established. Peter Scott largely agreed. He thought our experience since we started showed that there were great variations in the approaches adopted by institutions and he would like to see greater uniformity. He also reflected on the anomaly that the teaching profession had its hands on the raw material for its own recruitment yet seemed to do little to attract able sixth-formers into teaching; some teachers actually discouraged them. He imagined how other professions might use this opportunity. David Shadbolt did not seek to excuse poor selection techniques but pointed out that the kind of methods advocated by Michael Dixon were very expensive. Michael countered this by saying there was a greater cost in wastage from training and in the damage that a poor teacher could do. The Chairman agreed that there was a lack of what might be called manifest disaster criteria in teaching, such as the effect of crossed wires. (An aircraft on a domestic flight had recently crashed, allegedly for this reason.) More work on predictive testing had been done in the States, though Bernice Martin thought it would be a mistake to suppose that the Americans had all the answers; human beings were still more sensitive about interpersonal relations than computers. David Winkley thought that all the emphasis should not be on initial selection and final assessment; assessment should be continuous throughout initial training. However, we seemed to be of one mind concerning the desirability of being more specific about what makes a good teacher and more rigorous about recruitment.

The Chairman then moved us on to consider the area of educational and professional studies. A criticism now sometimes made was that the education element had become so attenuated that there was too little theory; had we got it right? David Winkley argued that if theory were to be useful it needed to be related to practice, and perhaps teachers got more out of it after they had acquired some teaching experience. David Shadbolt was rather dismissive of the kind of theory to be found in most courses; students merely dabbled in it. In response to a question from the Chairman about what Groups discovered on the ground I observed that here was a curious gap: HMI surveys revealed that almost all ITT courses contained some mix of the same elements — subject studies, curriculum studies and subject method, education studies, professional studies and school experience — and the Criteria had much to say about all of these except education studies. About what these should include, and in what quantity, or how they should be related to practice they were almost completely silent; consequently we had no cause to investigate this aspect of the courses which came before us. The Chairman agreed that it was residual. Michael Pipes said he thought much of the criticism we heard of the subject studies criterion was not about the amount of subject studies as such but of what they squeezed out, and this included education. Renford Bambrough took a somewhat different view, and considered that there were principles involved in professional issues which his Group frequently discussed. I felt myself that this part of our discussion lacked clarity because there was confusion among speakers between educational studies in the sense of theoretical disciplines such as psychology, philosophy and sociology, professional issues such as special educational needs and multicultural education, and the methodology of subject studies. This seemed to be confirmed when Mary Hallaway made the point in this context that when the Council had referred in Catenote 3 to 25 per cent of subject studies in primary courses being for methodology this had been intended to establish a maximum; now there was a tendency to feel that there was something wrong if there were less than 25 per cent. The Chairman observed that the debate on subject studies had been going on for at least 100 years and he did not suppose we should solve it that day.

This was a cue to move us on to his third topic for the day. CATE had been given minimal administrative support and only the professional support provided by HMI. Was this enough? What should we be recommending for a successor body? I remarked that this question seemed to call for the same kind of response as Renford Bambrough and I had given at the previous meeting in relation to local committees: we needed to know what the new body would be called upon to do before we could judge what support structure it would require. Nevertheless, Bernice thought we had a responsibility to point out that the Government had got CATE on the cheap. The Chairman said he had done a few sums based on the not unreasonable assumption that if members' time was charged out by our various employers it would be at a rate of about £400 a day. On this basis each Council meeting would cost about £8000 and the work of CATE as a whole about £20,000 a month or £250,000 a year in members' time alone, all of which was in fact given free. Bernice also thought that as the field was constantly changing, with courses being revised and revalidated, any new Council should have staff resources adequate to maintain links with other relevant bodies, and David Shadbolt considered that essentially there was need for a professional input and a policy input. Gillian Murton felt that in any new structures there should be some provision for evaluation; otherwise there was an enormous waste. Michael Pipes shared this view and believed there should be some way in which the knowledge and experience which CATE had accumulated could be retained. But here time again caught up with us and the Chairman brought the discussion to a close, saying that there was now enough material for a draft CATE paper to be produced.

Accompanying the minutes of this February 1989 Council meeting was a postscript saying that notes of the two discussions on 'the CATE experience' were being amalgamated and would be circulated in due course as an aide-memoire to the Council in formulating a response to the awaited consultative paper on revised criteria and machinery for accreditation.

The Consultation Document

This document *Future Arrangements For the Accreditation of Courses of Initial Teacher Training*, was published on 3 May 1989. In summary it made three proposals to take effect from 1 January 1990. The first was to replace the existing criteria for ITT courses by what were described as 'more detailed and clearer criteria' supplemented by a commentary on the lines of a Catenote; the second was to reconstitute CATE 'with a wider remit, fewer members, and a strengthened secretariat'; and the third was to give clear terms of reference and formal constitutions to the local committees, each of which should cover between five and ten institutions in England, with one committee each for Wales and Northern Ireland. The local committees, working within CATE guidelines on principle or precedent, would give detailed consideration to new or amended courses and monitor existing ones, reporting annually to CATE on their activities; CATE itself, leaving detailed scrutiny to the local committees, would supervise their work and have a monitoring and developmental role. (A point of some interest was the source of the stress laid on the role of the local committees: was it Branch or the politicians? One head of a UDE whom I knew formed the impression that the DES saw themselves as covert champions of enlightenment holding back ideological centralization by inserting a degree of local control; about HMI he was not sure, since they perhaps saw the local committees as encroaching on their own powers.)

With regard to the Criteria, the aim was to bring them up to date, particularly with regard to the National Curriculum, and to put more stress on the expected outcomes of courses, with, where applicable, a checklist of competences. Much of the substance of the Criteria was unchanged. One addition was to include the requirement that all primary phase courses should contain 100 hours devoted to science and design and technology as well as to English and mathematics and to specify that in each of the three sets of 100 hours there should be a minimum of 60 hours' contact time. Another change was to quantify the 'recent and relevant' requirement so that teacher trainers should undertake school teaching experience equivalent to one term in every five years. The structure of students' school experience was to be more tightly controlled, with a requirement for a 'sustained period of teaching practice' in the final year and for a written policy statement about the roles of all concerned. The subject studies criteria were virtually unchanged, though it was now required that courses for intending secondary teachers should include at least a third of a year on the application of students' subject specialisms. The accompanying commentary suggested that since in smaller primary schools teachers might need to act as curriculum leaders in several subjects the most useful form of training would be one that enabled intending primary teachers to specialize in more than a single subject; but since the subject study programme ought not to be too broad it should not normally comprise more than two subjects in the National Curriculum, or if three were studied they should be related. Outcome criteria for subject studies and for curriculum studies in primary courses included ability to assess, and in the case of the latter to 'teach to the level required by the National Curriculum', and institutions would be expected to inform their students' first employers which subjects had been studied only in short introductory units. The criteria relating to educational and professional studies were rewritten in fairly specific outcome terms — for example, 'on completion of their course students should have developed the capacity to identify gifted pupils and pupils with special educational needs'.

With the agenda for the June Council meeting came a paper from Gillian Murton on issues raised by the Consultation Document, and when we reached *Future Arrangements* at the meeting the Chairman indicated that he proposed to structure our debate by reference to this issues paper. Gillian had suggested in it that the Criteria themselves, while clarified, emphasized and extended, were substantially unchanged. 'The part of the Consultation Document most likely to arouse debate among all interested parties is that concerned with the machinery of accreditation and, in particular, the redefinition of the nature and role of local committees to bring them more formally into the accreditation process.' She went on to identify those aspects of the document which we might wish to welcome and to draw attention to those changes which had been made to the Criteria, especially the development of the 'output' approach, and to the proposed remit, membership and operation of CATE and the local committees. There was an appendix by Stephen Dance outlining points arising from the two Council discussions in February, but this was very much a summary. Introducing our discussion, the Chairman said that since the Council would not be meeting again before the end of June — the date by which comments on the Consultation Document were to be submitted — our response would need to arise from what was said that day. He also remarked that there had been at least ten previous versions of this document, and the DES Assessor, when appealed to for confirmation, said he thought more like twenty. It had been very carefully worked over. Nevertheless it was on specific points that several members wished to comment, and Gillian's issues paper, while clearly useful, was largely bypassed in the debate.

Mary Hallaway pointed out that the proposed new wording of the criterion on subject studies made the half-year equivalent of subject application for primary teachers a minimum, whereas, as she had previously reminded us, CATE had introduced the notion of a half-year's application as a maximum since some previous BEd courses had been almost wholly application. The DES Assessor agreed that this was a shift in emphasis in that the new wording would allow for more than half a year. Mary then wondered why, if application was seen as so important, the draft criterion did not specify a minimum time for applications in a primary PGCE, and I added that the contrast was highlighted by an explicit statement in the document that no minimum time was specified for applications work in postgraduate primary courses. The DES response was to plead (a little lamely, I felt) the difficulty of specifying a precise requirement in so full a year and the need to say that there was no requirement in order to avoid everybody asking.

There was a general welcome for the emphasis on outcomes and for the proposal that science and design and technology should have 100 hours in primary course, though Peter Scott felt that this amount of time should be devoted to science on its own, and Andrew Collier would have omitted 'design'. Andrew, who made a number of detailed comments, would have liked to see all lower primary courses covering age 4, and Marian Giles Jones regretted the absence of a European dimension. We spent some time on resource implications, especially those arising for institutions from the harder line on staff development and for schools in relation to teacher participation in selection and supervision of students. We were somewhat concerned by the suggestion that primary students should normally study no more than two subjects.

The debate up to this point had taken so long that the Chairman now sought agreement for an extension of the meeting in order to allow for some discussion of the machinery proposed in the consultative document. David Shadbolt had to leave, but before doing so expressed his disagreement with the suggestion in the document that the proposed new structure of local committees would require smaller financial contributions from institutions. On the more general question of their proposed new role, the Chairman commented that it was a big job; would they do it? It was clear that most members present had considerable misgivings about this. We in our work for CATE had been motivated by our national brief and the fact that we were directly responsible to the Secretary of State for enforcing the Criteria in a consistent manner; what inducement would there be for a local committee to apply the same kind of rigour to one of its 'own' institutions? Andrew Collier and Derek Mortimer made it clear that they would sooner move in the opposite direction and do away with local committees altogether. In view of what I had said on this subject in February I felt that I must make some comment at this point. I reiterated my view that to have a national body continuing as we had done to involve itself in the detail of every ITT course in the country would be a highly centralized and bureaucratic way of proceeding. But I thought there were difficulties in the model in the document. What would be the possible outcomes of local committee review of courses? To those with which we had worked would be added a fifth: 'refer to CATE'. This would be a very difficult system to monitor or operate consistently. What I had had in mind was the delegation to local committees of certain relatively unproblematic aspects of the Criteria. But I still thought that in principle the notion of involving local committees in the accreditation process had quite a lot to recommend it. The Chairman surprised me when I had concluded by saying that we all brought our own perspective to these matters and perhaps what I had said was more understandable in Northern Ireland than it would be in England. I said I didn't think I was saying it from that point of view. He said he was sure I wasn't, but perhaps unconsciously...At any rate he asked whether there was any other support for what was proposed in the document. This was greeted with total silence. The Chairman turned to the DES Assessor and said he supposed the proposals had really taken the form they had on grounds of cost; he agreed that this was so.

And that effectively brought the debate to an end. The Chairman indicated that if we had any points of detail which had not been covered we should send these to the Secretary in writing.

The Council's Response

Accepting the Chairman's invitation, I wrote to express concern that if the CATE submission merely said that the great majority of members saw little merit in the proposed new machinery and would sooner move in the direction of doing away with local committees altogether, but the DES nevertheless went ahead as planned, then absence of comment from us on the nuts and bolts of the machinery might lead to its producing more squeaks and grinding noises than were necessary. I analyzed the consultative document to show that the way the proposed model would work was unclear, and suggested that this was due not just to a lack of detail but to a fundamental flaw; it was a recipe not for delegation and streamlining but for confusion and additional bureaucratic procedures. I spelt out my view that the only sensible way to bring local committees into the formal accreditation process was to decentralize responsibility for approving some but not all the new criteria, and I suggested which these might be and how this model would work in practice. When Group A met three weeks after the Council debate Gillian told me that three members including myself had sent in written comments and another had made some by telephone. She was going to take them all away and work on them but she made it clear that the Chairman would be much involved in what went into the CATE response. Tony Becher and Bill Wright, who had not been present at the June 1989 Council, were both surprised by my account of what had happened and indicated that if they had been there mine would not have been a lone voice in expressing some degree of support for the DES thinking. The Chairman himself made a brief appearance at lunch-time and when Tony commented on the outcome of the Council discussion he said I would have noticed that he had reserved his own position.

With the agenda for the July 1989 Council meeting came the CATE response to the Consultation Document which Gillian and the Chairman had written. A covering note referred to the Council debate and to subsequent contributions from various members and expressed the hope 'that the resulting response strikes the right constructive balance'. The paper had already been sent to the DES but could still be amended if Council wished. It followed the earlier version in expressing a general welcome for many aspects of the document, including the move towards output criteria, but adding that the Council would not wish to see the existing 'input' criteria dismantled too soon. It suggested that greater emphasis should be given to two aspects — the promotion of positive partnership and the application of the Criteria in alternative routes into teaching. Attention was firmly drawn to the resource implications. Tactful doubt was cast on the assumption in the document that 'following CATE's initial review of all ITT courses, the necessary adherence to the Criteria can be secured by a somewhat less intensive process of local monitoring and central sampling'. It was suggested rather that the period of rapid change marked by the introduction of various new types of course 'requires the firm and unambiguous application of clear central guidelines if standards are to be maintained and quality assured'.

The remainder of the paper dealt with the reconstitution of CATE and of local committees — the aspect which, as the Chairman said in introducing the paper at the meeting, was clearly the most controversial within the existing Council. It was suggested that the new Council would need no fewer than fifteen members and that the secretariat would have to be strengthened adequately to deal with work coming forward from local committees as well as that generated by the Council itself; the respective roles of the Council and local committees would need to be clearly defined. The idea that the new local committees should each be associated with up to ten institutions was 'not without difficulty': it could result in a 'bureaucratic sub-structure' leading to delay, expense and distraction. There was also the difficulty of moving to the new system from the existing one of seventy-five local committees for ninety-three institutions 'on 1 January 1990'. In the light of our experience and of impending developments it seemed essential for the reconstituted Council to be involved initially in new course scrutiny. One model would be for local committees to have no more formal involvement than at present and for institutions to certify compliance with basic criteria, notify major changes and provide material for monitoring. An alternative model would be for a sharing of responsibility between a reconstituted Council and reconstituted local committees on a negotiated basis: initially the Council itself would scrutinize some, if not all, new or substantially amended course proposals but gradually the local committees would undertake responsibility for the quantitative criteria and those which involved specific links with schools. The paper implied that the latter, being both practicable and flexible, was the preferred model, one which would facilitate the monitoring role of the Council. Some more detailed points about the Criteria and the commentary, mainly reflecting members' contributions to the Council debate, were made in an appendix.

Introducing the paper, the Chairman was clearly anxious to defend it as the nearest approach to a consensual response we were likely to achieve. He drew attention to the paragraph which argued that there was still much to be done in establishing the Criteria and thereby maintaining public confidence in the quality of teacher preparation through all the new routes now being developed. We had to be conscious of the political realities in suggesting changes from the proposals in the Consultation Document and he felt that the notion of a negotiated relationship between the new CATE and the local committees might be the best answer in view of differing views within the Council. When he invited comments no one at first seemed eager to speak. Michael Pipes had not been present at the previous meeting and had therefore read the paper from cold; he said it struck him as discreet to the point of being slightly tentative. However, most of the comment was broadly in support. I remarked that while I accepted that the paper drew together members' views about local committees as well as could be done it could say rather more clearly that nobody liked the model in the Consultation Document; even those, of whom I was one, who saw some merit in an enhanced role for local committees, considered that version to be a recipe for bureaucracy and confusion. Tony Becher said that if the new Council were to perform its developmental role it would need time to think — it would need to delegate — and he thought the model in the paper to be a good one.

In September 1989 we were sent a copy of the final text of the response to the Consultation Document which had been submitted to the DES on our behalf. It differed little from the July draft. A sentence had been added calling on the Department to provide mechanisms for ensuring that the release of teachers for involvement in initial training was accepted as a proper call on school budgets. In relation to structures another new sentence read: 'Council does not believe that the model proposed in the Consultation Document is appropriate'; the paper then went on to outline the alternatives as before. An added advantage of the negotiated model was now said to be that it would enable the Council to undertake its broader developmental role in initial teacher training. The paper was not further discussed but at the September Council the Chairman surmised that the recent arrival in the DES not only of a new Secretary of State (John MacGregor having replaced Kenneth Baker in a July reshuffle) but of a new Permanent Secretary had caused some delay in decisions about the new Council. At our October meeting the DES Assessor explained that the continuing delay was largely due to the resource implications of the new criteria and the need for these to be taken into account in the current PESC round. He seemed to suggest that this hurdle had now been overcome. With regard to the new criteria he expected that we would find some small changes from the draft version in the Consultation Document; he instanced the time specified for science and technology and the place of RE. He also indicated that, in recognition of the amount of travel which in some parts of the country would be entailed by larger groupings, the minimum size of cluster of institutions which could be looked after by a single local committee would be reduced to three.

The New Circular

Circular 24/89 (*Initial Teacher Training: Approval of Courses*) eventually bore the date 10 November 1989. It did not contain many substantive changes from the draft version of the Criteria in the Consultation Document. The most significant, as the Department's Assessor had foreshadowed, occurred in the section on curriculum studies in primary courses: it was science on its own which now joined English and mathematics as requiring 100 hours to be devoted to its teaching; design and technology were relegated to a place among the other subjects of the curriculum for which students should be prepared. The change affecting RE, which the DES Assessor had also mentioned, was merely to reflect its inclusion in the National Curriculum. A new stipulation that in primary undergraduate courses the subject studies should be in not more than three subjects was in a sense a concession to our view that the guidance given in the Consultative Document had been too narrow; nevertheless, it was still more restrictive than the 1984 permissive reference to 'a wide area of the curriculum'. The section on educational and professional studies included an elaborated reference to cross-curricular dimensions, themes (which now included Marian's European dimension) and skills; and another addition was the insertion in the list of skills which students should have developed by the end of their course of the ability to set appropriate objectives for their teaching and their pupils' learning. One or two small changes had been made to the Commentary in response to suggestions from CATE — for example, the reference to 'short introductory units' in foundation course subjects in which an intending primary teacher was not specializing had been omitted — but the paragraph commending the delay of selection of subject studies until the second year of primary courses had been retained in spite of our view that it was unhelpful. Nor had Andrew's point about the primary age-phase been accepted.

So far as structures were concerned, the terms of reference given to both the new Council and the local committees were virtually unchanged from those set out in the Consultation Document, though the minimum number of institutions to be associated with a local committee had indeed been reduced to three. The main concession made to CATE's observations was that the new Council would 'negotiate a gradual transfer of responsibility to local committees for certain aspects of the criteria', but these were not specified, nor was it made clear how complete the delegation might be. It was only from the DES press release that another aspect of the new dispensation became clear: Professor William Taylor, Vice-Chancellor of the University of Hull, had been reappointed as Chairman of CATE until June 1993.

The existing Council's penultimate meeting in November 1989 provided the last opportunity for us to comment on the new arrangements. Our Branch Assessor told us that there were fifty changes from the Consultation Document, though he again mentioned the references to science and RE as the major ones. The Chairman referred to a statement in the DES release that CATE's new membership would be announced later; the Assessor agreed that it would be fourteen or fifteen. The Chairman asked if we had any further comments on the Circular, but did so in such a way as to leave no real opportunity for anyone to say anything. In the afternoon a representative of the National Curriculum Council appeared, expecting a debate on the new Circular, and so we had to revert to the subject. Discussion, however, was somewhat desultory. Members were probably suffering from some degree of fatigue on the subject of 'life after CATE', if indeed it was still appropriate to use that phrase; and in any case it was clear that for good or ill the decisions had now been made. There had recently been a UCET conference at which, we were told, Professor Ted Wragg had referred to the new criteria as the most prescriptive document since the Koran. Alan Marshall had asked him whether he did not see any scope for discretion in them; the reply had been that it was like being asked whether you would prefer two whip lashes or three.

Chapter 31

The Impact and the Future

On the day of CATE's last meeting, in December 1989, it fell to my lot to make a presentation to the Chairman. I observed that CATE had at least this in common with the French Revolution, that it was still rather early to know what its lasting effects would be. The point was more soberly put in November 1990 by Education Minister Tim Eggar when he said: 'It is important to recognise that the vast bulk of the teachers now teaching trained in the 1970s and early 1980s. We are living with the product of the past... The changes that have been made to teacher training by this government will take time to work through', (DES, 1990b). The passage of a few months to the time at which I write has obviously not changed the situation, and in any case the only people who could offer any informed assessment would be HMI and teacher trainers themselves — later, no doubt, the schools. In the meantime one can only note such straws as may be in the wind. Some published accounts of being Cated are now beginning to appear. Professor Norman Graves of the University of London Institute of Education found his experience of HMI inspection to be a pleasant one, albeit an invitation under duress, and he compares the Inspectors' report with one from a management consultant; but having had to supply CATE with all the details we required, 'I am left wondering whether the effort was worthwhile, except in the purely formal sense of acquiring the stamp of approval'. He sees CATE review as 'essentially a bureaucratic process' (Graves, 1988). Professor Ted Wragg of Exeter, claiming that CATE 'nowadays requires an 18-page form to be filled in for every new course', adds: 'It is enough to inhibit creativity for life' (Wragg, 1990).

In CATE's early days the Chairman was wont to contrast what we should be about with an MoT test for used cars. Accreditation was not the application of a checklist: the Criteria were handles for review. It may be, however, that the experience was perceived rather differently at the receiving end. There was no escape from the reality of CATE's having to satisfy itself that the specified conditions were being met. In doing this, as

I pointed out in Chapter 10, we were largely dependent on what was written down. Nor were we well placed to distinguish between what was formally included in a course and what was done well or even covered adequately. I have asserted my belief that members of CATE did not approach their task from any overtly ideological standpoint but neither did we discuss philosophical issues such as the relationship between educational theory and the practice of teaching. A committee cannot be blamed for behaving like a committee; CATE tried hard to be a sensitive and flexible one within its terms of reference.

In a paper prepared by the secretariat for the press conference in February 1989 it was pointed out that the proportion of favourable recommendations made to the Secretary of State had increased. In 1985 the Council had been turning back about half the courses submitted for review; in 1986 the proportion fell to about a third, and in 1987/88 only about one in six was deferred or rejected. This is evidence at least of courses being modified in ways that more readily satisfied the Criteria. While we were at work we heard both of institutions which considered such changes to be improvements and of ones which thought the reverse. HMI, however, seem prepared to be initially positive. I have referred in chapter 28 to their perception, reflected in the Annual Report for 1987/88, of 'a considerable change for the better' in ITT; the corresponding document for 1988/89 found that:

> The general picture is encouraging. Institutions continue to respond constructively to the requirements of the Secretary of State's criteria for teacher education, and the work of CATE. In particular, institutions are improving staff development, most importantly by including opportunities for lecturers to work in schools...there are indications that initial teacher training is beginning to tackle the need — perennially reiterated in HMI reports — to take far greater account of individual differences in the classroom and to differentiate the work accordingly. (DES, 1990)

On the other hand the challenges of the National Curriculum and recent national reports were creating problems; treatment of cross-curricular issues was often superficial; the 'positive and important trend towards more school-based courses' was coming under financial strain.

The Consultation Document of May 1989 noted a 'substantial' improvement in the overall quality of ITT since 1984, and the subsequent issue of Circular 24/89, announcing new arrangements for accreditation on broadly the same lines, confirmed the commitment of the Government to the process. The Circular pointed out that the revised criteria were 'directed more towards outputs: towards statements of what students should be able to show they know, understand and can do by the end of their training'. This approach had been presaged in November 1988 when CATE received the latest version of the HMI survey, *The New Teacher in School*. Our attention had been specifically drawn to the statement that 'More attention needs to be given to defining the levels of competence in different professional skills which may reasonably be expected of teachers at the conclusion of their training' (DES, 1988c). The survey (of teachers who had completed training in 1986) found shortcomings in the support given to newly qualified teachers during their induction year — which all members of CATE believed to be critically important — and the two issues were seen as being linked: induction could be organized more effectively if the outcomes of ITT were clarified. This shift of attention to outcomes was welcomed at the widely representative conference on the future of teacher education at the University of Lancaster in December 1988, and in the Inspectorate's report for 1988/89 the point was also related to ensuring that the new routes of entry to the profession did not jeopardize 'the new, hard-fought improvements in quality' (DES, 1990).

The Chairman more than once pointed out to CATE that there was now a substantial body of research literature, much of it American, on teacher training and teacher effectiveness, and he expressed regret that this was not more widely known. At a meeting of Group Convenors in September 1989 he referred to a large project being undertaken in the States on output measures and we were told that HMI had produced a document on competences in the context of licensed teachers, though this was still internal. In October Tony Becher outlined a proposal from the University of Sussex for a profiling system linked to QTS assessment. It seemed clear that the 1990s would see a developing trend away from sole reliance on input measures, which is what the criteria given to CATE in 1984 essentially were, and towards the skills and standards to be expected at the end of the training process. There must be a lot of sense in such an approach, though if I were expressing my own views I should be tempted to add a quotation.

> The language we use to report, to describe and to explain, not only reflects the times we live in — input, throughput and output instead of growth and development, mechanistic, cybernetic and technological metaphors rather than those of agriculture, botany or biology — but also influences what we regard as educational reality.

The words are from the Sir John Adams Memorial Lecture delivered in May 1983 by Dr William Taylor, then Director of the University of London Institute of Education. Had he been speaking a few years later he might have added management and the business school to the sources of contemporary imagery. The warning is no less apposite.

From time to time during the life of CATE reference was made to the aspiration for a general teaching council. The functions of such a body might in theory encompass both the determination of the qualifications for entry to the profession and criteria for courses of initial training, though Bill Taylor claimed that there was no country where control of QTS or its equivalent was not retained by government. No farther away than Scotland, however, a situation has been achieved in which the Secretary of State is called in to the process of accrediting courses of pre-service training only when the governing body of a college of education refuses to accept any recommendations from the General Teaching Council (made after visit and report) for change in the general content or arrangement of its courses. The General Teaching Council for Scotland is responsible for ensuring that pre-service courses offered by the country's training institutions are professionally appropriate and relevant; in effect the colleges are accountable through the Council to the teaching profession, and the principle of professional partnership and collaboration is highly valued. In the United States of America there is a National Council for Accreditation of Teacher Education (NCATE) which describes itself as providing —

> a mechanism for voluntary peer regulation of the professional education unit [in UK terms an institution or department providing ITT] that is designed to establish and uphold standards of excellence, to strengthen the quality and integrity of professional education units, and to ensure that requirements for accreditation are related to best professional practice. It is a process by which the profession of education declares its expectations for professional education and applies these expectations to units. (NCATE, 1990)

A mechanism for the accreditation of teacher education in England, Wales and Northern Ireland has been in place since 1984 and with some changes that mechanism was reinstated in 1989 for the nineties. Whether it will continue throughout that decade, whether its mode of operation will become harder and more centralized or move towards the more professionally-based Scottish and American models must be a matter for speculation. The answers will depend in part on changes in the general political climate, in part on the effects of the exercise on education in the schools as these gradually become manifest. In part too they will depend on the practical efficiency of the structures provided — on the whole against the advice of its predecessor — for the reconstituted CATE.

Chapter 32

Epilogue (Daughter of CATE)

The reconstituted Council met for the first time on 16 February 1990. In addition to the Chairman, now Sir William Taylor, it had sixteen founder members (only two fewer than CATE 1) and of these there were four from the original Council — Renford Bambrough, Derek Mortimer, Michael Pipes and David Shadbolt. Gillian Murton continued as Secretary. At least for its first few months in office CATE 2 enjoyed a notably lower public profile than its predecessor, with little news of its doings appearing in the press. The indications were that it made a business-like start to its work. It recognized that this must involve close liaison with the new local committees. Their grouping, terms of reference and membership were given initial approval. A representative of CATE attended an early meeting of each and an induction seminar for local committee chairs and secretaries was held at the Royal Festival Hall in May 1990.

It was intimated to the Council that after consultation the Secretary of State would ask it to consider some specific issues in ITT. In the meantime, in order to tackle its essential work, the Council established two sub-committees — a Monitoring Group and a Good Practice Group. Its responsibilities for monitoring related in part to its specific inheritance from CATE 1, in part to the need to ensure that courses approved under Circular 3/84 conformed with the new criteria and in part to the general maintenance of standards after courses had been accredited. The last aspect had an obvious bearing on the developmental role given to CATE 2, and the Good Practice Group was asked to consider how this part of the Council's remit might be discharged and to suggest topics and themes for early attention. CATE 2 was also given the duty of keeping the Criteria themselves under review and began to consider this in the light of its growing experience.

Appendix 1

Membership of CATE (1984–1989)

Chairman: Professor W. (Bill) Taylor

Group A

Mr T.P. (Peter) Snape (Convenor until June 1985; resigned December 1985)

Dr D.R. (David) Shadbolt (Convenor from July 1885 for remainder of first period)

Mr W.H. (Bill) Wright (transferred from Group C September 1986; Convenor for second period)

Mr D.G. (Gordon) Macintyre (joined Council July 1985; Convenor for third period)

Professor R.A. (Tony) Becher

Councillor F.J. (Frank) Cogan (resigned May 1986)

Mr M. (Michael) Dixon

Mr P. (Peter) Ward (resigned January 1988)

Miss A.L. (Lesley) Abbott (joined Council September 1988)

Mrs A.G. (Anne) Cattoor (joined Council September 1988)

Group B

Mr A.J. (Andrew) Collier (Convenor for first period)

Mr D.J. (Derek) Mortimer (Convenor for second period)

Dr B. (Bernice) Martin (Convenor for third period)

Mr A. (Angus) Clark

Mr P. (Peter) Griffin

Mr P.J. (Peter) Scott

Dr D.R. (David) Winkley (joined Council October 1986)

Mrs A. (Ann) Rees (joined Council November 1988)

Group C

Dr H.M. (Mary) Hallaway (Convenor for first period; resigned September 1989)
Mr J.R. (Renford) Bambrough (Convenor for second period)
Dr M. (Marian) Giles Jones (Convenor for third period)
Dr D.H. (David) Hargreaves (resigned September 1985)
Councillor P.J. (Pat) Mullany
Mr W.H. (Bill) Wright (until transfer to Group A September 1986)
Mr M. (Michael) Pipes (joined Council October 1986)
Mr A.J. (Alistair) Lawton (joined Council January 1987)
Mr J. (Julian) Greatrex (joined Council February 1989)

Appendix 2

Events Contemporary with CATE

	Chronology of CATE	External events
March 1983		White Paper *Teaching Quality*
June 1983		General Election, Conservatives returned; Sir Keith Joseph Secretary of State for Education and Science
April 1984	Publication of Circular 3/84	
August 1984	Membership of CATE announced	
September 1984	First meeting of CATE	
January 1985	Publication of Catenote 1 (Accreditation) Publication of Catenote 2 (Local committees)	
March 1985		Publication of the Swann Report
May 1985	Announcement that Northern Ireland to be associated with CATE	
August 1985	Publication of Catenote 3 (Subject studies)	
January 1986	Publication of Catenote 4 (Links with schools)	
February 1986	Verbal evidence by CATE to Select Committee	

	Chronology of CATE	**External events**
May 1986		Five ITT institutions asked to enter into academic association with universities Kenneth Baker succeeds Sir Keith Joseph as Secretary of State
September 1986	First general change of Reporting Group Convenors	NAB invites proposals for special courses in shortage subjects Report of Select Committee on primary schools
December 1986	First conference for local committees	
April 1987		White Paper on higher education
June 1987		General Election, Conservatives returned; Kenneth Baker reappointed Secretary of State
July 1987		Consultative document on national curriculum
October 1987	Visit from Minister of State	
November 1987	Withdrawal of 25 per cent criterion for exceptional entry	Publication of Education Reform Bill (England and Wales)
March 1988		Publication of proposals for educational reform in Northern Ireland
April 1988	Parliamentary briefing	Publication of Kingman Report
May 1988	Second conference for local committees	Publication of HMI report on UDEs Publication of DES proposals for QTS including licensed teacher scheme

	Chronology of CATE	**External events**
June 1988	Publication of Catenote 5 (Student selection) Retirement of E Grogan; Mrs Murton becomes Secretary	
July 1988		Education Reform Bill becomes law
September 1988	Second general change of Reporting Group Convenors	
October 1988		Publication of Government's decisions for educational reform in Northern Ireland Publication of *The New Teacher in School*
January 1989		Report of Select Committee on Under Fives
February 1989	Special meeting on future arrangements Press conference	Publication of HMI report on New Jersey program
March 1989		Orders for maths and science in National Curriculum laid before Parliament
May 1989		Publication of the Elton Report
June 1989		Publication of consultative paper on future arrangements for accreditation Publication of Draft Order in Council: 'Education Reform (NI) Order'
July 1989		Invitation from DES for articled teacher schemes
November 1989		John MacGregor succeeds Kenneth Baker as Secretary of State

Chronology of CATE	**External events**
November 1989	Publication of Circular 24/89
December 1989 Reception by Secretary of State Final meeting	

Institutions Reviewed by CATE

The letter preceding the name of each institution listed below indicates the Reporting Group of CATE which was primarily responsible for reviewing its ITT courses. The page numbers which follow serve as an index for specific references to that institution.

References

BAMBROUGH, R. (1990) Editorial: '1984 and all that', *Philosophy*, January.

BAYLISS, S. (1988) 'Tutors lack "relevant" experience', *TES*, 4 November.

BOLTON, E. (1985) *Education Policy: The Role of HMI* (transcript of talk given to NATFHE conference), 10 January.

CATE (1985a) *The Council's Approach to Accreditation* (Catenote No. 1), London, CATE.

CATE (1985b) *Local Committees* (Catenote No. 2), London, CATE.

CATE (1985c) *Subject Studies* (Catenote No. 3), London, CATE.

CATE (1986) *Links between Teacher Training Institutions and Schools* (Catenote No. 4), London, CATE.

CATE (1988) *Selection of Students for Admission to Initial Teacher Training Courses* (Catenote No. 5), London, CATE.

CENTRAL ADVISORY COUNCIL FOR EDUCATION (1967) *Children and their Primary Schools* (the Plowden Report), London, HMSO.

COMMITTEE OF ENQUIRY INTO DISCIPLINE IN SCHOOLS (1980) *Discipline in Schools* (the Elton Report), London, HMSO.

COMMITTEE OF ENQUIRY INTO THE EDUCATION OF CHILDREN FROM ETHNIC MINORITY GROUPS (1985) *Education for All* (the Swann Report) (Cmnd 9453), London, HMSO.

COMMITTEE OF INQUIRY INTO THE ARRANGEMENTS FOR THE EDUCATION, TRAINING AND PROBATION OF TEACHERS (1972) *Teacher Education and Training* (the James Report), London, HMSO.

COMMITTEE OF INQUIRY INTO THE TEACHING OF ENGLISH LANGUAGE (1988) *Report* (the Kingman Report), London, HMSO.

DENI (1985) *Teacher Education: Approval of Courses of Initial Training*, (Circular 1985/20), Bangor, DENI.

DES (1973) *Development of Higher Education in the non-University sector*, (Circular No. 7/73), London, DES.

DES (1975) *The Reorganization of Higher Education in the non-University sector: The Further Education Regulations 1975*, (Circular No. 5/75), London, DES.

DES (1977) *Education in Schools* (Consultative Document), London, HMSO.

DES (1978) *Primary Education in England* (HMI Survey), London, HMSO.

DES (1979) *Aspects of Secondary Education in England* (HMI Survey), London, HMSO.

References

DES (1981) *Teacher Training and the Secondary School* (HMI Discussion Paper), London, HMSO.

DES (1982) *The New Teacher in School* (HMI Report), London, HMSO.

DES (1983) *Teaching in Schools: The Content of Initial Teacher Training* (HMI Discussion Paper), London, HMSO.

DES (1984a) *Initial Teacher Training: Approval of Courses* (Cmnd 8836), (Circular No. 3/84), London, DES.

DES (1984b) *Training in a Second Subject for Intending Secondary Teachers*, (Teacher Training Circular Letter 7/84), London, DES.

DES (1985) *Increasing the Supply of Ethnic Minority Teachers* (Consultation Paper), London, DES.

DES (1986) *Quality of Education Vital Says Sir Keith* (News), 3 April.

DES (1987a) *Quality in Schools: The Initial Training of Teachers* (HMI Survey), London, DES.

DES (1987b) *The National Curriculum 5–16* (Consultation Document), London, DES.

DES (1988a) *Education Observed 7: Initial Teacher Training in Universities in England, Northern Ireland and Wales* (HMI Review), London.

DES (1988b) *Qualified Teacher Status* (Consultation Document), London, DES.

DES (1988c) *The New Teacher in School* (HMI Survey), London, HMSO.

DES (1989a) *The Provisional Teacher Program in New Jersey* (HMI Paper), London, HMSO.

DES (1989b) *Standards in Education 1887–88* (HMI Annual Report), London.

DES (1989c) *Future Arrangements for the Accreditation of Courses of Initial Teacher Training* (Consultation Document), London, DES.

DES (1989d) *Design and Technology for Ages 5 to 16*, London, HMSO.

DES (1989e) *Initial Teacher Training: Approval of Courses* (Circular No. 24/89), London, DES.

DES (1990a) *Standards in Education 1988–89* (HMI Annual Report), London, DES.

DES (1990b) '*Teacher training a priority area*' — *Tim Eggar* (News), 29 November.

DONOUGHUE, B. (1987) *Prime Minister: The Conduct of Policy under Harold Wilson and James Callaghan*, London, Jonathan Cape.

EDUCATION (1986) CATE: 'Criteria come under attack at SHRE Conference', 30 May.

EDWARDS, A.D. (1990) 'Schools of education — Their work and their future' in THOMAS, J.B. (Ed.) *British Universities and Teacher Education: A Century of Change*, London, Falmer Press.

EQUAL OPPORTUNITIES COMMISSION (1989) *Formal Investigation Report: Initial Teacher Training in England and Wales*, London, EOC.

FORD, R. (1987) 'Storm looms over plan for new teachers: Baker aims to recruit retired executives', *The Times*, 29 December.

GENERAL TEACHING COUNCIL FOR SCOTLAND (1989) *The Role of the General Teaching Council in the Accreditation of Pre-Service Training Courses*, Edinburgh, GTC.

GRAVES, N. (1988) *The Education Crisis: Which Way Now?*, London, Christopher Helm.

HALLETT, J. (1987) 'What CATE is doing to schools', *Forum*, spring.

HANSARD (1986) Council for the Accreditation of Teacher Education (Written Answers), 30 October.

HARGREAVES, D. (1989) 'Out of BEd and into practice', *TES*, 8 September.

HMI (1988) *A Survey of Information Technology within Initial Teacher Training in the Public Sector*, London, DES.

HMI (1989) *The Renewed Teacher Experience Scheme at Trent Polytechnic, Nottingham*, London, DES.

HOUSE OF COMMONS (1986a) *Achievement in Primary Schools: Minutes of Evidence of the Education, Science and Arts Committee*, 14 February, London, HMSO.

HOUSE OF COMMONS (1986b) *Third Report from the Education, Science and Arts Committee. Session 1985/86. Achievement in Primary Schools*, London, HMSO.

INFORMATION TECHNOLOGY IN INITIAL TEACHER TRAINING EXPERT GROUP (1989) *Report* (the Trotter Report), London, HMSO.

LANCASTER UNIVERSITY SCHOOL OF EDUCATION (1989) *A Future for Teacher Education?* (Conference Report), Lancaster.

LODGE, B. (1987) 'An unloved baby grows into a bearable child', *TES*, 25 September.

LODGE, B. (1989) 'Someone to mind the shop', *TES* 10 February.

MCGUCKIN, J.A. (1987) 'CATE and the reshaping of initial teacher training: The publications of its first year 85–86', *Journal of Further and Higher Education*, 11, 1.

MIDGLEY, S. (1987) 'Teachers' leader attacks plan to use pensioners', *The Independent*, 30 December.

MOON, R.E. (1988) 'Licensed to support', *TES*, 3 June.

NCATE (1990) *Standards, Procedures and Policies for the Accreditation of Professional Education Units*, Washington, NCATE.

NEWMAN, C.V. (1987) 'Open mind' (Letter), *THES*, 13 November.

O'CONNOR, M. (1986) 'Why anxious academic eyes are trained on a watchdog', *Education Guardian*, 4 June.

ROSS, A. (1990) 'Give a teacher a voice', *The Times*, 7 March.

RUDDOCK, J. (1986) 'Ingredients of a good partnership', *TES*, 18 June.

SANTINELLI, P. (1986) 'Titanic to the rescue!', *THES*, 22 August.

SHARPS, J.G. (1989) 'A bureaucratic brake on good training' (Letter), *THES*, 22 September.

SRHE (1986) *The Impact of CATE* (Conference Report).

SPENCER, D. (1986) 'Inspector turns from training to technology', *TES*, 26 September.

SWANWICK, K. and CHITTY, C. (1989) *Teacher Education and the PGCE*, London, University of London Institute of Education.

TAYLOR, W. (1983) 'Teacher education: Achievements, shortcomings and prospects', *TES*, 13 May.

TAYLOR, W. (1986) 'CATE: Consistent, not curst' (Letter), *THES*, 10 October.

TAYLOR, W. (1987a) 'Time lapse' (Letter), *THES*, 18 September.

TAYLOR, W. (1987b) 'Half teacher courses approved so far' (Letter), *Daily Telegraph*, 18 October.

TAYLOR, W. (1989) 'Sterling Work' (Letter), *THES*, 29 September.

TES (1985) Recent experience of CATE (Editorial), 1 November.

THES (1986) CATE on trial (Editorial), 3 October.

References

WARNOCK, M. (1987) 'Teacher power', *New Society*, 2 October.
WHITE PAPER (1972) *Education: A Framework for Expansion* (Cmnd 5174), London, HMSO.
WHITE PAPER (1983) *Teaching Quality* (Cmnd 8836), London, HMSO.
WHITE PAPER (1985) *Better Schools* (Cmnd 9469), London, HMSO.
WHITE PAPER (1987) *Higher Education: Meeting the Challenge* (Cmnd 114), London, HMSO.
WOOD, N. (1988) 'Bosses tired of stress may find new job in classroom', *The Times*, 11 May.
WRAGG, E.C. (1990) 'Educating Teacher' (Book Review), *TES*, 25 May.

Index